Social Factors in the Personality Disorders

A Biopsychosocial Approach to Etiology and Treatment

JOEL PARIS

Professor of Psychiatry
McGill University
Montreal, Québec, Canada

Foreword by PETER J. TYRER

Published by the Press Syndicate of the University of Cambridge
The Pitt Building, Trumpington Street, Cambridge CB2 1RP
40 West 20th Street, New York, NY 10011-4211, USA
10 Stamford Road, Oakleigh, Melbourne 3166, Australia

First published 1996

Printed in the United States of America

A catalog record for this book is available from the British Library

Library of congress cataloging-in-publication data

Paris, Joel.
   Social factors in the personality disorders : a biopsychosocial
approach to etiology and treatment / Joel Paris.
      p.   cm. — (Studies in social and community psychiatry)
   Includes bibliographical references.
   ISBN 0–521–47224–5
   1. Personality disorders—Social aspects.   2. Personality disorders—
Etiology.   3. Personality disorders—Treatment.
   I. Title.   II. Series.
   [DNLM: 1. Personality Disorders—etiology.   2. Personality
Disorders—therapy.   3. Social Environment.   4. Social Medicine.
WM 190 P232s 1996]
RC554.P37—1996
616.85'8—dc20
DNLM/DLC
for Library of Congress   95-16586   CIP

ISBN 0-521-47224-5 Hardback

This book is dedicated to the memory of my father, who taught me the importance of a skeptical mind.

Contents

Foreword

The study of personality disorders was once thought to be a subject that should be abhorred by psychiatrists, as these disorders were not part of mainstream psychiatry. These conditions were considered untreatable and, as they were a measure of social deviance, they should occupy the attention of the legal and social service systems rather than the healthcare one. If psychiatrists were alienists (their old title) among other doctors then personality disorders were the aliens of psychiatric classification.

We are glad to say that this attitude has changed in recent years and the change in no small measure has been a consequence of opinion-formers such as Joel Paris, who has played a major part in dragging personality disorder to centre stage to be examined in the spotlights of scientific criticism, validity, reliability and utility. Professor Paris manipulates these spotlights well and shows that the psychiatric classification of personality disorders, despite several imperfections that need attention, has improved and that they can be discussed with confidence as an observable and reliable entity rather than as a pejorative prescription of someone the clinician does not like.

He also shows that personality disorders have many facets and that biological and social hypotheses need to be integrated to explain them. Genetic endowment, early and late childhood experiences, the quality of attachments to key figures, and consistency of upbringing are all influences that modify temperament into fully formed personality and Joel Paris shows how healthy processes can easily be distorted into maladaptive ones. We live in a specialised age and psychiatrists are no exception. It is now rather rare to find someone with the breadth to cross from the psychodynamic literature to the latest biological theories but Joel Paris achieves this with confidence and élan, showing the true value of eclecticism in giving an unbiased account of the range of important influences that affect the presentation treatment and outcome of personality disorders.

In addition to this all around perspective, Professor Paris has provided a wealth of factual and research information and a comprehensive list of references which will be invaluable to the reader who wishes to know more about this interesting and expanding subject. This book should open the door to those wishing to learn more about this challenging area of enquiry and its biosocial model should help to maintain a balanced interpretation of the sometimes conflicting information coming from many sources.

Peter J. Tyrer
Professor of Community Psychiatry
Imperial College School of Medicine
London

Introduction

What is a personality disorder?

Mental disorders produce a wide range of distressing symptoms. Patients may suffer from the profound gloom of depression, the terror of a panic attack, or the disturbing unreality of psychosis. By and large, psychiatric symptoms are experienced as alien and painful.

Personality disorders, in contrast, may or may not cause subjective distress. Their core features are maladaptive patterns of behavior. Some patients report painful inner experiences, but others may not even agree that they have pathology. Some behaviors lead to consequences that make individuals unhappy, while other behaviors, at least in the short run, are more likely to make other people unhappy.

In essence, personality disorders are characterized by inflexible, pervasive, and stable behaviors that cause significant dysfunction in the life of the patient. They begin early in life and are enduring. We can illustrate these basic attributes with two clinical vignettes, describing one patient with distress, and one with almost no distress.

Case 1

A 23-year-old woman was undergoing training for a professional career. In spite of her external success, she thought about suicide nearly every day. In her personal life, she had many unsuccessful love affairs, in which she became overly attached to men who showed insufficient interest in her. When these relationships ended, she would become despondent.

Her problems had begun early in life. At age 13, she had attempted suicide with an overdose of pills. By the time she was 18, she had experimented with a variety of drugs, and was sexually promiscuous. As an adult, although she could not bear to be alone, most of her intimate relationships were highly conflictual. As a last resort, she decided to seek consultation from a psychiatrist.

Case 2

A 26-year-old man had been unable to hold any job for more than a few months. His intimate relationships were unstable, but he could exploit the women in his life, to the extent that several of them had provided him with financial support. He had a long history of petty criminality, including repeated credit card fraud, for which he had received a suspended sentence.

He began to be truant from school at age 9, and dropped out entirely at age 16. His criminality began with shoplifting in childhood, and continued with minor burglaries during adolescence.

In spite of these problems, he had never voluntarily sought help. He presented to a psychiatrist only because he was facing a criminal charge. His lawyer had advised him that if he could prove that the frauds were due to a mental disorder, he would be more likely to stay out of jail. As far as the patient was concerned, the problem lay not in himself, but in society. His view of his life was that he always had good intentions, but had never "been given a break".

What do these two cases have in common? Both had patterns of behaviors that caused significant impairment in their social or occupational roles. For both patients, their difficulties began early in life, and then became characteristic of their long-term functioning.

Personality disorders take a number of different clinical forms. Experienced clinicians will have no trouble recognizing the two patients described above as prototypical, respectively, of borderline personality disorder, and of antisocial personality disorder. The borderline patient was chronically depressed and suicidal, and had more of the symptoms usually associated with mental disorders. The antisocial patient, in contrast, had few symptoms at all. Yet, as will be discussed later in this book, these patients are classified in the same cluster of personality disorders, since their clinical pictures may reflect two different forms of the same pathological process.

Not all clinicians would recognize these patients as having personality disorders. The first patient would be seen as ill, but might be thought to be suffering from depression. The second patient might be seen as a criminal, rather than as a patient. We need to consider the place the personality disorders have in contemporary psychiatric practice.

Personality disorders and contemporary psychiatry

Hirschfeld (1993) has described personality disorders as "the stepchildren of psychiatry". Like stepchildren, they often go unrecognized. In clinical practice, there are three reasons why personality disorders may not be diagnosed. The first is that these conditions are not well understood. There has been less research on their etiology, outcome, and treatment than on other psychiatric diagnoses, such as schizophrenia or mood disorders. The second reason is that personality problems may not be seen as mental disorders. Clinicians focus on symptoms, and personality pathology may be viewed as secondary to depression. The third reason is that clinicians may consider patients with personality disorders to be untreatable. This perception leads to a reluctance to make these diagnoses (Lewis & Appleby, 1988).

These preconceptions are only partly due to misinformation. Each of them contains at least a grain of truth. There *is* a dearth of hard data on the etiology and treatment of personality disorders. There *is* no absolute boundary between normal and disordered personality. Personality disorders *have* a high comorbidity with other diagnostic entities. Patients with personality disorders *are* difficult to manage.

Patients with personality disorders do not appear in "pure culture". Their "comorbid" symptomatology, such as anxiety or depression, is usually the initial focus of clinical attention and intervention. Many patients with personality pathology do not present in mental health settings at all, but are common among problematic medical patients (Emerson et al., 1994).

Nevertheless, personality disorders demand the attention of clinicians. The construct describes patients who are seen commonly in practice, and who suffer from serious morbidity. By themselves, personality disorders are associated with levels of dysfunction comparable to major psychiatric disorders (Nakao et al., 1991). Patients in whom personality disorders coexist with other psychiatric diagnoses are considerably more impaired, and otherwise effective methods of treatment are less often successful for them (Shea et al., 1989; Reich & Green, 1991; Reich & Vasile, 1993). Comorbidity for personality pathology is far from rare: in a very large sample of both outpatients and inpatients, Koenigsberg et al. (1985) found that nearly half of psychiatric patients have a personality diagnosis in addition to a symptomatic disorder. In addition, some categories of personality disorder are associated with a significant rate of suicide (Perry, 1993). Individuals with personality dysfunction may even tend to have a shorter life span (Vaillant & Vaillant, 1990). A comprehensive approach to psychiatric theory and practice must therefore take the personality disorders into account.

The purpose of this book

Books on psychiatry are written to summarize the present state of knowledge on a subject, and to bring this information to the attention of clinicians. Although many books on the personality disorders have been published over the last 15 years, four have taken an approach parallel to the present volume. Each of these books applied a different perspective to the subject: personality theory (Millon & Davis, 1995), research (Tyrer, 1988), treatability (Stone, 1993), or cognitive therapy (Beck & Freeman, 1990). The perspective of the present volume will be to develop a biopsychosocial theory of personality disorders.

This book will aim to be comprehensive. It does not pretend to be entirely original. The theory to be presented here is, in fact, similar to ideas already developed in the four volumes listed above. What could distinguish this book from its predecessors is a detailed presentation of a model taking into account the complexity of interactions between biological, psychological, and social factors. In addition, the social factors in the personality disorders will receive stronger emphasis.

The present book will maintain a strong empirical orientation. Medicine is increasingly becoming less of a clinical art, and more "evidence-based" (Evidence-Based Medicine Working Group, 1992). Psychiatry must take the same direction. In the past, clinicians have published too many speculations, based on experiences with small numbers of patients in treatment. For example, there have been frequent claims that early life experiences account for personality pathology, ideas quoted in certain quarters with undue reverence. However, to establish whether we can generalize clinical observations to larger populations, they *must* be confirmed by research findings. Ideas that have not been, or cannot be, subjected to empirical investigation have no place in a scientific psychiatry.

In recent years, the personality disorders have become the subject of a good deal of systematic research. Wherever possible, empirical studies will buttress the theoretical structure of this book. However, since this research is still in its early stages, we do not have an overall explanation for the development of personality pathology. Inevitably, these pages will contain some degree of speculation. Many ideas in this book will be consistent with theory, but remain unsupported by hard data. The reader will note that throughout the text, conclusions with strong empirical support have been kept separate from ideas not yet subjected to investigation. The ultimate goal of this book is to offer testable hypotheses for future research.

A model of the personality disorders

For a long time, it was commonplace among clinicians to assume that individuals with personality pathology in adulthood must be suffering from the effects of an unhappy childhood. This idea is, at best, a half-truth; at worst, it is simplistic and misleading. Psychological factors are indeed associated with personality disorders. However, one of the main thrusts of this book will be to show that negative experiences, by themselves, do not account for abnormal personality.

The idea that "the child is the father of the man" is alive and well, and has recently taken on a new form. One only has to open a newspaper to see how pathological behavior can be explained by traumatic experiences, even in the absence of memories for such events. Trauma theory leads to a narrow perspective on the personality disorders. This book will take a broader view.

In recent years, psychiatry has also moved in a diametrically opposite direction, by accounting for the etiology of many mental disorders entirely in terms of biology. We can now see patients with personality disorders who explain their behavior as due to "a chemical imbalance". Many clinicians have fallen into a simplistic reductionism, and some psychiatrists are prescribing drugs for almost every type of behavioral problem.

We might also address another common idea, that there is no such thing as a disordered personality, but only societies that do not allow certain types of individual to flourish. As will be discussed later in the book, this is also a half-truth. Personality pathology does involve conflicts between individuals and society, but some traits are universally maladaptive.

All of these models are unidimensional. Neither biological, psychological, nor social factors, by themselves, can explain the development of mental disorders. Only a *multidimensional* theory can provide a comprehensive approach to their etiology. Multidimensional theories are more complex than linear etiological models. Even in general medicine, very few diseases can be explained by simple models, such as the germ theory of infectious diseases, or the one gene–one enzyme theory of hereditary illnesses (McHugh & Slavney, 1983). Most forms of illness require an etiological model that assumes that only the cumulative and interactive effects of many causal factors are sufficient to produce a disorder, and that single factors can only account for a certain percentage of the overall risk.

Multidimensional models are also consistent with a basic principle of epidemiology, that the etiological influences on any disorder consist of risk factors that make illness more likely, and protective factors that buffer the effects of risks (Mausner & Kramer, 1986). Finally, multidimensional models are in line with research in developmental psychopathology, in that single risk factors in children rarely lead to mental disorders in adults (Rutter, 1987; Rutter & Rutter, 1993).

The cumulative effects of the multiple factors that lead to psychopathology can be understood through a model that Engel (1980) has called *biopsychosocial.* This is the most influential multidimensional theory in modern psychiatry. It has been applied most frequently to schizophrenia (Carpenter et al., 1990), in which biological factors are necessary but not sufficient causes (Carson & Sanislow, 1993). The biological vulnerability behind schizophrenia can express itself in various ways, on a continuum from personality traits to psychosis

(Meehl, 1990), while social factors affect the severity and outcome of schizophrenic illness (Murphy, 1982a; Gottesman, 1991).

This book will apply a biopsychosocial model to the personality disorders. There is a theoretical basis for postulating a role for biological factors in these conditions. The greatest amount of data thus far supports the importance of psychological factors. The evidence for the role of social factors remains indirect. However, it will be argued that all of these factors are necessary for the development of a personality disorder.

The original formulation of biopsychosocial theory by Engel (1980) was a general systems theory, in which no etiological factor had primacy over any other. More likely, many factors determine whether or not individuals become ill, but biology determines the specificity of mental disorders (Cloninger et al., 1990). Differences in biological vulnerability explain why individuals do not necessarily develop mental illness when they experience stress, as well as why, under the same stress, one person will develop one type of illness, and another person will develop a different type of illness.

This emphasis on biological vulnerability is an essential element of *diathesis-stress theory* (Monroe & Simmons, 1991). Diatheses (also known as predispositions) determine what kind of illness patients can develop, while stressors activate this potential. After a long period of neglect, diathesis-stress theory is in the process of being revived in psychiatry. Similar models were common in the nineteenth century, and Kraepelin (1905) defined the categories of mental disorder in terms of both phenomenology and biological predispositions. Diathesis-stress models in psychiatry have been called "neo-Kraepelinian" (Klerman, 1986). Neo-Kraepelinian theory has become the predominant paradigm of modern psychiatry, and is associated with the primacy of biological psychiatry. Diathesis-stress models have been applied to a number of psychiatric diagnoses, including schizophrenia (Gottesman, 1991), affective disorders (Brown & Harris, 1978), and anxiety disorders (Shear et al., 1993).

The theoretical framework of this book will make use of all these models. Personality disorders have a multidimensional etiology, including contributions from biological, psychological, and social factors. Their development depends on both diatheses and stressors.

The theoretical model to be developed in the forthcoming chapters can be outlined as follows:

1. Personality traits are strongly influenced by genetic factors.
2. Personality disorders are pathological amplifications of traits.
3. The amplification of traits to disorders is mediated by biological, psychological, and social factors.
4. Personality traits can be more or less adaptive, depending on the social context.
5. Personality disorders are more likely to arise when there is a discordance between personality traits and social expectations.

The basic argument of the book will be that although biological, psychological, and social factors are all necessary, none of them by themselves are sufficient to produce personality disorders. Biological factors, by shaping individual differences in personality traits, would determine the specific forms that personality pathology can take. Psychological and social factors would have a more nonspecific effect in determining whether underlying vulnerabilities lead to overt disorders.

The model would not apply in the same way to all disorders. Not every form of personality pathology would have the same etiology or respond to the same form of treatment. It is for this reason that each category will be examined separately in the course of the book. In order to do so, this heterogeneous group of disorders must be sorted into meaningful entities. As a result, a fair amount of attention will have to be paid to problems of classification.

The argument of this book

Chapter 1 begins with a historical review of how the construct of personality disorders became accepted in psychiatry. We will then compare two major systems of classification: ICD-10 and DSM-IV. Individual personality disorders can be clustered in three groups described by DSM; these clusters are a useful frame for the examination of individual categories of disorder.

Chapter 2 concerns the relationship between personality traits and personality disorders. Every individual is characterized by specific traits, or "dimensions" of personality. These traits are derived from both temperament and social learning. We will review the major systems that describe the dimensions of personality. Each trait is a behavioral strategy, which could be adaptive under a given set of environmental conditions. Personality disorders are maladaptive variants of these strategies.

Chapter 3 reviews biological factors in personality disorders. Research suggests that genetic factors have a much stronger influence on traits than on disorders. Nonetheless, there are theoretical reasons to expect that patients with personality disorders may have unusual or extreme temperamental characteristics.

Chapter 4 reviews psychological factors in the personality disorders. We will examine the question as to what extent childhood influences adult personality. There are serious methodological problems in conducting research on childhood experiences. The theory that trauma accounts for personality disorders will be subjected to criticism. We will show, nonetheless, that negative childhood experiences, related to a common factor of family dysfunction, are common in personality disordered patients.

Chapter 5 turns to social factors in the personality disorders, and to epidemiological methods that can be used to identify them. We need an accurate measurement of the prevalence of personality disorders in the community. We could then measure social effects on prevalence from indicators of social factors, such as demography, culture, or changes over time.

Chapter 6 concerns the mechanisms by which social factors could affect risks for developing personality disorders. Culture may influence the prevalence of personality traits but the main effects of social factors lie in their interactions with psychological risks. The most important of these interactions involve the prevalence of family breakdown and of parental psychopathology. We will introduce two theoretical constructs to describe how the social context might influence rates of psychopathology: social integration-disintegration, and rapid social change.

Chapter 7 will combine biological, psychological, and social factors in a general theory of the etiology of personality disorders, and show that it can account for many essential features of these conditions.

The next three chapters will apply the basic model to specific categories of disorder.

Chapter 8 examines personality disorders in the "odd cluster". Many of these conditions fall within a "schizophrenic spectrum", in which biological risk factors are particularly important. Social factors play a role in determining the degree of dysfunction associated with this group.

Chapter 9 examines the "dramatic" or impulsive cluster. Two categories in this group, antisocial and borderline personality disorder, have been the subject of extensive research, and we will examine them in more detail. It will be argued that the social context has a particular relationship to impulsivity.

Chapter 10 examines the "anxious cluster" of personality disorders. Trait vulnerability (anxious temperament) and psychological factors (anxious attachment) contribute to this form of pathology. Social factors play a role in amplifying social anxiety to pathological proportions.

Chapter 11 reviews empirical findings concerning the treatment of personality disordered patients. Outcome research shows that certain categories of disorder improve naturally over time. There is little evidence at present that pharmacotherapy is useful for personality disordered patients. Psychotherapy is best applied to a subgroup of patients with higher levels of functioning.

Chapter 12 will present an overall approach to psychotherapy. In order to improve their social adaptation, patients need to be taught to make more adaptive use of their personality traits. Recognizing the social context for psychotherapy with personality disordered patients has practical value. Case examples will be presented to demonstrate the clinical application of these ideas.

The Epilogue will review the major themes of this book, and suggest research to test its hypotheses.

Acknowledgments

The idea for this book was supported at an early stage of its development by Peter Tyrer, the editor of this series. Peter Tyrer was also crucially helpful in guiding the revision and expansion of an earlier version of the manuscript. Dr. Richard Barling of Cambridge University Press provided specific assistance, both in developing the original plan and in making the revisions. The structure and design of this book was refined through the benefit of suggestions made by Allen Frances.

The time required to write the text was provided by the Department of Psychiatry of the Sir Mortimer B. Davis Jewish General Hospital, and its Psychiatrist-in-Chief, Dr. Phillip Beck, as well as by the Department of Psychiatry of McGill University, and its Chairman, Dr. Gilbert Pinard. Ruth Stillman, Librarian at the Institute of Community and Family Psychiatry, provided indispensable help in obtaining references.

I am indebted to colleagues who took the time to read earlier versions of this manuscript. Hallie Zweig-Frank has been my collaborator in many research projects, and has also been, for many years, a strong influence on my thinking about the etiology of the personality disorders. Her searching and incisive comments led to many important revisions of the text. Laurence Kirmayer, who has helped me to understand the principles of social psychiatry, provided me with a "close reading" of Chapter 6.

Whatever the ideas of an author, they must be communicated to the reader in readable prose. I am deeply grateful to my wife, Rosalind Paris, who took the time to read the entire manuscript, and whose feedback has made this book much more comprehensible. Where I had been unnecessarily obscure, her suggestions led to important clarifications. Where my sentences had been convoluted, she helped me make major improvements in the flow of the text. Where I had failed to document my ideas, she led me to examine the issues in adequate detail.

Many members of the personality disorders research community have stimulated my thinking on the issues addressed in this book. In recent years, the number of investigators in the field has reached a critical mass. Two organizations now hold regular meetings to review current research activity: the International Society for the Study of the Personality Disorders, and the Association for Research on the Personality Disorders.

I would particularly wish to thank four colleagues, all of whose ideas on the personality disorders have influenced mine, and with whom I have also had the privilege of having a personal relationship. Over the last 20 years, Ted Millon has written with great originality and profundity about the personality disorders. Many of the ideas developed in this book are elaborations of his formulations concerning the social factors in personality pathology. John Livesley's work on the relationship between traits and disorders was crucial for the theory of this book. Marsha Linehan is probably the most original contemporary researcher on borderline personality, and her biosocial approach to personality pathology has helped to shape my theoretical ideas. Finally, any writer on the personality disorders must be indebted to Michael Stone, who was the first to apply a biopsychosocial approach to the personality disorders.

I would like to acknowledge a special debt to two other researchers. My model of personality disorders parallels earlier work by Aaron Beck. My theoretical approach also reflects the strong influence of the work of Sir Michael Rutter, whose course on developmental psychopathology I had the pleasure of attending at Cape Cod in 1993.

I wish to thank my family for their strong personal support. My wife, Rosalind Paris, has consistently believed in my potential and my career, and has provided the grounding that has made it possible for me to write this book.

Some of the ideas developed here appear in an earlier volume focusing on borderline personality disorder (Paris, 1994).

From this book, with the permission of American Psychiatric Press, Inc., Figure 1 has been reproduced. The quotation in Chapter 4 from Rutter and Rutter appears with the permission of Basic Books. Some of the material in this book, in earlier versions, has been published in journal articles, including the biopsychosocial theory of personality disorders (Paris, 1993), the role of social factors in personality disorders (Paris, 1992), and the validity of childhood memories in personality disordered patients (Paris, 1995).

1

Overview

Personality disorders: the history of an idea

In the past, most of the present categories of personality disorder were not considered to be mental illnesses. We need to explain how people with characterological problems came to be seen as meriting psychiatric diagnoses.

Personality disorders are exaggerations of normal personality traits. At some point, these exaggerations produce significant levels of dysfunction, and can therefore be considered pathological. The problem is where to draw the line between normality and pathology.

All medical illnesses lie on a continuum with normality. The determination of what is a "case" is in many respects a social construct (Eisenberg, 1986). If we consider the two examples of personality disorders presented in the introduction, these patients might be considered, in the first case, unwise or unlucky in love, or, in the second case "more bad than mad". What justifies seeing these people as having mental disorders?

The acceptance of personality disorders as valid diagnoses reflects a change in psychiatric ideology. In order to understand this change, we need to know its historical context.

The classification of personality has a long history that can be traced back to the Greeks (Frances & Widiger, 1986; Tyrer & Ferguson, 1988; Tyrer et al., 1991). A theory describing four temperaments (choleric, sanguine, phlegmatic, and melancholic), associated with the Roman physician Galen (Kagan, 1994), dominated thinking about abnormal personality for many centuries. In fact, if one considers Galen's temperamental types as descriptions, and if one ignores his anachronistic physiological speculations, the four temperaments still have a certain validity (Frances & Widiger, 1986).

Abnormal personality types have been considered throughout most of history to be variants of normal personality. It is therefore not surprising that disorders of personality have lain outside the purview of psychiatry. It was in the nineteenth century that clinicians first became interested in whether, at some point, these variations become forms of mental illness (Fabrega, 1994). At that time, psychiatrists recognized only one form of pathological personality as a valid diagnosis. They termed this entity "moral insanity", defined by an inability to control criminal actions (Pritchard, 1837, quoted in Livesley et al., 1994).

The gradual acceptance of personality disorders as diagnoses over the next 100 years reflects the broadening of the scope of practice. In the early part of the century, psychiatry was based in mental hospitals, and concerned itself almost exclusively with psychoses. The construct of "moral insanity" appeared at a time when the field was expanding. Specialists might now be consulted in criminal cases. Cases seen in psychiatric hospitals were no longer exclusively psychotic. In the course of the nineteenth century, as the major forms of mental disorder were reclassified, influential theoreticians (e.g., Kraepelin, 1905) hypothesized that pathological forms of personality are occult forms of psychoses. This view became the foundation of a European, phenomenological approach to the personality disorders (Schneider, 1950).

By the beginning of the twentieth century, psychiatrists no longer restricted themselves to the treatment of the psychoses, but expanded their clinical practice into outpatient clinics and private offices. Many clinicians became interested in understanding problems in interpersonal relationships, and in treating these problems with psychotherapy. Their practice profile largely consisted of patients who would, today, be classified as suffering from personality disorders.

In the present century, psychoanalysis has been the driving force behind the acceptance of personality disorders as diagnostic categories. Ironically, psychoanalytic theory was not at first very interested in problems of personality pathology, but concentrated on the treatment of symptomatic neuroses. The early psychoanalysts tended to assume that the personality behind symptoms was intact (Jones, 1953). Early psychoanalytic therapies were therefore brief and not geared to characterological change. Over time, analysis changed and began to view all psychiatric symptoms as rooted in personality. One of the main reasons for this evolution was that experience with analytic methods showed that neurotic symptoms were not easily removed, even with increasingly lengthy treatment (Freud, 1937).

The analytic construct of "neurosis" became gradually broader, coming to include abnormalities of personality structure. In the postwar heyday of psychoanalysis in North America, characterological change became the overt goal of analytic therapy. More recently, the success of biological psychiatrists in treating symptomatic neuroses with drugs has reinforced this trend, with the personality disorders left as a residual domain for dynamic psychotherapy (Gunderson, 1985).

Wilhelm Reich (1933) was the first psychoanalyst to develop an explicit method for treating character pathology. He described the function of maladaptive personality as "character armor", by which he meant that personality traits protect the patient against neurotic symptoms. This theory was a forerunner of the modern construct of defense mechanisms. Reich thought that if the therapist could remove the character armor, the patient would experience more symptoms, which could then be more readily treated! Therefore character disorders, characterized by "egosyntonic" personality traits, required "character analysis" to convert them into "egodystonic" neurotic symptoms.

Since most European psychoanalysts had been forced to emigrate to North America for political reasons, the 1930s and 1940s were a period when the sociopolitical climate had a strong influence on psychological theories. A number of analysts were interested in understanding personality pathology in social context. Karen Horney (1940), combining clinical observations with social criticism, suggested that excessive individualism in Western culture was a cause of "neurotic personality". Erich Fromm (1955), a committed socialist, thought that neurotic personality structures reflected excessively acquisitive economic behavior associated with capitalism.

The transplantation of analysis across the Atlantic converted it from a more conservative European idea into a radically environmental American theory (Torrey, 1992). Europeans have strong historical traditions, and are generally more likely to believe that character is fixed. Americans are descended from immigrants who rejected Europe to start anew, and are therefore more likely to believe in the importance of the environment (Frank & Frank, 1991).

During the period before the Second World War, European psychiatry took a very different direction from the ideas then prevalent in North America (Berrios, 1993). Psychoanalytic theories of the etiology of mental illness were not generally accepted. Mental disorders were seen as largely determined by constitutional factors. The leading European psychiatrists were not interested in looking for putative psychological causes, but in classifying mental disorders, based on systematic phenomenological observations.

Kurt Schneider (1950) developed a classification system for the personality disorders that was influential in Europe. He defined ten forms of "psychopathic personality", each of which has specific abnormal behavioral patterns. His categories resemble those later developed for the DSM, and some of Schneider's terminology, such as "anankastic", and "emotionally unstable" personalities, are still in the ICD classification.

During the postwar period, theoretical differences created a divergence in psychiatric classification between North America and Europe. The DSM-I (American Psychiatric Association, 1952) was strongly influenced by the ideas of the Swiss-born psychiatrist Adolf Meyer (1957). Meyer saw psychopathology not as a series of disease categories, but as a set of reaction patterns. Although he accepted in principle that biological factors influence predispositions to mental illness, in practice, Meyer was an environmentalist, with a theory that strongly emphasized psychosocial factors. In this respect, Meyerian "psychobiology" was typically American.

DSM-II (American Psychiatric Association, 1968) made an effort to make American classification accord with international standards, creating categories of personality disorders more similar to those described in ICD. In the ensuing years, European psychiatry began to have greater influence in North

America. The phenomenological tradition emphasized studying the clinical symptoms of mental illness, and postponing etiological speculation until hard data become available. This approach gained popularity across the Atlantic, due to a reaction against the excesses of psychoanalytic speculation, as well as the inefficiency of psychodynamic therapies.

Psychoanalysis had proclaimed itself to be a comprehensive theory of mental illness, as well as an effective treatment for a wide range of mentally disordered patients. It became increasingly obvious that there was no scientific basis for either of these claims. In retrospect, social and historical factors influenced the dominance of the psychodynamic approach in American psychiatry. First, the analysts who had emigrated from Europe, as well as their students, became prominent and prestigious. Second, in the postwar political climate, North Americans were relatively isolated from European thought. Finally, Americans are highly idealistic, and tend to be suspicious of constitutional theories of human nature, preferring to believe that new beginnings in life are always possible. For example, theoretical developments in biology, such as ethology and sociobiology, emphasizing the strong influence of genes on human behavior, caused little controversy in Europe, but became the target of violent opposition in America (Barkow et al., 1992)

As recently as 25 years ago, it was possible to train in psychiatry in North America, and to be unfamiliar with the work of Emil Kraepelin. Yet, Kraepelinian psychiatry remained as dominant as ever, if not more so, in Europe. In North America, psychiatrists committed to developing an empirical base for their specialty revived Kraepelin's ideas. This group was centered in the Midwest, where psychoanalytic ideas had never been as popular as in coastal regions. The influence of "neo-Kraepelinian" theory grew (Klerman, 1986), and was the conceptual basis of DSM-III (American Psychiatric Association, 1980). This diagnostic system used observable criteria to operationalize all constructs, including the personality disorders.

With empiricism dominating American psychiatry, psychoanalysis was displaced and left in a peripheral role. In retrospect, psychoanalysis became isolated because it remained a clinical and not a scientific method. Instead of developing links with researchers to test its hypotheses, psychoanalysis clung to an inadequate epistemology. Its conclusions were drawn not from systematic empirical studies but from historical information provided by patients, the interpretation of which is not open to verification (Grunbaum, 1984). Over the last 20 years, classical analysis has become intellectually isolated. Some of its practitioners responded by withdrawing entirely from the scientific enterprise and promulgating, as an alternative, a "hermeneutic" model (Spence, 1992). Hermeneutics does not even claim to be in accord with scientific methodology, but only describes the process by which analysts interpret the stories that patients provide.

There have, however, been psychoanalysts who have responded more positively to the changes in modern psychiatry. Many of them continued to work in hospitals, remaining open to new developments in general psychiatry. Some have also chosen to enter the empirical mainstream. It is important that psychotherapists become seriously involved in research, since most scientific work in psychiatry is biologically oriented. There is a great and relatively unfulfilled need to subject psychological factors in mental disorders to systematic research. Clinical impressions, drawn from the practice of psychotherapy, can only be tested by quantitative observations.

Beginning in the 1970s, a group of investigators in North America, led by John Gunderson at Harvard, began to study personality disorders with empirical methods. As researchers, they worked within the epistemological rules of neo-Kraepelinian psychiatry, but expanded them, in order to study constructs from the psychodynamic tradition. Psychotherapists trained in research methodology have been responsible for some of the most important research on personality disorders.

In addition to psychoanalysis and phenomenology, a third stream of ideas, derived from psychology, has influenced present concepts of personality disorders. Academic psychologists had long been involved in the measurement of personality traits. This psychometric tradition can also be applied to the psychopathology of personality. The result is a "dimensional" approach to personality disorders, which will be discussed in detail in Chapter 2.

Although the study of personality disorders has had its greatest flowering in North America, it has also flourished elsewhere. A great deal of research has been carried out in Scandinavia (Dahl, 1993; Simonsen & Parnas, 1993), where psychiatry tends to combine American with European traditions. There has also been research activity in Britain (e.g., Tyrer, 1988; Coid, 1993); Ireland (e.g., Casey et al., 1986; Casey & Tyrer, 1986); on the continent of Europe (e.g., Maier et al., 1992; Andreoli et al., 1993; De Jong et al., 1993; Lepine et al., 1993; Lingiardi et al., 1994) as well as in Japan (e.g., Nakao et al., 1992).

In summary, the history of the personality disorders begins with their acceptance as valid mental disorders, and ends with their becoming the subject of empirical research.

The major obstacle to further progress is the absence of a reliable and valid system of classification for the personality disorders (Tyrer, 1987; Livesley, 1995a). Classification might appear to be a tedious matter, and in some respects it is. However, the history of science demonstrates that proper classification is a precondition for the understanding of the basic mechanisms that underlie phenomena. In biology, for example, without the detailed classification of organisms pioneered by Linnaeus, Darwin could have never developed an evolutionary theory. Unless we properly classify the personality disorders, we cannot know what we are studying.

Defining personality disorders

There are two major systems used for the classification of personality disorders: (1) the Diagnostic and Statistical Manual of Mental Disorders (DSM), published by the American Psychiatric Association; and (2) the International Classification of Diseases (ICD), published by the World Health Organization. These two schemata differ very little about how they define a personality disorder, but have different criteria for some categories.

DSM-IV (American Psychiatric Association, 1994) defines a personality disorder as an enduring pattern of inner experience or behavior that deviates markedly from the expectations of the individual's culture. This pattern must be manifest in at least two of the following sectors: cognition, affectivity, interpersonal functioning, or impulse control. In addition, the pattern must be inflexible or pervasive across a broad range of personal or social situations. It must lead to clinically significant distress or impairment in social, occupational, or other forms of functioning. Finally, the pattern must be stable and of long duration, and its onset traced back at least to adolescence or early adulthood.

ICD-10 (World Health Association, 1992) defines personality disorders more succinctly, as a severe disturbance in the characterological constitution and behavioral tendencies of the individual, usually involving several areas of the personality, and nearly always associated with considerable personal and social disruption. The disturbance appears early in life, and continues to be manifest in adulthood.

The most salient points of both definitions are a behavioral disturbance, a significant effect on functioning, an early onset, and a chronic course. The DSM definition is somewhat broader, in that it allows for not only behavior (interpersonal functioning, and impulse control) but also the cognitive and affective aspects of personality. The ICD definition is more focused on maladaptive behaviors, which are the core features of any personality disorder.

The placement of personality disorders on a separate "Axis" in DSM-III had the aim of encouraging clinicians to consider the role of personality factors in symptomatic diagnoses (which are placed on Axis I, whereas the categories of personality disorder are placed on Axis II). In ICD-10, however, these disorders are only one of many groups of mental illness.

The DSM categories are "algorithmic", in that they have been designed using formal rules for diagnosis based on criteria sets. For each personality disorder, a list of clinical features is provided, and a positive diagnosis is made when a given number of these criteria are present. This approach increases the reliability of diagnosis, and lends itself to revisions when criteria are insufficiently specific and/or sensitive to the final diagnosis. This use of formal criteria in DSM has made it popular outside North America (Spitzer et al., 1983).

The ICD system, on the other hand, lists the most characteristic features of a disorder, and leaves it to the clinician to determine if enough of them are present to justify a formal diagnosis. This procedure might run the risk of being unreliable, since it depends on clinical judgments. However, in a recent report (Merson et al., 1994), most of the personality disorder criteria in ICD-10 were found to have reasonable interrater reliability. In any case, clinicians are not as systematic as researchers, so that most diagnoses in practice are made on the basis of an overall "gestalt".

The categories of personality disorder

There is no universally accepted way to define the categories of personality disorder. Psychiatrists are much in the same position as Linnaeus, who classified plants and animals by their external appearance. In the absence of an etiological theory, psychiatrists have had to use clinical phenomena to describe specific categories of illness.

There is also no way to decide how many personality disorders we should accept into our classification. As we will see in Chapter 2, personality characteristics can be broadly defined so as to identify only a few dimensions, or narrowly defined so as to measure many traits. There is no theoretical basis on which to decide whether to have three personality disorders, or 300.

The DSM classification has ten categories, and the ICD has nine. Ten is a convenient number for classification. However, whether each category was included in either system was based largely on *clinical traditions*. This means that the diagnoses are either those frequently described in the literature, or those with some base in research.

It should also be noted that many patients meet the general criteria for a personality disorder, but cannot be assigned a diagnosis from any of the specific categories. In one study, which used DSM criteria in a large sample, about one third of patients meeting the overall criteria for a personality disorder, could only be diagnosed as "personality disorder, not otherwise specified" (Loranger, 1991).

We will now briefly examine the specific categories of personality disorder. (Chapters 8, 9, and 10 will examine the clinical features of all the diagnoses listed in DSM in greater detail, as well as provide case examples of each, while Chapter 12 will describe several cases in depth.) The most salient characteristics of the categories in the ICD and DSM systems are summarized in Table 1.1.

Both systems have categories that have traditionally been considered to have a relationship to schizophrenia. Schizotypal personality in DSM is characterized by reduced capacity for relationships and cognitive-perceptual distortions. This category is classified by ICD as "schizotypal disorder", and is placed, not among the personality disorders at all, but among the psychoses. (This issue will be further addressed in Chapter 8). Both systems describe a schizoid personality disorder, characterized by detachment from relationships and restricted emotions, and a paranoid personality disorder, characterized by suspiciousness.

Both systems also describe personality disorders with either poor impulse control, or a dramatic interpersonal style. The best known of these categories is "psychopathy", characterized by a pervasive pattern of disregard for the rights of others. This older term has been replaced by antisocial personality disorder in DSM, and by dissocial personality disorder in ICD. A second category, borderline personality disorder, is characterized by impulsivity and unstable relationships. This DSM diagnosis was accepted into ICD-10 under the label of emotionally unstable personality disorder, borderline subtype. ICD also includes an additional subtype of emotionally unstable personality disorder not described in DSM: impulsive personality disorder, characterized by uncontrolled aggressive behavior. The DSM category of narcissistic personality disorder is not in ICD. Both systems describe histrionic personality disorder, characterized by excessive emotionality and attention seeking.

Finally, in both systems, there are disorders characterized by anxiety. One category, termed avoidant personality disorder in DSM, and anxious personality disorder in ICD, is characterized by social inhibition. Another category, termed dependent personality disorder in both systems, is characterized by

Table 1.1. *Features of DSM and ICD definitions of the personality disorders*

DSM-IV Diagnosis	Main Clinical Features	ICD-10 Diagnosis	ICD vs. DSM
Schizotypal	Acute discomfort in close relationships Cognitive or perceptual distortions Eccentricities of behavior	Schizotypal disorder	Psychosis in ICD Personality disorder in DSM
Schizoid	Detachment from social relations Restricted range of emotional expression	Schizoid	No important differences
Paranoid	Distrust and suspiciousness	Paranoid	No important differences
Antisocial	Disregard for and violation of the rights of others	Dissocial	Few differences: DSM requires prior conduct disorder
Borderline	Instability in interpersonal relationships Instability in self-image Instability in affects Impulsivity	Emotionally unstable, borderline subtype	Few differences: DSM includes cognitive symptoms
Histrionic	Excessive emotionality and attention seeking	Histrionic	No important differences
Narcissistic	Grandiosity Need for admiration Lack of empathy		Not listed in ICD
		Emotionally unstable, impulsive subtype	Not listed in DSM
Avoidant	Social inhibition Feelings of inadequacy Hypersensitivity to negative evaluation	Anxious	No important differences
Dependent	Submissive, clinging Excessive need to be taken care of	Dependent	No important differences
Compulsive	Preoccupation with orderliness, perfectionism, and control	Anankastic	No important differences
Not otherwise specified	Meets general criteria for personality disorder but not any of above specific criteria	Unspecified or mixed	

excessive dependence. A third category, compulsive personality disorder in DSM, or anankastic personality disorder in
ICD, is characterized by an excessive need for control.

There are serious problems with having two systems of classification. Most of the diagnoses in DSM and ICD derive from
the same constructs, even when their specific criteria differ;
from the point of view of face validity, the differences between
ICD and DSM appear minor. However, when Blashfield (1990)
asked American clinicians to unscramble a mixture of crite-
rion-based descriptors from both systems, he found a poor
correspondence between similarly defined categories (anxious
vs. avoidant, impulsive vs. borderline, and even ICD histrionic
vs. DSM histrionic). In cross-cultural research on the diagnosis
of personality disorders (Loranger et al., 1994), the differences between ICD and DSM were sufficient to prevent them
from being interchangeable in research.

Whatever the final outlines of a universal system of classification for the personality disorders should be, it will need to
be valid across cultures. A research group under the sponsor-
ship of the World Health Organization (Loranger et al., 1991,
1994) took the first step, conducting an international study of
personality disorders in multiple sites on several continents.
The criteria used were primarily those of ICD, although DSM
diagnoses were also examined. The method involved developing an interview (the International Personality Disorders
Examination) that measures ICD categories in countries all
over the world.

The DSM clusters

The idea that the categories of personality disorder can be
clustered is one of the more useful aspects of the DSM system.
The diagnoses described in DSM-III were placed in three
groups, called "odd", "dramatic", and "anxious". However,
in DSM-IV, the clusters were labeled only by the letters "A",
"B", and "C", since there is an absence of agreement as to
how to describe their commonality.

In the present book, the older, more descriptive terms will
be retained. However, we will replace the term "dramatic" for

the B cluster with a different label: *"impulsive"*. Although this usage might be criticized as idiosyncratic, impulsivity is a better description for the traits common to this group. In later chapters, we will also present evidence that specific biological, psychological, and social factors are associated with the dimension of impulsivity.

Returning to Table 1.1, the ten disorders in DSM-IV can readily be placed in clusters, with the odd group consisting of the schizoid, schizotypal, and paranoid categories, the dramatic (or impulsive) group consisting of the antisocial, narcissistic, histrionic, and borderline categories, and the anxious group consisting of the compulsive, avoidant, and dependent categories. (A fourth category in the anxious cluster, passive-aggressive personality, was dropped in DSM-IV.)

From the point of view of phenomenology, the disorders in each cluster have clear overlaps. The validity of the DSM clusters can be examined more formally, by carrying out factor analysis or cluster analysis on the symptoms of personality disordered patients. Studies derived from structured interviews tend to confirm the DSM clusters (Stangl et al., 1985; Kass et al., 1985). In a review of studies applying factor analysis to clinician ratings used to make DSM diagnoses (e.g., Kass et al., 1985; Hyler & Lyons, 1988; Zimmerman & Coryell, 1989), Bagby et al. (1993) concluded that a three-factor solution, corresponding to the present clusters, provides a reasonable fit. On the other hand, studies using symptoms derived from self-report questionnaires have supported the validity of the clusters (Morey, 1988; Livesley et al., 1989). But since clinical diagnoses are made from interviews, confirmation of the clusters by structured interviews demonstrates that they are at least relevant to practice. It was for this reason, after some debate, that the clusters were retained in DSM-IV.

Validity of the categories of personality disorder

Many of the categories in both the DSM and the ICD diagnostic systems have problems with reliability (Zimmerman, 1994). As will be discussed in Chapter 5, diagnostic instruments have been used to identify specific disorders, most of them based on the structured criteria of DSM. Even when these instruments attain acceptable reliabilities, different measures for the same purpose have not necessarily been reliable with each other (Perry, 1992).

Even if personality disorder diagnoses were highly reliable, validity would remain a problem. A set of general criteria for the diagnostic validity of any mental disorder was developed by Robins and Guze (1970), and have since then been considered as benchmarks. These criteria are (1) clinical delimitation, (2) family history, (3) biological markers, (4) a defined course, and (5) a specific treatment response. None of the personality disorders meet all these criteria, although, as we will see in Chapters 8, 9, and 10, some disorders meet some of them.

Clinical delimitation

The categories of personality disorder, as presently defined, overlap each other to an unacceptable degree. If one uses an atheoretical system of classification, one inevitably ends with unclear boundaries. Moreover, the definitions do not *require* any particular feature to be present. DSM simply lists a set of criteria, from which a given number are required to make a diagnosis. This "polythetic" approach might be justified by having no empirical basis for favoring one criterion over another, but it makes for fuzzy diagnoses.

Family history

The personality disorders, as presently defined, lack a specific pattern of inheritance.

Biological markers

The personality disorders lack markers to show that they are well-defined biological entities. (These issues will be addressed in detail in Chapter 3.)

Course

Some of the personality disorders have a specific outcome, and longitudinal data may be the most promising source of validation for these diagnostic categories (Perry, 1991). Although personality disorders are defined as stable over time, they need not last for a lifetime. For example, the impulsive cluster of disorders, which are more common in youth, "burn out" with time. (This subject will be reviewed in detail in Chapter 11.)

Treatment

No specific treatment response has been described that would support a biological validity for personality disorders. In fact, they are consistently resistant to conventional forms of psychiatric treatment. (This subject will also be reviewed in Chapter 11.)

None of these difficulties with diagnostic validity should lead us to discard the present categories of personality disorder. In all fairness, hardly any of the diagnoses of symptomatic conditions in either DSM or ICD, including common and important entities such as depression, meet the stringent criteria proposed by Robins and Guze! However, the present system also suffers from another set of problems, concerning their overlap with symptomatic mental disorders, and their overlap between each other.

Patients with personality disorders usually present when they are significantly distressed. As a result, neurotic symptoms often accompany personality disorders, a phenomenon that, in the jargon of DSM, is termed "Axis I comorbidity". The concept of comorbidity refers to the presence of more than one disease in the same patient, but is also the artifact of a system that prefers to divide mental disorders into narrow categories, rather than lump them together into broader classes.

The advantage of applying multiple diagnoses to the same patient lies in defining subgroups within the broader categories, who may resemble each other more closely than if they only had a personality disorder diagnosis in common. The disadvantage of multiple diagnoses is that they can obscure the possibility that one disorder is primary, and others secondary.

The most common form of Axis I comorbidity is depression. On the one hand, since symptoms distort the personality, it can be difficult to decide whether depressed patients have an enduring pattern of dysfunction (Frances & Widiger, 1986; Tyrer et al., 1990). On the other hand, dysfunctional behaviors bring patients into conflict with other people, which eventually causes symptoms. Patients with recurrent depressions or dysthymia have been shown to have a high prevalence of personality disorders (Mezzich et al., 1987; Pilkonis & Frank, 1988; Pepper et al., 1995).

Another interpretation of comorbidity is that the same diatheses underlie symptomatic disorders and comorbid personality pathology. Akiskal et al. (1983), following European psychiatric traditions, proposed that personality disorders are variants of the major psychiatric diagnoses, such as mood disorders. Yet it is equally possible that symptoms of depression or anxiety can be secondary to personality disorders. Some patients have multiple and changing symptoms, none of which correspond to classical descriptors (Gunderson & Phillips, 1992). If these symptoms are only epiphenomena, and derived from character pathology, it makes clinical sense that a personality disorder should be the primary diagnosis.

Overlaps between categories of personality disorders, or "Axis II comorbidity", is another major problem for the validity of our diagnostic classifications. Studies using structured diagnostic instruments (Pfohl et al., 1986; Nurnberg et al., 1991) have shown that, in the DSM system, if patients receive one personality diagnosis, they are also likely to meet criteria for at least one more. This "comorbidity" between personality disorders is largely artifactual, since it reflects overlap between definitions of specific disorders. Most of the overlaps fall within the clusters, although there are also "crossovers". Although this problem has not been systematically studied for the ICD categories, it is probably much the same.

In the international study by Loranger et al. (1994), there were very few overlapping personality disorder diagnoses. It is possible that clinicians outside North America are more pragmatic, even when using standard instruments, and readily satisfied with one predominant diagnosis. In practice, most clinicians use prototypes that do not exactly correspond to the official criteria (Morey & Ochoa, 1989), and tend to make only one diagnosis per patient.

If categories share common traits, some degree of diagnostic overlap is probably inevitable. Revisions in the criteria for specific diagnoses made in DSM-IV have attempted to reduce spurious co-occurrences (Gunderson et al., 1991), but the problem is far from being solved.

In order to conduct research, we need a better system of classification. There are several possible ways to accomplish this. One would be to improve the criteria for each disorder, by carrying out research aimed at maximizing the "hit rate" of each criterion. The committee that revised the classification of personality disorders for DSM-IV (Gunderson et al., 1991) generated studies of this type, designed to increase the sensitivity and specificity of all criteria. This approach might, at least, reduce the overlap between diagnoses.

A second approach would be to develop a better theory of the origins of the personality disorders, so as develop a classification based on etiology. A theoretical model is what is most lacking in our attempts to establish the validity of any classification system. Until we obtain sufficient data as to their etiology, the categories of psychiatric disorder will have no basis in theory. Our present diagnoses therefore remain syndromes, not true diseases. Unfortunately, we are far from achieving a comprehensive understanding of any mental illness, and it is unlikely that we will soon develop an encompassing theory of the personality disorders. We will probably have to muddle along for many decades to come.

A third possibility would be to reduce the number of categories to a manageably smaller number so as to reduce their comorbidity (Tyrer, 1988). This solution would be similar to using clusters rather than categories.

A fourth possibility would be to start from scratch, and develop categories of personality disorders that derive from a classification of personality traits (Livesley & Jackson, 1992; Costa & Widiger, 1994). The advantages and disadvantages of that approach will be addressed in the next chapter.

2

Personality traits and personality disorders

The nature and origin of personality traits

Every individual has a set of unique behavioral characteristics, popularly called "personality". Psychologists define personality *traits* as consistent patterns of behavior, emotion, and cognition. These characteristics vary greatly between one individual and another. Personality traits can be identified early in life, and are highly stable over time. The broadest characteristics of personality change very little between the ages of 18 and 60 (McCrae & Costa, 1990).

Let us consider an example. Perhaps the most basic of all individual differences in personality is extraversion vs. introversion (McCrae & Costa, 1990; Eysenck, 1991). Extraverts need to be around people, and require a higher level of stimulation. Introverts need more time alone, and require a lower level of stimulation. These differences are rooted in temperament. Extraverts and introverts, if they go on to develop personality pathology, will have different types of disorders.

Both genetic and environmental factors play a role in shaping personality. Rutter (1987) suggested that two factors influence the development of traits: temperament and social learning. Temperament describes those behavioral dispositions present at birth. Observations of newborn- infants show that they differ from each other in how active they are, in how sociable they are, in how easily they get upset, and in how readily they can be calmed down (Kagan, 1994).

Within normal ranges, infantile temperament is not notably continuous with later personality. The only consistent finding of long-term follow-up studies of children with different temperamental dispositions is that a "difficult" temperament, i.e., being easily upset and hard to calm down, makes psychopathology in adulthood more likely (Chess & Thomas, 1990). Yet even this association is rather weak; most children with difficult temperaments never develop mental disorders.

Extreme temperaments are more stable predictors of psychopathology. Studies of children who were unusually "difficult" as infants (Maziade et al., 1990), and of children with extreme levels of shyness (Kagan, 1994), show stronger relationships with psychiatric symptomatology. Moreover, temperamental effects need not be limited to characteristics present at birth, since a number of genetic effects on personality only "switch on" at later periods of development (Rutter & Rutter, 1993).

Although temperament "bends the twig" by setting limits on the predominant characteristics of any individual, environment plays an important role in shaping personality. The most useful model to explain environmental effects is social learning theory (Bandura, 1977). This theory hypothesizes that behavioral patterns in children are shaped in two ways: by positive and negative reinforcement, and by the modeling of behaviors that children observe in adults. However, there are individual differences in the process of social learning, which reflect the influence of temperament (Rutter, 1987).

Individuals vary widely in personality. Most trait differences are entirely compatible with normality. There is room in the world for both extraverts and introverts. It is only when traits significantly interfere with functioning, and when behaviors are used rigidly and maladaptively, that one can speak of a personality disorder. The relationship between temperament, traits, and disorders is summarized in Figure 2.1.

Dimensional theories of personality

The traits that define individual differences in personality can be measured quantitatively. These measurements are based on the assumption that although personality traits covary, they are also independent of each other. Personality as a whole can be thought of as consisting of a set of traits, each of which could

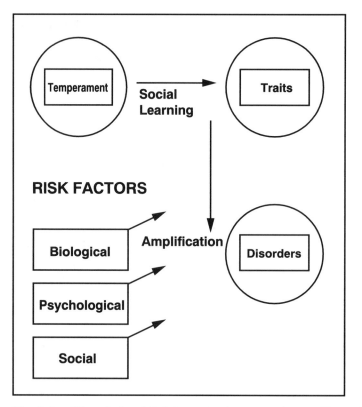

Fig. 2.1.   The relationship between temperament, personality traits, and personality disorders. (From Paris J. American Psychiatric Press, 1994.)

be pictured as a dimension in space. It is for this reason that traits are called the *dimensions* of personality.

Many personality characteristics are "ego-syntonic". This means that, in contrast to psychiatric symptoms, which are alien to the self, or "ego-dystonic", "ego-syntonic" traits are considered as normal, or not even apparent, to those who have them. For this reason, studying personality entirely through self-report presents a problem. Certain traits might not even be reported at all. There are advantages in using observations from interviews, or data from informants. However, the practical problem is that interviews are cumbersome and have serious problems in reliability. Most of the research on personality dimensions has been carried out using self-report instruments, in which the questions are cunningly designed to allow people to describe themselves in a neutral and therefore relatively accurate fashion.

The questionnaires that measure personality traits are composed of a large number of items that describe a wide range of behaviors and attitudes. The dimensions of personality are identified from these scores, using a statistical procedure called factor analysis. This method gathers together intercorrelated items on the questionnaire into "factors", which can then be labeled by describing the characteristics they have in common.

Factor analysis can either be used to describe a smaller number of broadly defined factors, or a larger number of narrowly defined factors. Therefore, dimensional models fall into two general types. A few broad dimensions or many narrow dimensions can be used to describe personality. Each method has its advantages and disadvantages. Broad dimensions, such as the five-factor model of personality (Costa & McCrae, 1988), are closer to temperament. Narrow dimensions, such as the schema developed by Livesley et al. (1994), describe traits closer to the pathological phenomena seen in personality disorders. The two approaches are inherently compatible, since broader factors can be divided into "facets", while narrower factors can be grouped into "superordinate" dimensions.

Dimensional models of personality can test the hypothesis that personality disorders are exaggerations of normal traits. Livesley et al. (1994) have found strong evidence in support of this relationship. In both community and clinical populations, his group found that traits and disorders are continuous. Personality disorders become diagnosable at a cutoff point, beyond which traits are maladaptively intense (Livesley, 1987; Livesley et al., 1992). Unusually high or low dimensional scores could be used for clinical diagnosis. An analogous situation would be hypertension, which is defined by a cutoff point, beyond which elevated blood pressure has been shown to be more likely to cause complications.

Yet even if there is no sharp cutoff between traits and disorders, they could still be distinct. The studies of extreme temperament reviewed above show how quantitative differences, at a given point, become qualitatively meaningful. An analogy offered by Kagan (1989) is that in evolutionary theory, small differences between individual organisms eventually lead to the formation of new species. The questions are whether personality traits and disorders are influenced by the same factors, and whether these factors have the same weight.

We will now examine systems that have been developed to describe the dimensions of personality. The most important of these models are summarized in Table 2.1

Eysenck (Three-factor model)

This model (Eysenck, 1991) describes three broad factors in personality: extraversion, neuroticism, and psychoticism. The Eysenck Personality Inventory (EPI) is the instrument used to measure these dimensions. Eysenck (1991) hypothesized that these dimensions reflect biological variability, on a neurophysiological level, which affects personality structure. He has also shown that these traits are heritable.

Extraversion and neuroticism are the most important dimensions of personality. They appear, either under the same name or under different names, in nearly every classification. Taking into account their interactions, one can re-create Galen's four temperaments (Eysenck, 1987)!

Extraverts are sociable, lively, and impulsive. Extraversion reflects individual differences in the need for interpersonal stimulation. This dimension is hypothesized to derive from baseline levels of arousal: introverts have a high level, which leads them to limit their interpersonal contacts, while extraverts have a low level, which leads them to seek out interpersonal contacts.

Neuroticism measures emotional stability. Individuals high on this dimension are easily upset, while those low on this dimension are, using Galen's term, "sanguine". Neuroticism was hypothesized by Eysenck to reflect levels of limbic system activity.

The third dimension, "psychoticism", describes interpersonal insensitivity. This trait is not well named, since it is more related to psychopathy than to psychosis.

Table 2.1. *Dimensional models of personality*

Authors	Type	Theoretical Base	Dimensions	Heritability
Eysenck	Broad, factor analytical	Neurophysiology	Extraversion Neuroticism Psychoticism	Strong
Costa & McCrae	Broad, factor analytical	Empirical	Extraversion Neuroticism Openness to experience Agreeableness Conscientiousness	Strong (except for agreeableness)
Buss & Plomin	Broad, factor analytical	Temperament	Emotionality Activity level Sociability	Strong
Cloninger	Broad, factor analytical	Neurochemistry	Novelty seeking Harm avoidance Reward dependence	Strong
Siever & Davis	Broad, theoretical	Neurochemistry	Cognitive-perceptual Impulsivity-aggression Affective instability Anxiety-inhibition	Unknown, indirect evidence
Wiggins	Broad, factor analytical	Interpersonal theory	Affiliation Dominance	Unknown
Benjamin	Clinical	Interpersonal theory	Triple circumplex	Unknown
Tyrer	Clinical	Personality pathology	24 dimensions	Unknown
Livesley	Clinical	Personality pathology	18 dimensions	Strong for most traits
Torgersen	Clinical	Personality pathology	18 dimensions	Strong

Eysenck (1987) points out that the three dimensions of his system correspond broadly to the three clusters of Axis II, with Cluster A patients having high introversion, Cluster B patients having high psychoticism, and Cluster C patients having high neuroticism.

Costa and McCrae (Five-factor model)

In North America, this model (Costa & McCrae, 1988) has largely replaced the Eysenck system. It describes five personality factors: neuroticism, extraversion, openness to experience, agreeableness, and conscientiousness. The first two dimensions are, of course, the same as Eysenck's. The third and fourth dimensions separate two aspects of Eysenck's "psychoticism": agreeableness, an interpersonal construct related to emotional warmth vs. coldness, and conscientiousness, related to behavioral control vs. impulsivity. The fifth dimension, openness to experience, is a new construct, describing imaginativeness vs. constriction. The research instrument to measure these traits is the NEO-PI-R, whose name derives from the initials of the five factors (Costa & McCrae, 1992). Four of the dimensions have been shown to be highly heritable (Costa & Widiger, 1994), but agreeableness, as with other measures of social intimacy, has a stronger environmental component (Bergeman et al., 1993).

Temperamental model

Based on temperamental variations that can be observed in early childhood, the "EAS" model (Buss & Plomin,1984) describes three dimensions: emotionality, activity level, and sociability. Sociability parallels extraversion, while emotionality parallels neuroticism. These traits are scored retrospectively for children by their parents; they have not been used extensively in research on the personality disorders.

Neurochemical models

These models describe personality traits hypothesized to correspond to variations in neurotransmitter levels. Cloninger

(1987) developed a schema with three dimensions: novelty seeking, harm avoidance, and reward dependence. Novelty seeking involves a need for high levels of stimulation, and is therefore similar to extraversion. Harm avoidance involves concern with the consequences of actions and is the converse of impulsivity. Reward dependence involves concern about the reactions of other people to one's behavior, and is similar to agreeableness.

Cloninger hypothesized that each of these dimensions corresponds to the activity of a major neurotransmitter (dopamine, serotonin, and norepinephrine, respectively). Although all three traits are heritable (Cloninger, 1991), there is little empirical evidence at present for their hypothesized link to neurobiology. More recently, Cloninger et al. (1993) proposed a fourth temperamental dimension, termed persistence. (In order to account for environmental effects on personality, his group also expanded the theory to include three additional, and nontemperamental, dimensions of adult character.)

Siever and Davis (1991) developed a model that hypothesizes a relationship between levels of neurotransmitter activity and four personality dimensions: cognitive-perceptual, impulsivity-aggression, affective instability, and anxiety-inhibition. Each dimension would be mediated by specific variations in neurotransmitter interactions: the cognitive-perceptual by dopaminergic pathways, impulsivity-aggression by serotonergic pathways, affective instability by an interaction of noradrenergic and cholinergic pathways, and anxiety-inhibition by pathways that could involve either γ-aminobutyric acid (GABA) or norepinephrine. Each dimension could reflect a diathesis for either symptomatic or personality pathology. Thus, using the terminology of DSM, each group of Axis II disorders would have Axis I counterparts, schizophrenia for the cognitive-perceptual dimension, impulse disorders for the dimension of impulsivity-aggression, mood disorders for affective instability, and anxiety disorders for anxiety-inhibition.

Interpersonal models

These models are based on the interpersonal theory of personality, which describes characteristic modes of relating to other people. The "circumplex" model, originally proposed by Leary (1957) and revised by Wiggins (1982), defines two dimensions that describe patterns of adult interpersonal behavior: affiliation and dominance. The term "circumplex" refers to the interaction of these two factors, which are measured graphically in a series of concentric circles that reflect the strength of each dimension. The circumplex model is probably too simple to account for personality pathology, since it is entirely concerned with interpersonal behavior and does not take into account internal states, such as affective or cognitive phenomena.

Benjamin (1993) proposed a more intricate circumplex model, with added dimensions intended to account for the clinical symptoms seen in personality disorders. Her instrument, the Structural Analysis of Social Behavior (SASB), is a triple circumplex that describes how behavior reflects internal models: of self, of others, and of introjects. In view of its complexity, this model might be more applicable to research than to clinical diagnosis.

Clinical models

These schemata use narrowly defined dimensions, which derive from the symptoms of personality pathology. Each system is designed to be an alternative to categorical diagnosis.

In Canada, a series of studies in both community and clinical populations (Livesley et al., 1989, Livesley & Schroeder, 1990; Livesley et al., 1992, 1994) led to the development of an instrument called the Diagnostic Assessment of Personality Pathology (DAPP). Livesley's 18 dimensions provide a comprehensive description of the symptoms of the categorically defined personality disorders, and can therefore be used to make dimensional diagnoses.

In Norway, Torgersen and Alnaes (1989) and Torgersen (1991) developed the Basic Character Inventory (BCI), in which 17 dimensions of personality describe the common symptoms of personality pathology, and which can be converted to broader dimensions through factor analysis (Torgersen & Alnaes, 1989).

In Britain, Tyrer (1988) developed the Personality Assessment Schedule (PAS), a self-report instrument describing 24 dimensions to account for all aspects of personality pathology. This instrument can be used either for clinical diagnosis or for research.

Dimensional diagnosis of personality disorders

Are dimensional models of normal personality good alternatives to the categorical diagnosis of personality disorders? Of the broader schema, the five-factor model accounts best for clinical phenomena (Wiggins & Pincus, 1989; Costa & Widiger, 1994). Costa and Widiger (1994), the leading proponents of the five-factor model as a clinical instrument, argue that if we give up categorical diagnosis in favor of dimensional measures, the problems of diagnosing personality disorders would be largely solved. But making this change might lead to equally thorny problems. Critics of the five-factor model express the concern that the differences between pathology and normality will be obscured (Millon, 1994; Rutter, 1995). As discussed above, the important point is that we do not know whether the factors that influence traits are the same for disorders.

It is worth reviewing how the five-factor model proposes to describe the personality disorders. The following list, drawn from Widiger et al. (1994), describes the most salient aspects of profiles on the five factors for each of the DSM categories:

Schizotypal: high introversion, high neuroticism.
Schizoid: high introversion, low neuroticism.
Paranoid: low agreeableness, low openness.
Antisocial: low neuroticism, low agreeableness, low conscientiousness.
Borderline: high neuroticism, high extraversion, low agreeableness.
Histrionic: high neuroticism, high extraversion, high openness.
Narcissistic: high neuroticism, low agreeableness.
Avoidant: high introversion, high neuroticism.

Dependent: high neuroticism, high agreeableness.
Compulsive: high neuroticism, low agreeableness, high conscientiousness.

A number of empirical studies have been conducted to test these predictions (Costa & Widiger, 1994). Some methods involve examining scores on the NEO-PI in nonclinical samples and comparing them with scores on other self-report instruments that measure personality pathology. This approach has the disadvantage that normal subjects do not have personality disorders. There have also been studies of scores on the five factors compared to clinical diagnoses in personality disordered patients (Trull & McCrae, 1994; Clarkin et al., 1993). In such studies, the correlations between personality dimensions and the categorical diagnosis of personality disorders have not been very high, and different types of categorical disorders have similar dimensional profiles (Yeung et al., 1993).

The clinically based models developed by Livesley and Tyrer offer a more practical alternative to categorical diagnosis. These schemata, derived from observations on patients, describe more accurately the phenomena seen by clinicians. Livesley's model has generated a particularly large body of research. The main findings, as already discussed, are that there are no discontinuities between personality traits and disorders, either in normal populations, or in patients (Livesley et al., 1992, 1994), and that most pathological traits are heritable (Livesley et al., 1993).

Let us now examine the relative advantages of dimensional and categorical models for the diagnosis of personality disorders.

The first advantage of the dimensional approach is that diagnosis retains more information (Widiger & Frances, 1994). When personality disorders are diagnosed categorically, a single diagnostic decision places patients either inside or outside their boundaries. Reducing diagnosis to a simple yes-no decision loses data about the unique characteristics of patients. The additional information provided by dimensional scores could be helpful in understanding the outcome and treatment of the personality disorders.

A second advantage concerns etiological studies. If personality traits are heritable, and if personality disorders are on a continuum with personality traits, etiological studies of the personality disorders could proceed by measuring the dimensions of personality, and then attempt to account for the pathways by which traits develop into disorders.

There are, nonetheless, theoretical and practical advantages in retaining the present categories of personality disorder (Millon, 1994). First, medicine has always approached illness categorically. Dimensional scores can be unwieldy, and the increased data provided by dimensional methods might lead to information overload. In clinical practice, diagnostic labels are a useful shorthand. One simply needs to remember that there are important differences between individuals with the same diagnosis. Second, a therapeutic plan for a patient based on a series of scores would only make sense if treatment could be shown to be specific to these dimensions. Finally, most of the research on the psychological factors in the etiology of the personality disorders has examined categories.

The problem of defining what is a case, and what is not, always involves a cutoff point. Therefore, all disease entities are simultaneously categories and dimensions (Eisenberg, 1986). Categorical classification is needed when continuously varying quantities have important discontinuities, since quantitative differences between traits and disorders become qualitative when they fall at the extreme end of continua. Research on personality development might miss important relationships unless categories are used to measure pathological and extreme variants. Millon (1994) calls the categories of illness "latent taxons", i.e., constructs that describe differences at the pathological end of a spectrum.

The conclusion of Chapter 1 was that the most important reason for the lack of valid categories for the personality disorders is that we do not have enough data to derive our classification from biological research. Until we are able to do so, both categories and dimensions will reflect abstractions, and not reality. Dimensional measures of personality should, ideally, be based on biological differences between individuals. In this respect, Siever's group may offer the most promising approach. However, there are many problems with this model (to be further discussed in Chapter 3), and it will have to be modified by further research. While waiting for biology to provide us with better ways to measure personality traits, the best strategy for carrying out research on the etiology and treatment of personality disorders might be to obtain both categorical and dimensional data on all patients.

3

Biological factors

In the next four chapters, we will examine biological, psychological, and social factors for the personality disorders. Any of these could be associated with mental disorders: if they make the illness more likely, they are risk factors; if they make the illness less likely, they are protective factors.

In a diathesis-stress model, diatheses are inborn individual differences that influence the vulnerability to mental disorders. The biological risk factors to be examined in this chapter could be diatheses for personality disorders. However, they do not, by themselves, explain their etiology.

The biological factors in mental illness can be measured either through genetic studies, or by the identification of biological markers.

Genetic predispositions to psychiatric disorders are identified by family history methods, by adoption studies, or by twin studies. Family history methods, which determine how frequently a disorder is found in the close relatives of patients, provide information that can only be suggestive of genetic influence, since they cannot separate heredity from environment. On the other hand, adoption and twin studies offer much stronger evidence for biological factors. Adoption studies examine whether the children of parents with psychiatric disorders will develop the same disorder if raised in another family. Twin studies, which determine whether identical twins are more concordant for a disorder than are fraternal twins, are the most common way to measure heritability.

Biological markers are an indirect measurement of heritability. Although they could, in principle, reflect either the causes or the consequences of psychopathology, their presence, particularly in combination with other evidence, points to genetic diatheses in mental disorders (Gottesman, 1991).

At present, the role of biological factors in the personality disorders is based more on theoretical principles than on solid evidence. What this chapter will show is that, although it is not clear whether disorders are inherited, personality *traits* are strongly heritable. However, only the presence of biological risk factors can account for two important facts about the personality disorders: (1) individuals with *all* the psychosocial risk factors for these disorders do not necessarily develop them, and (2) the same psychosocial risk factors produce entirely different disorders in different individuals.

The genetics of personality

A relatively new discipline, behavioral genetics (Plomin et al., 1990) has produced a large body of research that demonstrates the influence of genetic factors on personality. The most common method for determining the heritability of personality traits is by comparing their frequency in monozygotic (MZ) and dizygotic (DZ) twins. These studies show that for almost any broadly defined trait, MZ twins have much higher concordances than do DZ twins.

A statistical measure called "heritability" can be derived from twin data (Carey & DiLalla, 1994). Rose (1992) criticizes the apportioning of variance by this method, arguing that multiple interactions between heredity and environment make them less than meaningful. Nevertheless, behavioral genetics provides us with a useful overview of the situation, especially when different traits have different levels of heritability.

Most personality traits have high heritabilities, usually in ranges between 40% and 50% (Plomin et al., 1990; Livesley et al., 1993). This means that approximately half the variance of most of the dimensions of personality can be attributed to genetic influence. Heritabilities determined by adoption studies yield slightly lower estimates (Plomin et al., 1990).

The mechanisms by which genetic factors influence personality are complex. First, personality traits are influenced not by single genes, but by the interaction of several genes. If genetic effects on behavior only appear when several genes are present at the same time, this explains why differences between MZ and DZ twins reflect genetic effects for traits that do not run strongly in families (Lykken et al., 1992). Second, each genetic effect is itself "pleiotropic", i.e., each gene influences more than one type of behavior. Third, the true proportion of personality variance accounted for by genetic influence could be greater than 50%, since some of the residual variance involves interactive effects between genes and environment. For example, children directly influence the quality of their environment, by shaping the responses of others to conform to their traits (Scarr & McCartney, 1983).

The Minnesota Twin Study offers the most striking findings on the heritability of personality. This project used a design combining the advantages of twin and adoption studies by examining personality traits in MZ and DZ twins raised together and apart (Tellegen et al., 1988; Bergeman et al., 1993). Correlations between scores on the personality measure (the 11 dimensions of the Multidimensional Personality Questionnaire) for MZ twins were just as high whether the twins were raised in the same family or separated at birth. Dizygotic twins have surprisingly little correlation between personality traits.

Although the heritability of most personality traits is high, there are important exceptions. In the five-factor model, agreeableness is less heritable than the other broad dimensions (Bergeman et al., 1993). In the Minnesota study, there was only a moderate (30%) heritability for a measure of social closeness or intimacy. This finding has been replicated, using a different instrument, by Livesley et al. (1993). Plomin et al. (1990) conclude that broader dimensions, such as extraversion or neuroticism, do not account for problems in intimacy, which are more open to environmental influence.

There is more evidence for differential heritability when one examines narrowly, more clinically defined traits. For example, Livesley et al. (1993; 1995b) found high heritabilities (> .5) for callousness, identity problems, narcissism, oppositionality, and social avoidance; but there were low heritabilities (< .3) for self-harm and submissiveness.

In spite of these differences, we can accept, as a general principle, that personality traits reflect strong genetic factors.

Two additional lines of evidence support the biological nature of personality traits. First, the broad personality dimensions are valid in cultures all over the world (Eysenck, 1991). Second, some personality traits are associated with specific biological markers, either blood groups (Eysenck, 1991), or variations in levels of neurochemical activity (Cloninger, 1987; Coccaro et al., 1989; Siever & Davis, 1991).

The biological factors in personality should be observable through the measurement of temperamental characteristics in children. There is evidence from longitudinal studies that temperament shapes the development of adult personality. Rothbart and Ahadi (1994) have reviewed many of these findings, which show that children with increased fearfulness and irritability are more likely to become neurotic, that children with increased activity level and positive affect become more extraverted, that children with attentional persistence become more conscientious, and that children who are easily prone to distress have more difficulties with attachment. (Chapter 10 will review the research on temperamental fearfulness in detail.) A recent report from New Zealand (Caspi & Silva, 1995) presents similar findings.

Two mechanisms could enxplain how abnormal temperaments lead to psychopathology. First, temperamental abnormalities in children become amplified by the difficulties they create for both parents and peers (Rutter & Quinton, 1984). Second, an abnormal temperament could make children more susceptible to environmental stressors. (Chapter 4 will further address this issue.)

Paradoxically, behavioral genetics also demonstrates the importance of the environment. Even if the variance of most personality traits accounted for by genetic factors is close to 50%, there remains 50% to be accounted for by environmental factors. One of the surprising findings of twin research concerns the source of these influences. The environmental contribution to personality is largely *unshared*, i.e., not related to living in the same family. Contrary to what one might expect, siblings growing up in the same family, like dizygotic twins, are hardly more similar in their personality than if they were perfect strangers (Dunn & Plomin, 1990).

The importance of the unshared environment could be explained in several ways. First, siblings may receive differential treatment from their parents. Second, differences in traits could lead individuals to perceive their environment differently. Third, experiences outside the family affect personality. Since these mechanisms are not easily disentangled, the source of unshared environmental variance requires further elucidation. We will return to this finding in Chapter 6.

Personality traits as adaptations

The genetic factors in personality traits point to their adaptive function. This theory, that individual differences in traits represent alternative forms of adaptation, has been discussed in three previous books on personality disorders (Beck & Freeman, 1990; Millon, 1990; Stone, 1993).

One caveat must be registered: individual differences, whether in anatomy, physiology, or behavior, cannot be assumed to be adaptive without specific empirical support. Variability may not be always adaptive, since it could also represent "genetic noise" (Bergeman et al., 1993). Nevertheless, if traits are adaptations, this would explain a great deal about the functional significance of individual differences in personality. The hypothesis can be understood in the context of how organisms cope with an environment that is itself highly variable. Individual differences in personality would be alternate strategies, each of which could be more adaptive under one set of environmental circumstances, and less adaptive under another set of circumstances.

Let us consider two specific instances, each related to the clinical phenomena seen in patients with personality disorders. The first concerns the trait of shyness or "behavioral inhibition". This characteristic, operationally defined by a child's reaction to strangers, has a strong genetic component (Kagan, 1994). Social avoidance could be adaptive under conditions where strangers present a real threat. In fact, through most of history, strangers *have* been dangerous, and continue to be so, in both large and small communities all over the world. The same trait would be maladaptive in a setting where threats from outsiders are rare, and in which shyness interferes with peer relationships, and even leads to social isolation.

A second example concerns impulsive traits. Impulsivity could reflect variability in autonomic activation affecting the timing of response to environmental challenges (Mednick & Moffit, 1985). Under conditions of immediate external danger, rapid responses are more adaptive. Impulsive traits become maladaptive when they continue to occur in the absence of real danger, and when they interfere with the development of rational judgments.

Genetic factors in the personality disorders

In contrast to the findings of behavioral genetics that traits are strongly heritable, as concluded by three recent literature reviews (McGuffin & Thapar, 1992; Dahl, 1993; Nigg & Goldsmith, 1994), there is at present no convincing evidence that genetic factors influence the development of personality disorders.

One likely explanation for these negative findings is the problems described in the previous chapter in developing a rational classification of personality disorders. If categories are not valid, or if they fail to correspond in any meaningful way to biological variability, then it would not be surprising that they fail to show heritability. Eventually, we need to redefine personality disorders on a biological basis. At present, the evidence shows that biological factors are more strongly related to dimensional measures of personality than to any specific diagnosis (Nigg & Goldsmith, 1994). Therefore, dimensional systems of classification should provide the most useful information on biological factors in personality disorders.

This reflection brings us back to a schema discussed in the previous chapter, that developed by Siever and Davis (1991). In this model, the dimensions of personality correspond to individual differences in neurotransmitter activity. A trait profile is unique to each individual. Some of these profiles would be more adaptive; others less adaptive. Interactions between traits would determine whether adaptive characteristics buffer the effects of less adaptive ones, or whether cumulative risks arise from the presence of multiple maladaptive traits. Some combinations of traits would create a higher risk for the development of personality disorders.

These hypotheses are consistent with the theoretical position of this book. However, models of the biological factors in personality will have to be *much* more complex. It is unlikely that levels of a few neurochemicals can explain the diathesis for complex conditions, such as personality disorders. New neurotransmitters are being identified, and each of the known neurotransmitters has different effects depending on the type of receptor it activates (Coccaro & Murphy, 1990). Research in neurochemistry cannot explain how the brain works until we understand how it is wired; changes in brain structure are also associated with learning (Rose, 1992). Neuroanatomical and neurophysiological pathways have not been factored in to biological models of personality, except in the most provisional fashion.

Nonetheless, Siever's schema points to a research strategy. Instead of examining the present categories of personality disorder for heritability, we might concentrate on the biological correlates of personality dimensions. If Siever's group were to develop precise scales to measure their theoretically derived dimensions, they could then examine their heritability. Thus far, they have concentrated on determining whether there are biological markers associated with different categories and dimensions of personality disorders.

Thus far, the evidence shows that wherever biological markers have been identified in personality disordered patients, they are related to comorbid symptoms, or to traits. As an example of markers that reflect the comorbidity of symptomatic disorders, abnormal dexamethasone suppression and decreased rapid eye movement (REM) latency in impulsive personality disorders are only seen when patients are also depressed (Gunderson & Phillips, 1991). As an example of markers that reflect traits, a study of men with Cluster B diagnoses (Coccaro et al., 1989) found that a decreased response to fenfluramine challenge (a measure of serotonergic activity) was strongly related to traits of impulsive aggression, but only weakly to diagnostic categories such as antisocial or borderline personality. Although it is possible that future advances in biotechnology will provide an increased variety of biological markers to study, most findings will probably continue to be associated with traits.

Direct measurements of the genetic factors in personality disorders also suggest that genetic factors act on the trait level. Adoption studies have shown some degree of heritability for criminality (Crowe, 1974; Cloninger et al., 1982; Mednick et al., 1984), but not for antisocial personality. Heritability has been demonstrated for trait anxiety, but not for anxious cluster personality disorders (Nigg & Goldsmith, 1994). There is a stronger heritability for mild forms of thought disorder than there is for the diagnostic entity of schizotypal personality (Kendler et al., 1981).

The most extensive twin studies of personality disordered patients have been carried out by Torgersen in Norway (1980, 1983, 1984, 1991). Torgersen's research strategy was to use measures of traits or disorders in the same patients. He showed that differences in MZ vs. DZ concordance are found in relation to traits, or even to symptoms, but not to disorders. For example, in the Cluster C disorders, social anxiety, but not avoidant or dependent personality, was heritable (Torgersen, 1983); while obsessiveness was heritable, but compulsive personality disorder was not (Torgersen, 1980, 1991).

That traits are under biological influence, while disorders are not, is a verdict that could change. For example, Siever's research group might succeed in finding a genetically determined high intensity for certain traits associated with certain personality disorders. Another line of evidence for biological factors in personality disorders that may bear fruit is further follow-up on children with extreme temperaments (Maziade et al., 1990; Kagan, 1994). As more data come in over the next decade, we should have a better idea.

If, however, no further evidence for biological factors in the personality disorders is found, we may have to conclude, that, as has been shown for intelligence (Bouchard et al., 1990), genes are more important in the normal range, while environmental factors are more important at the extreme ends of the continuum.

The following prediction seems reasonable: Personality disorders *are* associated with a high intensity of personality traits that are more likely to be maladaptive, but biological factors are insufficient by themselves to cause disorders. The explanation would be that even in the presence of biological risks, personality disorders will not develop unless individuals are also exposed to psychosocial risk factors. The view of this book is that psychological and social factors are the crucial determinants for pathways between traits and disorders. The nature of these risk factors will be the subject of the next three chapters.

4

Psychological factors

To what extent is personality shaped by childhood experiences?

Personality disorders begin early in life, and remit only slowly with time. These characteristics are, of course, intrinsic to their definition. Yet they still demand an explanation. Early onset and chronicity could be accounted for by two alternative theories: (1) the origins of personality disorders lie in temperament; (2) the crucial psychological risk factors for these disorders derive from childhood experiences.

The hypothesis that early experiences, particularly problems in parent-child relationships, can either shape or deform personality, has been taken for granted by generations of theorists. Psychoanalytic theory has explained the consistency of personality over time by assuming a primacy for early experience. The principle is that early learning should have a greater impact than later learning, since it occurs at a time when the child is more dependent on its parents (Millon, 1969). Psychodynamic models all assume that the more severe the pathology, the earlier in life is its origin (Paris, 1983).

In spite of their ubiquity, these assumptions have not been supported by empirical research. One of the most important findings of research in developmental psychopathology is that, by and large, single negative events do *not* usually cause psychiatric disorders (Rutter & Rutter, 1993). Given a reasonably favorable environment, most children are resilient. In vulnerable children, who lack resilience, stressors have a greater impact. The pathogenic effects of negative events therefore involve interactions with preexisting diatheses.

When negative experiences lead to psychopathology, it is usually because they are multiple. Negative events are not independent of each other, since one leads to another in a "cascade". The cumulative effects of multiple risks overcome the natural resiliency of the child.

In reviewing the empirical evidence on the long-term outcome of negative childhood experiences, we can do no better than to quote Rutter, whose conclusions have been summarized in a recent book:

> For many years there was a general belief that personalities were largely shaped and fixed by experiences during the first few years of life. It seemed obvious that this must be the case because of the frequency with which really bad experiences were followed by psychological problems in later life, and by the relative persistence of these problems in spite of later good experiences. However, it is now known that the sequelae of adverse or depriving experiences in infancy do not fix personality development. Provided later experiences are really good, the ill-effects of early deprivation or adversity are surprisingly evanescent in many respects. The *impression* of lasting effects stems from the very high probability that a poor early upbringing will be followed by a poor later upbringing. (Rutter & Rutter, 1993, pp. 32–33)

The reader is directed to Rutter's integrative literature reviews (Rutter, 1982, 1987a, 1989) for references to the large number of studies from which these conclusions are drawn. In the present chapter we will examine examples involving the childhood experiences that are most frequently associated with personality disorders.

At this point, let us underline the distinction between risk factors for disorders and causal explanations of illness. When there is an association between a risk factor and a mental disorder, that risk is most likely to be involved in the etiology of the illness if it precedes the development of pathology; if it is consistently, strongly, and specifically associated with the disorder, and if there is a plausible mechanism linking the risk with the illness (Regier & Burke, 1989). These criteria are rarely met in practice.

In fact, associations between risk factors and disorders may not have any etiological significance. As is well known, correlation does not mean causation. Associations between risks and disorders can be accounted for by other factors, sometimes called "latent variables".

Even when risks do have etiological significance, single factors usually account for only a small percentage of variance. Cumulative effects are needed to cross the threshold between diathesis and disorder. The identification of a risk need not mean that it leads in any predictable fashion to the illness. Most individuals exposed to the same risk factors may not develop any pathology. Moreover, many individuals with the same disorder have not been exposed to the same risk factors.

As an example of these principles, let us consider an example: the long-term outcome of divorce on children. Several factors determine whether children are damaged by the divorce of their parents. First, children often have to deal not only with the separation itself, but with a cascade of other consequences: decreased financial resources, changes of domicile, continued conflict between the separated parents, and the possibility of depression or preoccupation in the custodial parent (Tennant, 1988). It is difficult to determine whether the long-term effects of parental separation on children are due to marital breakdown itself, or these ensuing negative events. Second, experiences are processed by cognitive schema, i.e., their effects are different in different individuals, depending on personality traits. Finally, the effects of family breakdown depend on the child's social environment.

An equally important example of the relationship of negative events in childhood and later psychopathology involves the effects of traumatic experiences. We will examine this subject in depth later in the chapter.

The general principle to keep in mind is that the relationship between early experiences and later personality is highly complex. The theoretical position of this chapter can be summarized as follows:

1. Personality is shaped to *some* extent by childhood experiences but less by any single experience than by the cumulative weight of many experiences.

2. The psychological effects of childhood experiences can only be understood in the context of their interactions with biological and social factors.

Before examining which childhood experiences are risk factors for personality disorders, we need to address the question of whether we can determine that adult memories of childhood are accurate.

Methodological problems in studies of the effects of childhood experience on adults

Retrospective vs. prospective design

Most research on the psychological risk factors for the personality disorders has used *retrospective* designs. This means that the investigators ask adult patients to remember what happened to them as children. By contrast, a *prospective* design might gather a large cohort of children, and then follow them into adulthood. Prospective research would be a better way of establishing the role of risk factors, by predicting which of them determine whether children in the original sample go on to develop personality disorders. Unfortunately, the practical difficulties, not to speak of the expense, that such a major project would entail, have meant that this type of research has not been carried out. There have been several long-term follow-ups of normal children (e.g., Chess & Thomas, 1990) as well as of children at risk (e.g., Werner & Smith, 1992), but these studies did not examine personality disorders.

Research has therefore depended almost entirely on retrospective reports. Subjects are either interviewed, or are given questionnaires about their childhood. Patients with personality disorders are then compared with other diagnostic groups to determine whether they report negative experiences more frequently. These methods produce findings that are, at best, suggestive. They do not provide us with the definitive information that prospective research could provide.

Accuracy of memory for childhood events

The crucial problem with retrospective research is that no one can be sure that patients' memories of childhood are accurate. There are, in fact, serious problems in assessing memories of childhood in adults.

First, memories can be distorted, particularly in the light of the individual's problems later in life. When one's present is not going well, there is a strong temptation to blame the past.

Second, empirical studies of memory, particularly for events long in the past, have shown that life experiences are *never* registered with factual accuracy by the brain. This observation is over 60 years old (Bartlett, 1932). On the contrary, from the very time of an event itself, memories for life experiences are colored by cognitive schema, i.e., individual perceptions and biases (Loftus, 1993).

Some therapists seem to assume that one can access memories as if they had been recorded on a cassette. This idea has led to the use of adjunctive methods, such as hypnosis, to retrieve these "lost" memories. The assumptions behind this approach are mistaken. Hypnosis is, in fact, particularly likely to produce "false memories", as has been shown in many experimental studies (Orne et al., 1988; Spanos, 1982; Laurence & Perry, 1983; Pettinati, 1988; Baker, 1990; Barnier & McConckey, 1992; Ofshe & Watters, 1994).

Third, inaccuracies of memory are common among psychiatric patients, particularly in those with personality disorders. It has been observed by many clinicians, for example, that patients with borderline personality disorder distort recent interpersonal events, including both interactions with significant others, and with their therapists (Gunderson, 1985; Paris, 1995). How much more likely, then, are these patients to distort, most probably in a negative direction, memories of their childhood?

Fourth, therapists can elicit false memories of trauma in suggestible patients. False memories are most usually produced by suggestions during psychotherapy or through hypnosis (Loftus, 1993). The procedure to elicit "recovered memories" are based on the assumptions that traumatic experiences in childhood cause profound effects on the personality, and that memories of traumatic experiences are often repressed. As will be discussed below, these theories were based on little solid evidence.

Methods used to validate memories of childhood

How do we go about validating what patients tell us about their childhood experiences? One recent review (Brewin et al., 1993) underlined that it is possible to confirm certain types of retrospective data. For example, as Robins et al. (1985) showed, siblings give highly concordant reports about the factual aspects of childhood experiences, such as deaths and illnesses. On the other hand they tend to disagree about nonfactual variables, such as family atmosphere.

It follows that we can only place strong reliance on the factual data provided by our patients. In principle, traumatic events, such as childhood sexual or physical abuse, should be factual. There is no doubt that child abuse is much more common than we had been led to believe in the past (Finkelhor et al., 1990). Yet in clinical practice, we deal with individuals whose perceptions of reality may be impaired, and we need to differentiate reports of real experiences from exaggerations of less severe events, or even fantasies.

It has been particularly difficult to confirm the validity of child abuse. Many incidents are kept secret and not reported to others. Incest, in which many children can be exposed to the same perpetrator, may be verifiable through siblings. Herman and Schafzow (1987) used siblings to confirm these reports from patients in an incest survivor group. Unfortunately, they did not develop any systematic approach to verification; in addition, their conclusions are limited by their having depended on patients to report on the experience of siblings (Ofshe & Watters, 1994). Moreover, there has been no comparable research on the validity of reports of nonincestuous sexual abuse, even though molestation by non-relatives constitutes the vast majority of incidents of sexual abuse in children (Browne & Finkelhor, 1986).

The theory of repressed memories

Thus far, there is no good evidence that trauma leads to repressed memories. In the first place, the repression of memories has never been observed experimentally (Holmes, 1990; Bower, 1990). It is possible that repression is hard to measure because it only occurs under extreme circumstances. Yet this purported phenomenon must be very elusive, since all attempts to demonstrate it have failed.

Ofshe and Watters (1994) as well as Pope and Hudson (1995), examined those studies that might conceivably support repressed memory, and found them to be flawed. Adults do not always remember documented traumatic experiences (Meyer-Williams, 1994). However, since many abuse experiences are multiple, most of those who forget one experience report others.

Herman (1992) claims that the usual response to traumatic experiences in childhood is to repress them. This statement is not in accord with the evidence. On the contrary, prospective studies of children who have been traumatized show that the memories of these experiences are not repressed, but continue to trouble the child for years afterwards (Terr, 1988). Memories are more readily subject to *suppression*, i.e., a conscious effort is made not to think about them. Abuse victims may report that there were times in their life when they did not think about or seem to remember traumatic experiences, but this does not mean they were repressed. In contrast, painful reexperiences of the past are characteristic of post-traumatic stress disorder. This is a prime example of how traumatic memories are typically *intrusive*.

Ironically, Terr, who was one of the investigators who found that trauma in children leads to intrusive memories, later hypothesized that *chronic* trauma during childhood might follow entirely different rules (Terr, 1991, 1994). What she proposed was that in the presence of repeated trauma, particularly from a caretaker, memories of the experience become repressed to allow children to defend themselves against an intolerable situation. However, there has been no evidence thus far to support this hypothesis (Loftus, 1993).

A great deal of harm can be done when hypotheses become ideological convictions, and when scientific methods are not used to test clinical impressions. The manufacture of false memories by well-meaning therapists, particularly in North America, has done much in recent years to bring psychiatry into disrepute (McHugh, 1992). Several well-publicized cases have involved suggestible patients who were influenced by clinicians into reporting traumatic memories for which there was no external validation (Loftus & Ketcham, 1994; Ofshe & Watters, 1994; Wright, 1994). Since false memories more frequently emerge under hypnosis, this procedure has been ruled out as a source of evidence by the American courts (Loftus & Ketcham, 1994).

The shaping of symptoms

Psychiatric symptoms can be shaped, at least in some patients, by the suggestions of therapists. Dramatic presentations of hysteria were common in the nineteenth century. For example, the clinical demonstrations by the French neurologist Jean-Martin Charcot involved patients who were willing to please their physicians by producing symptoms on demand (Ellenberger, 1970). Even a cursory reading of the writings of Freud demonstrates that, from the inception of psychoanalysis, patients in analysis have been pressured to provide confirmation for the theories of their therapists, and that many of them have complied (Torrey, 1992).

These episodes in psychiatric history are currently repeating themselves. Psychiatric patients with high levels of dissociation can have their symptoms shaped into a syndrome termed "multiple personality disorder" (MPD). It should be noted that this term does *not* refer to a personality disorder, as defined in psychiatric nosology. MPD is classified as a dissociative disorder, and has recently been given the new name of "dissociative identity disorder" (American Psychiatric Association, 1994).

Dissociative disorders had, up to recently, been considered as rare. Therapist suggestions are the most likely cause of the recent reported increase in the prevalence of the symptoms of MPD (Merskey, 1992). Moreover, the extremely traumatic experiences during childhood that these patients report (Putnam, 1989) could also be attributed to suggestions by therapists (Frankel, 1993).

In summary, all the research on the role of negative experiences in the development of personality disorders has been hampered by methodological problems. Retrospective designs depend on memories for events in the distant past that may not be accurate, and the methods for validating them are shaky. There is little evidence for the theory of repressed memories, and the symptoms associated with negative childhood experiences can, in some cases, be shaped by therapists.

Even if memories of negative events are accurate, an association between childhood experiences and later psychopathology does not prove that there is a causal link between them. In particular, even research showing that childhood sexual or physical abuse in adult patients is unusually frequent in patients with personality disorders does not prove that childhood abuse is the cause of this form of psychopathology. It is equally possible that such events could be epiphenomena, reflecting other, less obvious variables.

The role of trauma in psychopathology

Before reviewing research on the association between traumatic experiences in childhood and personality disorders, let us examine the overall status of trauma theory in psychiatry.

The main problem in ascribing the development of psychopathology to trauma is that the same experiences implicated as causes of mental disorders occur in large numbers of nonpatients. Most individuals with trauma, whether in childhood or adulthood, do not develop any observable psychopathology. To evaluate the pathogenic effects of any psychological factor in development, we need to carry out community studies. Such research can show how frequent such experiences are in the general population, and under what circumstances they are most likely to lead to a mental disorder.

Many studies have examined the long-term impact of childhood trauma in community samples. The largest number have concerned either childhood sexual abuse (reviewed in Browne & Finkelhor, 1986), or childhood physical abuse (reviewed in Malinovsky-Rummell & Hansen, 1993). This research shows that abuse experiences are, statistically associated with a wide range of psychological symptoms in adulthood. However, it would be incorrect to conclude that child abuse inevitably leads to mental disorders in adults. In fact, 80% of adults with such histories of sexual abuse have no demonstrable psychopathology, and similar findings apply to physical abuse.

What community research shows is that childhood trauma is a *risk factor* for mental disorders. What it does not show it that trauma *causes* mental disorders. One instructive example is a prospective community study of children who experienced violent physical abuse in childhood, examined for acts of violence in adult life (Widom, 1989). Statistically, physically abused children are more likely to grow up into violent adults; but, the vast majority do not.

What is the explanation for the discrepancy between childhood experience and long-term consequences in adulthood? One possibility is that only *severe* trauma leads to pathological consequences. In fact, a great amount of research shows that the impact of negative life experiences depends on their severity (Monroe & Simons, 1991).

Childhood sexual abuse is a good example. Its long-term outcome depends on its "parameters" (Browne & Finkelhor, 1986). The most important of these is the identity of the perpetrator. Father-daughter incest is the most damaging form of sexual abuse in childhood. Incest with any family member causes more sequelae than molestation by nonfamily members. The nature of the sexual act is also important, and children who have experienced penetration are more damaged. Other parameters associated with long-term consequences include higher frequency, longer duration, and the use of force. The findings for physical abuse (Malinovsky-Rummell & Hansen, 1993) are similar: children suffer the most long-term damage when they are beaten by their caretakers severely and frequently for long periods of time.

Fortunately, the vast number of incidents of reported child abuse in these community studies are of low severity. This fact explains a good deal of the discrepancy between the prevalence of abuse and the emergence of long-term consequences. Yet, even when severity is taken into account, the effects of trauma are difficult to predict. High-risk types of childhood sexual abuse, such as father-daughter incest or penetration, still have only a statistical relationship to outcome.

A second possibility to account for the variable effects of trauma is the influence of cognitive schema. The effects of negative events are influenced by how they are cognitively processed. For example, self-esteem is reduced when abuse experiences are felt to be stigmatic (Finkelhor, 1984).

A third possibility, as shown by a recent New Zealand study (Romans et al., 1995), is that sexual abuse leads to sequelae only when accompanied by other psychological risks.

A fourth possibility, very much in line with the theory of this book, is that traumatic experiences have greater effects on individuals who are already predisposed to psychopathology. There is a great deal of support in the literature for this idea, particularly from studies of trauma in adults. Whether individuals develop symptoms after a recent negative event depends, not so much on the severity of the trauma, but on underlying predispositions. For example, in a study of symptomatology in Australian firefighters after a bush fire (McFarlane, 1993), the degree of exposure to danger did not predict whether the survivors would develop post-traumatic stress disorder (PTSD). The presence of premorbid psychopathology was, however, highly predictive of long-term consequences.

Similar findings emerge from research concerning whether soldiers develop symptoms after combat. Most have no long-term consequences, while those who do tend to have had either a previous personal history, or a positive family history of psychiatric illness (Flach, 1990). Moreover, post-traumatic symptoms are associated with hereditary predispositions (True et al., 1993). Although community studies of PTSD in veterans point to some role for exposure to combat (Fontana & Rosenheck, 1994), the measures of trauma are retrospective accounts.

Unidimensional models of post-traumatic stress disorders focus only on the impact of stressors. They fail to take into account diatheses. Even the most traumatic experiences in adult life, such as concentration camps (Sigal & Weinfeld, 1989), did not lead to mental disorders in most of the survivors. If recent stressors do not predictably cause PTSD, then we must be more uncertain about the effects of stressors many years in the past.

Family dysfunction and adult psychopathology

Assessing the psychological sequelae of trauma is problematic. The nontraumatic factors in development present equally thorny difficulties. Researchers have tried to determine whether family dysfunction, since it affects the quality of a child's relations with its parents, produces adult psychopathology. However, the validity of this research is controversial.

The Parental Bonding Index (PBI), an instrument developed by the Australian psychiatrist Gordon Parker (1983), is probably the best known instrument measuring how adults perceive their childhood family environment. The PBI shows good concordance between siblings for descriptions of parental behavior. Abnormal scores on the PBI are associated with many mental disorders (Parker, 1983). The PBI, and a similar scale developed by Perris et al. (1980), the EMBU (an acronym of its Swedish name), derive their constructs from theories of child development. They define the tasks of parenting in terms of two basic dimensions: providing affection, and allowing autonomy (Rowe, 1981). The main problem is what these scales purport to measure, i.e., whether parents were loving or neglectful, and whether they encouraged autonomy, or were overprotective, is not just a matter of fact, but also a matter of perception.

What is remembered in adulthood about childhood experiences is a combination of reality and an interpretation of that reality. The way that we perceive our families is as much a function of cognitive schema, and therefore of personality, as of objective facts. This interpretation can be supported by a good deal of research. Nearly every measure of childhood environment that has been used in psychology contains a heritable component (Plomin & Bergeman, 1991). The explanation is that personality determines how we experience our relationships to our families, and personality itself is heritable.

In summary, associations between negative childhood experiences and adult psychopathology may or may not have a *causal* significance. The caveats include the unreliability of memory, the lack of predictable psychological effects from negative experiences, and the influence of personality traits on perceptions of these experiences.

Which psychological risk factors are associated with personality disorders?

We are now in a position to review empirical findings as to which negative childhood experiences are reported most frequently by patients with personality disorders. These risk factors include early separation or loss of parents, abnormal parenting, or traumatic experiences during childhood. All of these point to a common factor of family dysfunction.

Separation or loss

Early separation or loss is a common experience in patients with personality disorders. In a large sample of both males and females with various personality disorder diagnoses studied by the author and his colleagues, about half of them had lost a parent before age 16, and a quarter of them before age 5 (Paris et al., 1994a, 1994b). Since the subjects in this sample grew up prior to the "epidemic" of divorce in recent years, this rate is genuinely high.

Of course, divorce does not cause children to develop personality disorders as adults. Research has shown that the long-term effects of separation or loss from a parent during childhood depend on interactions with many other risk factors (Tennant, 1988; Rutter, 1989). A pathological outcome is most likely in the presence of multiple risks, which produce a cascade of negative experiences. It is also possible that family breakdown might have a different effect, not seen in normal populations, in those who are vulnerable to develop personality disorders for other reasons.

Abnormal parenting

Parental psychopathology

Abnormal parenting can be demonstrated in patients with personality disorders in a number of ways. The first is that many of these patients have had parents who themselves can be diagnosed with psychiatric illnesses. For example, the strongest risk factor for antisocial personality disorder is criminality in a parent (Robins, 1966). It has also been shown that the parents of patients with borderline personality disorder are more likely to have personality disorders themselves, as well as other chronic conditions, such as depression and substance abuse (Links et al., 1988b). Although these associations no doubt reflect common genetic vulnerabilities, it seems common-sensical to assume that living with a mentally ill parent is a stressor in its own right.

There might be a particular risk for children if one or both parents have a personality disorder. Unlike intermittent symptomatic disorders, personality pathology can have a continuous effect on parenting capacity. Long durations of exposure to any stressor are associated with more negative effects (Monroe & Simons, 1991). Direct studies of children provide additional evidence for the negative effect of having a parent with a personality disorder. In our own center (Weiss et al., submitted), we examined a high-risk sample of children whose mothers had been treated for personality disorders. Most of these children were quite symptomatic, more so if the maternal diagnosis was borderline personality.

Parent-child relationships

Another aspect of abnormal parenting involves the quality of parent-child relationships. Some clinicians (e.g., Adler, 1985) have hypothesized that adults with personality disorders have been emotionally neglected during their childhood. This possibility has been empirically investigated by giving patients with personality disorders instruments that retrospectively measure the quality of their parenting, such as the Parental Bonding Index.

This research shows that personality disordered patients, as compared to general clinical populations, more frequently report having had problems in bonding with their parents. The reported difficulties concern both lack of affection (neglect), and lack of autonomy (overcontrol) (Paris et al., 1991). These findings apply to patients with borderline personality (Paris & Frank, 1989; Zweig-Frank & Paris, 1991), but are generally applicable to personality disorders rather than to any specific category (Paris et al., 1994a, 1994b). Problems in parental bonding are not even specific to the personality disorders as a group, since they have also been reported for patients with various other psychiatric diagnoses (Parker, 1983).

Family structure

The quality of parenting can also be measured through the structural characteristics of families. The Family Environment Scale (FES) (Moos & Moos, 1986) is the best known self-report measure of family structure. The FES describes the cohesion and organization of the family, as well as other factors similar to those measured by the PBI, such as emotional expressiveness and the encouragement of independence. Studies using this instrument have found differences between diagnostic categories, in that patients with borderline personality disorder have low family cohesion (Ogata et al., 1990a; Feldman et al., 1995), while patients with dependent personality disorder have families with low emotional expression and overcontrol (Head et al., 1991). These findings might be explained by biological factors, such as common personality traits between parents and children, but there may be an etiological relationship between specific types of family experience and specific categories of personality disorder. (We will return to this issue in Chapters 9 and 10.)

Trauma

A large number of studies (Links et al., 1988a; Herman et al., 1989; Zanarini et al., 1989a; Brier & Zadli, 1989; Ogata et al., 1990b; Shearer et al., 1990; Ludolph et al., 1990; Westen et al., 1990; Byrne et al., 1990; Paris et al., 1994a, 1994b) have suggested that traumatic experiences, particularly sexual and physical abuse, are unusually common in borderline personality disorder. These associations have been interpreted as providing an explanation of the etiology of BPD, in that borderline personality could be a chronic form of post-traumatic stress disorder: a reaction to, and a reenactment of, these childhood experiences (Herman & van der Kolk, 1987; Herman, 1992).

Such claims, like most theories invoking single causes, are extremely attractive. The main problem in assessing their validity is that none of the studies on which these theories are based were prospective. Moreover, in some of the studies, conducted on patients in active therapy, the findings could have been contaminated by false memories, stimulated by therapists who *believe* that borderline personality disorder is caused by child abuse. The most serious problem, however, is that far-reaching etiological conclusions cannot be based on associations, which may or may not reflect causation. Interpreting the association between trauma and BPD as accounting for the etiology of the disorder flies in the face of community research, which shows that these experiences do not necessarily lead to psychopathology.

The diagnosis of a personality disorder has been considered somewhat pejorative. It is therefore tempting to promote a theory that views patients as having been shaped by events beyond their control, so as to conceptualize them as victims. The combination of this comforting shift of blame, and the charisma of a determined group of investigators who are personally convinced of a link between childhood abuse and personality disorder, has yielded a heady brew!

Our own research on this subject has led to a much more sober view of the matter. The associations between trauma and personality disorders demand a complex explanation. In a large-scale study carried out over a 4-year period by the author and Dr. Hallie Zweig-Frank, we examined a sample of 271 personality disordered patients of both sexes, half of whom were borderline, and half nonborderline (Paris et al., 1994a, 1994b). We took pains to minimize false memories by interviewing all subjects at length, and by excluding any reports that had emerged only in therapy, or under hypnosis.

In certain respects, our findings confirmed those of previous investigators. Thus, a large number of patients with borderline personality disorder reported childhood sexual abuse (70% of the females and 45% of the males). We used a personality disordered control group, which allowed us to determine that these experiences are not very specific to BPD, since they are far from uncommon in nonborderline personality disorders (45% of the females and 25% of the males). Our results concerning physical abuse by parents during childhood were similar, in that such experiences are more frequent in BPD, but common in personality disorders of all types.

The crucial finding of our research, however, was that patients reported *severe* abuse in only a distinct minority of cases. The range of reports of childhood sexual and physical abuse in our personality disordered patients resembles the spectrum of experiences found in community studies, with a wide variety of perpetrators. There were 15% of female patients, whether borderline or nonborderline, who reported father-daughter incest. This is indeed a high rate, about four times the prevalence in community populations (Finkelhor et al., 1990). However, most of our subjects who reported sexual abuse did not report incest with their fathers. The higher frequency of sexual abuse in the borderline group was attributable to perpetrators who were either relatives outside the nuclear family, i.e., uncles, cousins, or grandparents, or perpetrators not related to the patient.

Concerning the nature of sexual abuse, the reported experiences were identical in the BPD and non-BPD groups for most parameters, including frequency, duration, and age of onset. The vast majority of reports were for single incidents, which parallels the spectrum seen in community studies.

In both sexes, significant differences between the two diagnostic groups were related to severity. In females, a greater number of borderline than nonborderline patients reported sexual abuse with penetration (25% vs. 5%), and a significantly greater number of borderline than nonborderlines experienced abuse from multiple perpetrators (37% vs. 14%). In males, a significantly greater number of borderline than nonborderline patients reported both penetration (18% vs. 2%) and the use of force (44% vs. 25%). It should, nonetheless, be noted that all these differences derive from a minority of cases. Sexual abuse is indeed a risk factor for borderline personality disorder, but primarily in a subgroup with severe trauma.

We found that most of our personality disordered subjects, whether borderline or nonborderline, had also been exposed to other psychological risk factors, including family breakdown, parental psychopathology, and emotional neglect. Regression analyses showed, nevertheless, that sexual abuse, independent of other factors, discriminates borderline from nonborderline patients. This observation, which has been confirmed by Links and van Reekum (1993), suggests that once sexual abuse occurs, it sets into motion unique psychological mechanisms.

Nevertheless, the overall impact of trauma in our subjects cannot be understood without considering child abuse as one of many factors that, when taken together, involve cumulative effects. In community studies, the effects of sexual abuse can be partly accounted for by its correlation with family dysfunction (Nash et al., 1993). In addition, studies of pedophiles indicate that they choose children who seem lonely or vulnerable (Conte et al., 1989).

Herman and van der Kolk (1987) hypothesized that there are symptoms in adult patients that are "markers" for trauma during childhood. These authors attribute particular significance to the presence of symptoms of dissociation and self-mutilation. They propose that when children are traumatized and cannot escape from the traumatic situation, that they cope through dissociation, i.e., the splitting off of mental contents into separate compartments. They also hypothesize that when personality disordered patients self-mutilate, i.e., slash their wrists or otherwise injure themselves, that these actions function to counter painful aspects of dissociation.

Dissociation is also the characteristic feature of "multiple personality disorder", which has been claimed to be caused by childhood trauma. The significance of these reports depends, of course, as to whether there is really such a thing as multiple personality disorder, and whether the histories of abuse given by these patients are reliable. Higher levels of dissociation have also been reported in individuals with acute PTSD (Spiegel & Cardena, 1991). However, most of these patients have been Vietnam veterans with high rates of comorbidity for other psychiatric disorders (Young, in press) and particularly for personality disorders (Southwick et al., 1993). No community studies of veterans have examined the relationship of dissociation to trauma.

Nevertheless, the idea that there are symptomatic markers for trauma has had a wide influence. It has become quite common for clinicians with patients who dissociate to look for a trauma history and, if such histories are not obtainable, to search for repressed memories.

Dissociative symptoms have only recently become the subject of systematic scientific study (Kihlstrom et al., 1994). Yet, nearly 100 years ago, the French psychiatrist Pierre Janet (1907) developed a diathesis-stress theory of dissociation. Janet proposed that the tendency to dissociate was constitutional, but that stressful events were needed to bring on symptoms. In contrast, trauma theorists (Herman, 1992; Terr, 1991) have considered dissociation to be a defensive response that could occur in anyone exposed to extreme trauma.

The scientific evidence for the purported link between dissociation and trauma is a subject of dispute (Tillman et al., 1994). In our own research, when we examined dissociative symptoms in our sample of personality disordered patients, the findings supported the principles espoused by Janet. Dissociation and self-mutilation, although far more common in borderline than in other forms of personality disorder, had no relationship to a traumatic history above and beyond their frequency in borderline patients, either in our female sample

(Zweig-Frank et al., 1994a, 1994b), or in our male sample (Zweig-Frank et al., 1994c, 1994d). There have been findings elsewhere in the literature contrary to ours (e.g., Chu & Dill, 1990; Herman et al., 1989; van der Kolk et al., 1991), but these other studies did not take into account whether or not their patients met diagnostic criteria for BPD. Dissociative symptoms could be better markers for a borderline diagnosis than for any particular childhood experience.

The overall conclusions of our research on trauma in the personality disorders can be summarized as follows:

1. Histories of trauma are common in personality disorders.
2. Most reports of trauma involve incidents of low severity.
3. There is an association between childhood sexual abuse and borderline personality.
4. More severe trauma discriminates BPD from other categories of personality disorder.
5. Patients with histories of trauma are exposed to many other psychological risk factors.
6. There are no symptoms that can be used as markers for childhood trauma.
7. All associations between trauma and personality disorders are statistical, and may or may not have causal significance.

Our data did not, therefore, support the idea that traumatic experiences can be invoked in any simple way as an explanation for the development of personality disorders. If anything, our results point to the importance of taking into consideration the interactions between psychological factors and constitutional factors, most particularly personality traits.

Interactions between biological and psychological factors

There are several points of interaction between the psychological risk factors listed above and the biological factors discussed in the previous chapter.

First, it is unlikely that the effects of *any* of the psychological risks for the personality disorders are independent of biology.

Histories of separation or loss, of abnormal parenting, and of trauma can all reflect the presence of dysfunctional personality traits shared by parents and children. Impulsive parents are more likely to separate, more likely to be inadequate in parenting, and more likely to inflict trauma on children.

Second, children who are temperamentally more difficult are more likely to receive worse treatment from their parents (Rutter & Quinton, 1984). A difficult child can also make family dysfunction and breakdown more likely (Rutter, 1989).

Earlier longitudinal studies (Chess & Thomas, 1990) had shown that children with a "difficult" temperament are at somewhat greater risk for psychopathology as adults. These associations were weak, probably because, as pointed out by the authors, the outcome of an abnormal temperament depends on its "goodness of fit" with parental rearing practices. The children whom Chess and Thomas described as "difficult" required patient and consistent management, a principle applicable to many personality traits. As we will see in Chapter 9, children with an impulsive disposition need more limit-setting and structure, while, as will be discussed in Chapter 10, children with an anxious temperament need to be encouraged to overcome fear.

More recently, longitudinal follow-ups of children with extreme temperaments (Maziade et al., 1990; Kagan, 1994) have shown that temperamental abnormalities, in most cases, continue well into adolescence. Although these studies have not yet yielded findings on adult outcomes, they indicate that temperamental variability has a potentially profound effect on personality development. The most likely mechanism is that children with a "difficult" temperament are more difficult to calm down, and therefore more likely to come into conflict with their parents. These temperamental difficulties may be much more persistent when there is a poor fit between parent and child. Such children would be more likely, therefore, to suffer from the negative events in childhood so frequently reported by adults with personality disorders.

A third point is that the quality of life experiences is also a function of personality. Person-environment interactions strongly influence the degree to which life is stressful. Life experiences, including how many and what kind of negative events actually occur, have been shown to have a heritable component (Plomin, 1994). In other words, those who are most easily upset by life are also those who have the most negative things happen to them.

This principle has been supported by a great deal of research on adults. Kendler et al. (1993) and Plomin (1994) both report that monozygotic twins are more concordant for the frequency of stressful experiences than are dizygotic twins. The number of life experiences whose prevalence has been shown to have a heritable component is rather astonishing, and includes marital problems, divorce, friendships, social supports, problems at work, the use of drugs, as well as socioeconomic status and education.

In a large-scale Australian study, Poulton and Andrews (1992) found that the strongest predictor of negative interpersonal life events was Eysenck's dimension of neuroticism. It would be of interest to repeat this research on children, to see to what extent negative experiences during childhood are also a product of personality traits, rather than being simply due to ill fortune. In any case, the idea that measures of life stress reflect only environmental factors is misleading.

Personality traits make some children more sensitive to negative events, and others less sensitive. A great deal of evidence indicates that throughout life, even in the case of the most clear-cut environmental stressors, such as traumatic events, individual characteristics prior to the event determine whether symptoms develop (Flach, 1990).

The concept of "resilience" was developed to account for how children could grow up relatively normally in spite of having severe disadvantages (Werner & Smith, 1992). Resilience depends on biological factors, such as adaptive traits; psychological factors, such as positive experiences; and social factors, such as a favorable social environment. (We will return to this issue in Chapter 6.)

Purely psychological theories of the etiology of the personality disorders all suffer from the same fatal flaw: the failure to take into account person-environment interactions. Only the interactions of biological and psychological factors can account adequately for the role of childhood experiences in the development of personality pathology in adulthood.

What is not sufficiently emphasized in the literature is that all the psychological factors in the personality disorders are statistical risks. This means that even if they make the development of a disorder more likely, most of those exposed will either remain healthy, or develop a different illness.

In summary, the weakness of the associations between risks and disorders make sense in the light of two theoretical principles. The first is that psychological risks are most pathogenic when they interact with biological vulnerabilities. The psychological factors in the personality disorders can best be understood in the context of a diathesis-stress model, such that biological risk factors determine specific vulnerabilities, while psychological and social factors are the precipitants required for the development of diagnosable disorders. The psychological risk factors for personality disorders might consist of stressful events during childhood, but not necessarily single traumatic experiences. Although acute stressors do not always distort personality structure (Lazarus & Folkman, 1984), chronically stressful experiences have more impact (Monroe & Simons, 1991), with the greatest potential to amplify personality traits.

The second principle is that psychological protective factors, consisting of positive life experiences, buffer the effects of risk factors. Stressful experiences inside the family are buffered by extrafamilial attachments, which have been shown to protect children living with mentally ill parents (Kaufman et al., 1979), or children with severe psychosocial disadvantages (Clarke & Clarke, 1979; Werner & Smith, 1992). Psychopathological theories that focus exclusively on risk factors within the family underestimate the protective influence of factors outside the family.

This interpretation is supported by the findings of behavioral genetic studies, which point to the unshared environment as a determinant of personality. However, we must be cautious in generalizing from studies of normal personality to studies of psychopathology. It is possible that family dysfunction could be a more important factor in the development of personality disorders than it is for the development of traits.

Whatever the precise balance of risk factors and protective factors in the etiology of the personality disorders, the effects of psychological experiences on the individual have to be understood in a social context. This will be the subject of the next two chapters.

5

Social factors–methods

The present chapter is concerned with methods used to establish whether social factors are involved in the etiology of personality disorders. If the social context should prove to be crucial, important clinical implications would follow. Social factors might help explain why individuals exposed to similar psychological risk factors develop or do not develop personality disorders. The social context might also help explain why certain treatment strategies for personality disorders are effective, while others are not, and why some recover from personality disorders, while others do not.

The social context of mental disorders

Social psychiatry is concerned with the effects of social factors on the causes, course, and treatment of mental illness. However, the difficulty for empirical research in this area is that social risk factors for psychiatric disorders are difficult to measure. There is no practical way to conduct controlled experiments in which the role of social influences can be isolated from other etiological factors. Research in social psychiatry uses indirect methods, and its conclusions inevitably require some degree of inference.

The standard epidemiological methods for establishing etiological relationships are prospective follow-up studies or case-control studies. In prospective studies, general community populations, or populations at risk, are followed over a number of years to see which individuals develop a disorder. Case-control studies compare patients who have already developed an illness to those without the disorder for the presence of risk factors.

Both these methods are difficult to apply to social factors. The prospective method is ideal but is quite expensive. Moreover, prospective research is not always practical, since groups followed over time tend to suffer from attrition. In the case-control method, it is difficult to sort out precisely which factors account for any differences found between patient and nonpatient groups.

Social psychiatric research usually looks for differences in the prevalence of a diagnosis in different populations, and then infers from these differences what are the relevant risk factors for the disorder. The first step in such a process would be to determine the community prevalence of the diagnosis. The second step would be to show that prevalence levels vary with those indicators that are most probably related to social factors, such as demography, culture, or changes over time. If they do, one has presumptive evidence that suggests a role for social factors in the disorder.

Socioeconomic class

One of the best known findings in psychiatric epidemiology is the greater prevalence of major mental disorders in the lower socioeconomic classes (Dohrenwend & Dohrenwend, 1969). We could account for these social class differences in two contrasting ways. On the one hand, socioeconomic deprivation could be a risk factor for mental disorders. On the other hand, belonging to a lower socioeconomic class could be the consequence of having a mental disorder. These two possible explanations have been called "origin vs. drift" (Eaton, 1986). The direction of causality may depend on which disorder is being considered: in schizophrenia, the drift hypothesis best fits the evidence (Goldberg & Morrison, 1963), whereas in depression, there are data supporting the origin hypothesis (Brown & Harris, 1982).

Cross-cultural differences

The presence of cross-cultural differences in prevalence provides more convincing evidence for the role of social factors in mental disorders. Of course, even if there are strong differences in the prevalence of a disorder between one society and another, cross-cultural differences could reflect biological variability, rather than the social shaping of psychopathology. However, there are several reasons to be cautious about a biological explanation of cross-cultural differences. First, major mental disorders are found in all societies (Murphy, 1982a). This shows that the biological vulnerability for mental illness is widely distributed. Second, biological factors have been definitively shown to be associated with only a few psychiatric diagnoses. Third, differential prevalence can also be found between subcultural settings within the same society (Brown & Harris, 1978).

We can see the influence of culture most clearly in cases where the prevalence of a disorder has been low in a population, and then increases when its members emigrate to another society. An example is anorexia nervosa, which is rare in traditional societies, but common among emigrants from traditional to modern societies (DiNicola, 1990). Such findings, by controlling for biological factors, provide evidence for the social shaping of psychopathology.

Cohort effects

Changes in prevalence over time, or cohort effects, are the most powerful evidence for the presence of social factors in mental disorders. The increasing prevalence of a form of psychopathology, in the same population, and over a single generation, cannot be explained in any other way than by social change. Researchers have documented these cohort effects in several psychiatric disorders, particularly depression (Klerman & Weissman, 1989) and substance abuse (Robins & Regier, 1991).

Before examining research on social factors in the personality disorders, we will review findings on the major categories of psychiatric illness that have used the above methods.

Schizophrenia

Some of the best known research has been carried out on schizophrenia, which has been shown to be consistently more prevalent in lower socioeconomic groups. The weight of evidence suggests that this differential prevalence is due to drift, i.e., that schizophrenic patients move downwards in social class because of the social deterioration associated with their illness (Goldberg & Morrison, 1963). Cross-cultural studies have shown that schizophrenia exists in all cultures, although the severity of the disorder varies from one society to another (Murphy, 1982b; Cohen, 1992). The biological nature of schizophrenia is supported by the fact that there is no evidence that its prevalence is changing over time (Robins & Regier, 1991).

Depression

Mood disorders are more common in the lower socioeconomic classes (Brown & Harris, 1978), but depressive illness has a stronger psychosocial component in its etiology than does schizophrenia. Depression shows a notable difference in prevalence by gender, with rates two to three times higher among women (Weissman et al., 1986). It has been a matter of some controversy whether this difference reflects genetic differences between the sexes, the effects of hormones, or differential social risk factors among females (Engelsmann, 1982).

The interacting effects of gender, social class, and psychological experiences were examined in a well-known study of the risk factors for depression in working class women in Britain (Brown & Harris, 1978). Depression was associated with specific psychological risk factors, such as the early loss of a mother, and the lack of a confiding relationship in adult life. The Brown and Harris study demonstrated the importance of social factors in depression, as shown by higher rates among women in working class London, as compared to women living in a rural society (the Hebrides). These urban-rural differences in the prevalence of depression have also been consistently found in other settings, including the United States (Robins & Regier, 1991) and Canada (Kovess et al., 1987). In the Canadian study, increased rates of depression are concentrated in certain subgroups: unemployed males and single females living in large cities. This suggests that urbanization is a risk factor for depression.

The overall relation between urbanization and mental disorders is complex. There are no consistent differences between the prevalence of mental disorders as a whole in cities, as compared to the countryside (Srole & Fischer, 1980; Robins & Regier, 1991). Srole and Fischer (1980) called the tendency to idealize rural life "the myth of paradise lost". In fact, not all urban settings are pathogenic, nor are all rural settings good for mental health. In addition, there is a great deal of variability in the social integration of urban and rural life in different countries. For example, European cities, with their relatively stable populations, are different from Third World cities, where most of the population has recently emigrated from rural areas. In addition, for historical reasons, rural societies in Europe have been village based and tightly knit, whereas rural life in North America is characterized by the isolation of families.

Cross-cultural studies show that the clinical features of depression vary with culture. Guilt feelings and psychotic depression are more common in Northern Europe and North America, whereas shame, somatic presentations, and paranoid symptoms are predominant in the developing countries (Murphy, 1978; Kleinman & Good, 1985). Developing countries also vary between themselves in which symptoms are associated with depression (Engelsmann, 1982). These differences make it more difficult to carry out meaningful cross-cultural comparisons.

North American studies have found a rising prevalence of depression in the cohorts that have come of age in recent decades (Robins & Regier, 1989; Klerman & Weissman, 1989). These findings have been confirmed in a number of other countries, including Germany, Italy, France, Lebanon, Puerto Rico, Taiwan, and New Zealand (Cross-National Collaborative Group, 1992). The rate of suicide among the young has also increased dramatically in many Western countries, tripling in prevalence among North American youths between 1960 and 1980 (Sudak et al., 1984). These cohort effects are strong evidence that social change is affecting the prevalence of depression, and provide powerful support for the hypothesis that social factors play an important role in the etiology of mood disorders.

Alcoholism

Addiction to alcohol has a higher prevalence in the lower social classes (Robins & Regier, 1991). There is a striking gender difference, with male alcoholics outnumbering females by 4:1 (Helzer & Canino, 1992). There are also major cross-cultural differences in the prevalence of alcoholism (Helzer & Canino, 1992). In addition, the rate of alcohol abuse is increasing in North America (Robins & Regier, 1991). Alcoholism is a disorder that shows a great deal of sensitivity to social context.

Anorexia nervosa

Eating disorders are convincing examples of the role of social factors in mental disorders. As noted above, anorexia is generally unknown in developing countries, but is becoming increasingly common in more affluent countries, particularly among upper class women (Gordon, 1990). It therefore falls in a group of conditions that, unlike the major psychiatric disorders, occur only in certain cultures. Such syndromes have been called "culture-bound" (Prince & Tseng-Laroche, 1990). In the case of anorexia, social factors lead to the pursuit of thinness among young women (Gordon, 1990).

We will now consider how these methods for identifying social factors are applied to the personality disorders.

Epidemiology of the personality disorders

Epidemiological methods can be used to study personality disorders. Research into the prevalence of personality disorders in the general population shows that measures of whether an individual has *any* disorder is reasonably reliable, more so than for specific categories of disorder (Weissman, 1993). Since clinical diagnoses are more unreliable, psychometric instruments have been specifically designed to identify personality disorders. Earlier studies conducted prior to this development, both in North America (Leighton, 1959; Leighton et al., 1963; Langer & Michael, 1963) and in Scandinavia (reviewed in Weissman, 1993), had found an overall prevalence of between 6% and 10%. These rates may have been an underestimate, since later studies, using more precise instruments, found rates ranging between 10% and 13% (Weissman, 1993).

There has been less consensus on the prevalence of specific categories. This is primarily due to the problems with the validity of diagnosis discussed in Chapter 1. In the large-scale Epidemiological Catchment Area (ECA) study, carried out in several sites in the United States, only one personality disorder was considered, the antisocial type. This is because antisocial personality is the only disorder that has a clear-cut behavioral description, so that its criteria can be reliably identified in door-to-door surveys. The development of better criteria for personality disorders could be a stimulus for further epidemiological research (Weissman, 1993).

Before reviewing these findings, it would be worthwhile to examine the instruments used to diagnose specific categories. For large-scale epidemiological surveys, the most practical approach is self-report questionnaires. The validity of self-report in measuring "egosyntonic" personality pathology has been questioned (Perry, 1992). Two measures have been widely used in research: the Personality Disorder Questionnaire (PDQ) (Hyler et al., 1988), and the Millon Clinical Multiaxial Inventory (MCMI) (Millon, 1982, 1987, 1994). The PDQ is only a screening instrument, since it has few false-negatives for personality disorder, but many false-positives. The MCMI is much more sophisticated, and its concordance with diagnoses derived from structured interviews has increased with each of its revisions.

One might expect that the alternative method, structured interviews, would yield more valid diagnoses. The Diagnostic Interview Schedule (DIS), developed for the ECA study, only measures antisocial personality. There are four commonly used interview measures designed to diagnose all the Axis II disorders: the Structured Interview for DSM-III Personality Disorders (SIDP) (Zimmerman & Coryell, 1989), the Structured Clinical Interview for DSM-III-R Personality Disorders

(SCID-II) (Spitzer & Williams, 1986), the Personality Disorders Examination (Loranger et al., 1987) and the Diagnostic Interview for Personality Disorders (Zanarini et al., 1987). Unfortunately, these measures are not very concordant with each other (Perry, 1992). These difficulties are intrinsic to the limitations of categorical diagnosis. When there is no sharp cutoff between traits and disorders, clinical judgment becomes the ultimate determinant of when a patient is considered to have a diagnosable disorder.

In addition to research on disorders, there have been studies of the dimensional measures of personality in community populations (Eysenck, 1991; McCrae & Costa, 1986). We will discuss cross-cultural differences in the broader dimensions of personality in Chapter 6.

There have also been epidemiological studies of the narrower and more clinical dimensions of personality described in Chapter 2. A British community study (Casey & Tyrer, 1986) examined the prevalence of personality traits using the Personality Assessment Schedule (PAS), an instrument that has been shown to have cross-national validity between the United Kingdom and the United States (Tyrer et al., 1984). In Canada, Livesley et al. (1989) have carried out parallel community studies.

We have some preliminary data about the prevalence of the personality disorders. Community studies of the Axis II diagnoses in DSM have been conducted both in North America and in Europe. In North America, studies have used the PDQ (Reich et al., 1989), the PDQ, and the SIDP (Zimmerman & Coryell, 1989), or a structured clinical interview (Samuels et al., 1994). A European survey (Maier et al., 1992) was carried out using the SCID-II. In spite of the differences between these methods, the prevalence of the personality disorders as a whole was reasonably convergent, with rates ranging around 10%. These community surveys also examined the prevalence of specific personality disorders, but their findings were more discrepant, most probably because of differences between instruments.

Lifetime prevalence rates of personality disorders as a whole are consistent across age groups, with no differences in total prevalence between males and females, but with somewhat

higher rates in urban populations, and in lower socioeconomic groups (Weissman, 1993). These findings may not
apply to all the personality disorders in the same way.

Epidemiological research on the personality disorders is still
in an early stage of development. The basic method proposed
in this chapter for identifying social factors – the identification
of differential prevalence effects related to demographics, culture, and cohorts – has been systematically applied thus far
only to antisocial personality disorder. We need further research on the other categories.

While awaiting further data on prevalence, we need to develop hypotheses as to the mechanisms by which social factors
could influence the prevalence of the personality disorders.
This will be the subject of the next chapter.

6

Social factors – mechanisms

In the present chapter, we will suggest mechanisms by which social factors could either increase or decrease the risk for developing personality disorders. If the frequency of personality traits varies from one society to another, then the frequency of the disorders associated with these dimensions should vary accordingly. Therefore, in the first section, we will consider to what extent social factors can shape traits. In the second section, we will focus on mechanisms by which social factors could lower the thresholds for traits to develop into disorders.

We can only understand the influence of social factors, on either traits or disorders, in the context of social structures. Social scientists have many constructs to classify these structures, but at this point, we will introduce one basic distinction, which will pervade all the arguments to be made later.

Traditional and modern societies

Social structures can be dichotomized into "traditional" or "modern" types (Lerner, 1958; Inkeles & Smith, 1974). We can best understand this distinction from a historical perspective. Traditional societies are primarily characterized by slow rates of social change and by intergenerational continuity. Modern societies, in contrast, are characterized by rapid social change and by intergenerational discontinuity.

There are, of course, important differences between the traditions of all the societies that might be classified as "traditional". What we will argue here is that whatever the specific nature of traditions, they provide individuals with a set of predictable expectations. These expectations then form a structure. We will further hypothesize that these structures can buffer most forms of personality pathology. The breakdown of stable structures, and their replacement by less stable ones, as has been occurring in modern societies, creates conditions that can be termed rapid social change. We will argue that instability in the social fabric that results from these rapid changes is a risk factor for psychopathology in general, and for personality disorders in particular.

Although we will hypothesize that rapid social change is a risk factor for personality disorders, we will not, however, propose that all the risks for personality pathology are associated with modernity. The structures of traditional societies could also increase the frequency of certain types of pathology. These societies have less tolerance for deviance, and tend to "outgroup" individuals whose traits or behaviors fail to meet their expectations. Traditional societies provide relatively secure and predictable roles for every individual. But when conformity with the expectations of family and community is normative, social structures promote emotional inhibition and constriction. By contrast, modern societies demand a high level of autonomy. But when individuals are expected to create their own roles, social structures reward a more active and expressive personality style.

Social factors and personality traits

The dimensions of personality, as broadly defined, appear to be fairly universal. Cross-national studies using the three-factor model of Eysenck (1982), as well as the five-factor model (Costa & Widiger, 1994), have shown that the same personality traits can be found in all human societies. Lewis-Fernandez and Kleinman (1994) have criticized these studies for using Western categories and concepts to study non-Western societies. Nonetheless, this research offers empirical evidence for the universality of personality structure.

Eysenck (1982) found that variations in personality between individuals within a society are much greater than differences between one society and another. Although cross-cultural differences are relatively small, they have an order of magnitude of about half a standard deviation. For example, Iwawaki et al. (1977), in examining personality differences on the EPS between Japanese and English students, found that the Japanese students had higher neuroticism and introversion than did the British. These trait differences, if amplified, might lead to differences in the prevalence of specific personality disorders between the English and the Japanese.

Cross-cultural differences in personality admit of two explanations. The first is that they reflect biological differences between populations. Eysenck (1982) thought this the most likely explanation, supported by evidence of linkages between his personality dimensions and blood groupings. Kagan (1994) has also reported that Chinese infants are temperamentally quieter and more inhibited than those with Caucasian heredity. Shyness is also associated with Northern European physical features, such as blue eyes. It is possible that cultural factors in highly inbred groups lead to genetic selection for specific temperamental types (Durham, 1992).

An alternate explanation of these differences is that societies shape personality traits through behavioral expectations. Cultural anthropologists (e.g., Geertz, 1983) have strongly advocated the idea that culture shapes personality. The extent of this influence has probably been exaggerated. At one time, anthropologists (e.g., Benedict, 1938), as well as psychoanalysts (Erikson, 1950), thought that societies could shape personality to such an extent that each culture would be characterized by a modal personality structure. The empirical evidence from Eysenck's studies shows that this is not the case; there are wide individual variations in personality within all cultures, even if the frequency of traits varies from society to another.

Cultures value some forms of behavior more than others. By reinforcing or modeling different patterns of behavior, societies can reduce the frequency of traits that are contrary to social demands, and increase the frequency of traits that are in accordance with social expectations. Essentially, culture increases the level of social tolerance for some traits, and lowers the level of tolerance for other traits.

Several studies (reviewed in Weisz et al., 1993) have found consistent differences between the behavioral problems seen in children in traditional societies, as compared to modern societies. Children brought up in traditional social structures tend to suffer more from symptoms associated with overcontrol, while children raised in modern social structures are more likely to suffer from symptoms associated with undercontrol. These findings are consistent with the cross-cultural studies of Eysenck (1982), which found higher levels of extraversion and lower levels of neuroticism in Western societies.

Emotional expressiveness is a good example of a personality trait that demonstrates cultural variability (Leff, 1981). Family therapists working with different ethnic groups have consistently reported strong differences in how readily individuals communicated their feelings to others (McGoldrick et al., 1982). Families in traditional societies tend to encourage the repression of emotion more than those in modern societies (Murphy, 1982a). These differences reflect variations in how much societies value conformity to the group, as opposed to autonomy and individualism (Berry et al., 1992; Lewis-Fernandez & Kleinman, 1994).

In the past, the question of how strongly culture shapes personality had not been properly framed. Previous theories had often assumed that early childhood experience is the strongest determinant of personality, and that the mechanism of cultural influence therefore acts through child-rearing practices. The evidence from empirical research in support of these ideas is poor (Konner, 1987) and the associations between measures of child rearing and personality are inconsistent (Whiting & Edwards, 1988).

Contrary to previous received wisdom, extrafamilial factors are at least as important in the shaping of personality traits. Again, we must take into account the findings of behavioral genetic research, and the evidence that the "unshared environment" plays a crucial role in personality. This finding, discussed in Chapter 3, reflects, at least in part, the importance of socialization outside the family. Although culture affects family structures and child rearing practices (Whiting & Edwards, 1988), it also has profound effects on social learning outside the family.

The mechanism for this shaping of personality by culture would be social learning, involving the reinforcement and modeling of desired behaviors. The effects of social learning on personality traits could act in several mutually reinforcing ways. First, peer groups are important in the development of children (Rutter & Rutter, 1993). Second, children are influenced by authority figures in the community, particularly by teachers, as well as by the leaders of community organizations such as churches and ethnic associations (Rutter & Rutter, 1993). Third, the social context and community values influence personality development (Bronfenbrenner, 1979).

In summary, then, culture shapes personality. The Eysenck studies found cultural differences even for broadly defined personality dimensions, and there might have been many more differences if narrowly defined, clinical dimensions of personality had been measured. Also, even if cross-cultural differences in personality traits are small in normal populations, they could be greater in those subpopulations that are more vulnerable to personality disorders.

Social risk factors and social protective factors in the personality disorders

We will now propose a general theory describing mechanisms by which social factors could influence the development of personality disorders. In general, social risk factors are structures characterized by normlessness, and by a lack of useful social roles. Social protective factors are structures characterized by clear norms, and by adequate access to useful roles.

The risk factors, defined in this way, are more common in modern societies, while the protective factors are more common in traditional societies. The hypothesis of this chapter is that personality disorders as a group are somewhat less common in traditional societies. However, even if the overall prevalence of personality disorders were greater in societies characterized by modernity, one would still expect to see some degree of personality pathology in all societies. In the first place, there are traits, such as extreme levels of impulsivity or of social inhibition, which would be maladaptive in any society.

In the second place, individuals whose traits deviate too far from social norms are more likely to be rejected in traditional societies.

We will now describe the effects of social structure on the amplification from traits to disorders in terms of four specific mechanisms: (1) the interface of society with family structure; (2) cohort effects on psychological risk factors; (3) levels of social integration; and (4) rates of social change.

The interface of society and the family

One of the main ways by which social structures influence the risk for psychopathology is through effects on family functioning. First, social risk factors make family dysfunction more likely. Second, when family dysfunction is present, social risks further amplify their effects. Third, social protective factors buffer the effects of family dysfunction.

The evidence that family dysfunction is one of the major psychological risk factors implicated in the etiology of the personality disorders was reviewed in Chapter 4. However, families do not exist in isolation. It is entirely possible for families to be pathological in a well-functioning society. If that pathology is sufficiently severe, children growing up in that family will be more likely to develop mental disorders, but social buffering could protect against this possibility. Conversely, even in the most dysfunctional society, well-functioning families can raise healthy children. There would be an association with social factors for populations as a whole, but the quality of family functioning could still be a determining factor. (We will discuss the application of this principle to antisocial personality disorder in Chapter 9.)

The social factors that most affect family functioning are the availability of supports for members of the family. These supports include employment opportunities, extended family, and community membership (Leighton et al., 1963). The absence of these supports is associated with an increased frequency of many forms of psychopathology. For example, any breakdown in the social environment, such as unemployment (Eaton, 1986), or the breakdown of support networks in the community (Leighton et al., 1963), increases the prevalence of mental disorders. These associations might be accounted for, in part, by the loss of extrafamilial support systems that compromise the quality of life in nuclear families. When the family loses support, parents become more dysphoric, lowering the quality of their care, and their children are more at risk.

Lasch (1979a) has described the nuclear family in contemporary society as "a haven in a heartless world", or, alternatively, as "under siege". Modern families, as compared to families in traditional societies, are smaller and less stable.

Community studies show a strong relationship between family breakdown and the presence of a diagnosable mental disorder (Kramer et al., 1989). In addition to overt breakdown, modern nuclear families can more easily become overburdened. Geographical and social mobility uproots parents from their extended families, as well as from the larger community. The resulting lack of outside support makes family breakdown more pathogenic. Fisher (1992) has hypothesized that marriage may have been less stable in hunting-gathering as opposed to agricultural societies, but better support systems in the community would have buffered the effects on children of any marital disruption. Srole and Fischer (1980) suggested that one explanation for higher rates of psychopathology, as compared to urban populations, among those living in the rural areas of North America, was the greater isolation of these families.

Given the inevitability of conflict, even in the most functional families, it is, in many respects, fortunate that not all important relationships take place inside the nuclear family! This reflection brings us back to the question of resilience in children. Even in the most pathological environments, children will not necessarily develop mental disorders as adults. This is true of children growing up with a psychotic parent (Anthony & Cohler, 1979), and of children suffering the disadvantages associated with low socioeconomic status (Werner & Smith, 1992).

There are several possible explanations for these observations. One is that adaptive personality traits protect children against psychopathology. A second is that adult psychopathology depends on the severity of psychological risks: long-term consequences need not follow from most negative experiences. A third explanation of resilience is that while single risk factors can be more easily buffered, multiple insults are more likely to overwhelm defenses (Rutter, 1987a).

A fourth explanation, which is most relevant to the ideas in this chapter, is that the social environment buffers potentially damaging psychological experiences. Studies of "invulnerable" or "resilient" children point to social mechanisms that explain their relative lack of vulnerability (Kaufman et al., 1979; Werner & Smith, 1992). Resilient children recognize early on the pathology in their parents, and look elsewhere for attachments and models. In the larger society, there can be many potential opportunities for such alternate attachments, but social structures may determine how readily children can attain access to them.

Many important relationships outside the family protect children. Positive school experiences provide them with experiences of competence, as well as attachment to valued teachers. Good schools reduce the risk for delinquency (Rutter & Rutter, 1993). The same positive effects derive from other social structures, such as athletics and social clubs. These interfaces between attachments inside the family, and in the larger community, may be particularly important in contemporary social structures, in view of the changes in family structure that are occurring in every society, all over the world.

Cohort effects and psychological risk factors for personality disorders

Cohort effects in the frequency of mental disorders reflect social change, and are therefore the strongest evidence for the influence of social factors on psychopathology. The only personality disorder for which a cohort effect is firmly established is the antisocial category (Robins & Regier, 1991). There is also evidence, albeit indirect, for an increase in the prevalence of borderline personality (Millon, 1987, 1993; Paris, 1992). The other disorders have not been adequately studied. We do not know whether the prevalence of the personality disorders as a whole is changing. However, if the risk factors are becoming more frequent, then it is possible that many of the disorders associated with these risks could be increasing in prevalence.

There are two possible explanations for cohort effects on the prevalence of personality disorders. The first involves changes in the frequency of the psychological risk factors associated with them. The second involves changes in social structure. The latter possibility will be examined later in the chapter. At this point, we will examine whether there have been any changes in the prevalence of the psychological factors reviewed in Chapter 4.

Family breakdown

One risk factor stands out that has undergone a dramatic increase in frequency during the postwar era: family breakdown. In Western countries, about half of the children presently growing up in nuclear families will experience separation and divorce. This is a dramatic change that has occurred over only the last few decades, and it has also been accompanied by higher rates of illegitimacy (Riley, 1991).

Many factors mediate the long-term consequences of divorce for children, a good example of the principle that psychopathology develops only in the presence of multiple risks (Tennant, 1988). However, as discussed in Chapter 4, family breakdown is likely to initiate a cascade of other negative consequences, which then provide the requisite multiple risks. After divorce, the custodial parent is often economically worse off and the family more likely to become geographically uprooted (Riley, 1991). In addition, since the rate of divorce in second marriages is even higher than in first marriages (Riley, 1991), children of divorce may experience a second family breakdown. Finally, divorce is stressful for parents, making them psychologically less available to their children (Wallerstein, 1989), leading to relative emotional neglect, a risk factor in its own right for personality disorders.

Thus far the evidence for a consistent long-term psycho-pathological effect from the recent divorce epidemic is unclear. Twenty years ago, there was some tendency to minimize the effects of divorce on children, since it was assumed that parental conflict in an intact marriage could be at least as damaging as a parental separation. Some of the early research on divorce, which examined highly dysfunctional families, had pointed in this direction (Rutter, 1971). Rutter has often been quoted to support the idea that effects of divorce can be positive. However, Rutter (1993b), considering the mounting evidence that psychological complications follow from family dissolution, now states that "I have the right and the responsibility to say that I was wrong".

Different types of family breakdown have different effects on children. Divorces that occur in the presence of parental mental disorders, or in situations of family violence, have *relatively* positive outcomes, since children are relieved from being exposed to a traumatic environment. However, the majority of family breakdowns, which occur in the absence of either mental disorders or family violence, come as a disturbing and unpleasant surprise to children (Wallerstein, 1989). Whatever the parental conflicts had been, they were not necessarily apparent to most of the children in Wallerstein's cohort, who experience their intact family as positive, and the breakdown of the family as negative. Furthermore, one cannot make the bland assumption that if a divorce is positive for *parents*, that it is necessarily a useful or even neutral experience for *children*.

The best method of resolving these questions about the impact of divorce is to follow children from the time of parental separation to adulthood. These studies (Hetherington et al., 1985; Wallerstein, 1989) show that the most severe sequelae of divorce are short term, and that children tend to recover from the immediate effects. However, there is some intriguing but uncontrolled evidence that divorce has subtle but palpable long-term sequelae (Wallerstein, 1989). Although the absence of a control group limits the generalizability of Wallerstein's conclusions, her cohort had many difficulties during late adolescence and young adulthood. They were less likely to attain an educational level consonant with their economic background, found it more difficult to decide on a career, and had more problems in establishing stable relationships.

In our own center, we conducted a study that examined a subpopulation attending university, and who therefore had suffered less severe effects from parental separation. Even in this group, there were still measurable differences between children of divorce and children from intact families in their capacity for closeness and intimacy (Bolgar et al., 1995).

What research on the outcome of divorce has not addressed is whether family breakdown has a differential effect on biologically vulnerable populations. Most children of divorce are probably resilient enough to develop normally. This might not be the case for those with diatheses to mental disorders, such as extreme temperaments. Separation or loss may be more likely to lead to psychopathology in children who have trait vulnerabilities. These interactions between temperament and experience in the children of divorce have not yet been studied.

In summary, in looking for a psychological risk factor that could account for any cohort effects on the prevalence of personality disorders in modern society, the increased rate of family breakdown is the strongest candidate. Although we lack firm evidence at present to support this general hypothesis, there is an association between family breakdown and disorders in the impulsive cluster (see Chapter 9).

Family breakdown by itself is neither necessary nor sufficient for the development of personality disorders. Like all the other psychological variables reviewed in Chapter 4, it is not a cause, but a *risk factor* for psychopathology. This means that it could make the development of a personality disorder more likely, but that many individuals with such disorders will continue to come from intact families. It also means that the cumulative risk is probably only significant when combined with biological factors, with other psychological risks, and with the impact of social factors.

It is possible that research into the effects of divorce and single parenting may have been inhibited by the contemporary social climate, which is either tolerant of or favorable to divorce, and which assumes that traditional family structures are outmoded and can readily be replaced by alternate arrangements. The empirical literature reviewed above can be interpreted as supporting the idea that a two-parent nuclear family, whatever its inherent problems is, by and large, a better environment for children than other alternatives. The position taken here is that there is sufficient evidence for social psychiatrists to support the importance of "family values".

Emotional neglect

In theory, one could imagine two mechanisms that might lead to the increased emotional neglect of children in modern society. The first involves the uprooting of nuclear families; when parents receive less support, they might provide less care to their offspring. The second concerns social values; narcissism in parents might lead them to be less interested in their children.

There is, in fact, *no* evidence that children are receiving a lower quality of parenting in modern society. If anything, the historical evidence suggests that parents in the past probably had *less* interest in the lives of their children. One historian of the family (DeMause, 1974), reviewing quantitative data showing that children in premodern times were more frequently abandoned to foundling homes, concluded (paraphrasing James Joyce): "The history of childhood is a nightmare from which we have just begun to awake".

Trauma

Are traumatic experiences during childhood increasing in frequency in modern society? One might imagine, for example, that as the frequency of family breakdown increases, more children are being raised by step-parents, who are more likely than biological parents to be involved in either the sexual abuse (Browne & Finkelhor, 1986) or the physical abuse of children (Malinovsky-Rummell & Hansen, 1993).

Again, there is *no* evidence that child abuse is becoming more common. Empirical findings concerning the rates of childhood sexual abuse over time, such as an American national survey (Finkelhor et al., 1990), show that childhood sexual abuse was as frequent in women in their 60s as in women in their 20s. Finkelhor's group did find that sexual abuse was more common in women who grew up during the Second World War, when fathers were most often separated from children. However, in a national Canadian survey of childhood sexual abuse (Badgley, 1984), there were no cohort effects at all. On the whole, the evidence suggests that traumatic childhood experiences may be more *apparent* than they once were, but are no more common than they were 50 years ago.

Parental psychopathology

There is some evidence that some forms of parental psychopathology, including those associated with the development of personality disorders in children, are becoming more frequent. There have been marked cohort increases in both depression and substance abuse in recent decades (Robins & Regier, 1991). Parental depression leads to a higher risk of pathological sequelae in children (Downey & Coyne, 1990; Keitner & Miller, 1990), as does parental substance abuse (West & Prinz, 1987). Impulsive personality disorders are also increasing in prevalence, and, as will be shown in Chapter 9, when present in parents, they are strong risk factors for impulsive disorders in their children. There is direct evidence, derived from research in our own center (Weiss et al., submitted; Feldman et al., 1995), that children of parents with these disorders are highly symptomatic. Even if only some adults with depression, substance abuse, or impulsive personality disorders become parents, more children will be exposed to caretakers with significant psychopathology.

Since these disorders are more likely to be associated with family breakdown, cohort effects on psychological risk factors might involve interactions between a higher prevalence of parental psychopathology and an increased rate of parental separation. Nonetheless, even the presence of both these factors is insufficient by itself to produce a personality disorder. These risk factors would have their greatest effect on children who are already vulnerable by virtue of their personality traits. In addition, a pathological social environment amplifies the ef-

fects of psychological risk factors. We will now describe the
characteristics of such an environment.

Social integration and social disintegration

In a classical research project on the social factors in mental
disorders, "the Stirling County study", Leighton et al. (1963)
compared two Nova Scotia communities that varied in levels
of "social integration". One of these communities was relatively healthy, whereas the other demonstrated considerable
social pathology. The level of social integration in each setting
was measured by an index that was an amalgam of many factors, including broken homes, absence of social associations,
weak leadership, few patterns of recreation, frequent crime,
poverty, cultural confusion, secularization, migration, and social change.

The main finding of the study was that there was a higher
level of psychopathology in the more disintegrated of the two
communities. The authors hypothesized that sociocultural disintegration fosters psychiatric disorders by interfering with
physical security, by being more permissive in the expression
of sexual and aggressive impulses, by interfering with intimate
relationships and economic success, as well as with finding a
place in society, in a group, or in a moral order.

In many ways, the theoretical principles used in the Stirling
County study resemble those proposed by Durkheim (1951)
to account for changes in the prevalence of suicide. Durkheim
observed the varying rates in European societies over time,
and evolved a construct he called "anomie", or normlessness.
Similarly, the theory of social integration-disintegration predicts that societies that are more integrated, i.e., those with
clear norms, will protect individuals from psychopathology,
while in those characterized by social disintegration, psychopathology will be more likely.

The findings of the study supported this overall hypothesis.
The more socially disintegrated of the communities had
greater rates of mental disorder. There were methodological
limitations in this research, which prevent us from readily generalizing their results. By present standards the Stirling County

study was not quite rigorous in its methods and lacked a more precise measure of social disintegration. Given the fuzzy definitions of mental illness in use 30 years ago, it was not possible to study personality disorders separately. Nevertheless the concepts developed by Leighton's group represent a landmark in social psychiatry, and are relevant to contemporary phenomena.

Social disintegration is an organizing principle that helps to explain the effects of social factors on personality disorders. The mechanisms involve either the absence or the breakdown of the extrafamilial influences needed to buffer trait vulnerabilities and the effects of intrafamilial pathology. Those who are already vulnerable because of both personality traits and negative family experiences would be more susceptible to the effects of a pathological social environment.

This hypothesis might help to explain cohort effects on the prevalence of psychiatric diagnoses, and clinical symptoms. In North America, there has been an increase in phenomena associated with emotional dysregulation (depression, parasuicide, and completed suicide), and with impulsivity (substance abuse and criminality). Increases in emotional dysregulation could be due to the relative absence of secure attachments in contemporary society (Linehan, 1993), and a similar mechanism could lead to increased impulsivity (Paris, 1992). Siever and Davis (1991) have described these two dimensions as the core features of borderline personality disorder.

Anomie, which is a similar construct to social disintegration, helps account for variations in suicide rates. This association is well known, but several examples derived from research carried out in Canada illustrate the point. In a study of differential prevalence of suicide in Canadian provinces, Zakinofsy and Roberts (1987) found that the highest rates occurred in regions with the most economic development. This seeming paradox makes more sense if one considers that rapid development breaks down traditional values. Suicide was most frequent among those who were left behind by progress, i.e., the unemployed men. On the other hand, in more traditional societies, such as Newfoundland, the suicide rate remained low in spite of much higher levels of unemployment. In Québec, suicide rates are highest in mining communities, where people have few roots, and lowest in more traditional communities, where people have the strongest sense of cultural continuity (Charron, 1981). A recent study of the high suicide rates found in native populations, particularly in young males (Kirmayer, 1994), concluded that the causes lay with the breakdown of a traditional way of life, i.e., anomie. These results show that social disintegration leads to suicide in those who are unable to establish social roles and who lack social supports. These findings have been confirmed in societies all over the world (Jilek-Aall, 1988).

The breakdown of traditional social structures is often associated with family breakdown. Although the dissolution of families is one of the defining features of social disintegration, it is also a consequence of social pathology. When nuclear families are isolated from the community, there is less concern about whether families break up. Moreover, children from broken families, who might more readily find alternative attachments and models in an integrated society, would be less able to do so in a disintegrated society, in which they may either become socially isolated, or bond with pathological peer groups (Millon, 1993). These mechanisms might be more important for subcultural groups and in specific locations characterized by particularly high levels of social disintegration. Although there were few relationships between ethnicity and psychopathology in the Epidemiological Catchment Area study, the sites differed in the prevalence of diagnoses sensitive to social context, including antisocial personality disorder and substance abuse (Robins & Regier, 1991).

Rapid social change and personality disorders

Social disintegration is not a static concept. The breakdown of normative structures in society is more likely to occur under conditions of rapid social change. During the course of human history, most social structures have been "traditional", in that they have changed slowly and provided continuity across the generations. This type of society is historically normative, and is probably the most adaptive structure for most individuals.

Culture is itself an adaptive phenomenon. Anthropological theorists have proposed that, on the whole, there are biological advantages in relying on tradition rather than experiment in shaping social behavior (Boyd & Richerson, 1986). When social change is gradual, it is easier for individuals to adapt and to create new social roles. Culture normally changes in a gradual fashion, through quasi-evolutionary mechanisms (Dawkins, 1976; Durham, 1992).

"Modernity" describes those social and cultural conditions that characterize the twentieth century (Taylor, 1992). Modern societies have produced a number of progressive and valuable developments, particularly by offering a wider range of social opportunities. Most individuals have benefited from the greater availability of technology, as well as the freedom to develop new ideas. Women in particular have more options in modern society. Very few of us would consider living in any other type of social structure.

However, in the last 100 years, Western societies have experienced accelerating rates of social change, resulting in a breakdown in social norms (Westen, 1985). In the past, other societies have also undergone rapid evolution. What may be unique in modern society is a continuous *acceleration* of the rate of social change. Some historians (e.g., Johnson, 1992) date the emergence of modernity either to the French Revolution, or to the onset of the Industrial Revolution in the late eighteenth century. In the late nineteenth century, the German sociologist Tonnies (quoted in Lasch, 1991) hypothesized that there was a change in the structure of society, which he described as a shift from "gemeinschaft" (rewards based on group membership) to "gesellschaft" (rewards based on productivity). In the twentieth century the effects of modernity have become worldwide and are irreversibly changing traditional societies all over the globe (Inkeles & Smith, 1974). The concrete manifestations of this rapid transition from traditional to modern social structures involve smaller family size, high geographic and social mobility, and a fragmentation of social norms.

Rapid social change replaces predictable expectations with choices. In modern society, each individual has to create personal norms (Toffler, 1970). Contemporary historians have described the results of the breakdown of socially defined norms in contemporary North American society (Lasch, 1979a,b). The negative effects might be particularly important for young adults. When the rate of social change is sufficiently high, the norms for role performance that were valid for an older generation are no longer useful. Young people face a particularly stressful task, in having to forge a personal identity without being able to rely on models from the previous generation.

Empirical findings support the theory that stressful social environments can produce psychopathology in young adults. Recent increases in suicide (Sudak et al., 1984; Klerman, 1986) and in substance abuse (Rich et al., 1988) have affected mainly young males. Both suicide and substance abuse have increased even more strikingly among young men living in societies undergoing rapid acculturation (Jilek-Aall, 1988; Thorslund, 1990; Kirmayer, 1994). These findings point to the severe consequences when young adults cannot establish social roles.

In understanding the vulnerability of youth to "anomie", we might return to Erikson's (1950) concept that the developmental task of young adulthood is identity formation. In our society, young adults must develop a personal sense of self, as well as a unique direction to their lives. Young people have not always been required to form a personal identity. In fact, the idea that each generation must forge its identity is a new idea in social history. In traditional societies, the family and community, not the individual, would have been responsible for choices of work, partners, and community affiliations. In such societies, *not* allowing the young to choose their psychosocial roles ensures intergenerational continuity.

As with all the phenomena described in this chapter, defective identity formation would be associated with psychopathology only in vulnerable subpopulations. The basic hypothesis of this book is that the overall risk for personality disorders involves interactions between temperamental vulnerability, psychological risks, and social factors. In spite of rapid social change, most young adults successfully manage to develop both personal identity and social roles. The loss of intergenerational continuity is most stressful for young people with constitutional diatheses and negative psychological experiences.

The process of identity formation demands a high level of individuation and autonomy. These traits are not universal, and many individuals have temperamental characteristics that make them dependent on others. Attachment theory (Bowlby, 1969) predicts that the most autonomous individuals are those who have had more secure bonds in their families. Individuals with either temperamental diatheses that lead them to require stronger bonds, or who have lacked secure attachments in their families, will have the most difficulty in establishing their independence and their goals in life.

The problem of identity lies on an interface between society and the family. In order to develop a personal identity, young adults need family and social supports. Rapid social change makes the transmission of values from parents to children more difficult. In addition, the nuclear family is becoming highly unstable. The children of divorce are more likely to flounder during young adulthood due to a lack of a secure base for attachment and parental guidance (Wallerstein, 1989). The divorce epidemic is a reflection of a society that values individualism more than loyalty to the group, and which therefore sees dissolving a family as legitimate as long as it benefits the member who leaves.

Lasch's (1979b) description of contemporary society as "narcissistic" may not be far off the mark. Disintegrated or anomic societies are radically individualistic, and are therefore defective in providing a sense of meaning and belonging for their young. Modern society demands adaptation to a number of new challenges, including an increased life span, a decrease in family size, changes in family structure, new conditions of work, and ideological confusion (Westen, 1985).

One crucial caveat must be registered about these conclusions. In targeting aspects of modernity as risk factors, we must not idealize past societies, which had their own share of both social and family pathology (DeMause, 1974). Nor should we ignore the social tensions in existing traditional societies (Freeman, 1983; Edgerton, 1992). (Actually, it is no longer possible to find entirely traditional societies since, in most cases, their structures have not been able to cope with the powerful social forces behind modernity and are crumbling all over the world.) Every generation seems to believe that life was better in the past. There is a real danger of "cultural nostalgia", in which we imagine either the previous state of our own society, or that of other societies as "lost Edens". We must view the negative effects of modernization in the context of universal social tension and conflict.

There is, in fact, no reason to believe that the prevalence of mental disorders is greater in contemporary societies. The evidence rather suggests that social forces influence the *form* of distress (Al-Issa, 1982). For example, it is possible that symptoms formerly classified as "hysteria", which are decreasing in prevalence (Nandi et al., 1992), are being supplanted by personality pathology.

There is evidence from a study examining overall levels of mental health in New York City between the 1950s and 1970s, that the prevalence of psychiatric disorders decreased during this period (Srole & Fischer, 1980). The improvements primarily affected women. Social change can also be beneficial!

Modernization makes psychological development more difficult for some, but easier for others. Modern societies benefit those who can achieve a high level of autonomy, but there are many who are not able to cope with this expectation. These demands function as a social "selection pressure". Some benefit, the effects are neutral for the majority, but in a vulnerable minority, they lead to psychopathology.

Social risk factors and specific categories of personality disorder

Does social change increase the risk for all personality disorders, or does it have a specific effect that is more likely to lead to some disorders, but not others?

Chapter 3 developed the hypothesis that personality disorders develop out of discordances between trait variations and social expectations. The same traits could be maladaptive in different societies, depending on whether they have traditional or modern structure. Let us consider examples of the traits most closely linked to personality disorders.

Narcissism is defined as a grandiose concept of oneself, requiring constant external support and interfering with the perception of other people's needs (Gunderson et al., 1990). This constellation can lead to interpersonal difficulties, but is also associated with fierce ambition. When one reads clinical descriptions of narcissistic patients (e.g., Kohut, 1970, 1977; Kernberg, 1976), one has the impression that the population in therapy consists of successful people who feel empty about their accomplishments. Psychotherapists have been interested in narcissism, reflecting either a theoretical fad or a real increase in the frequency of narcissistic problems.

In many ways, modern society rewards narcissistic traits. It considers its most useful members to be those who become accomplished, not those who value their attachments. Since modern societies value individualism, the traits associated with high autonomy are considered pathological at a higher threshold, while traits that lead to dependence are considered pathological at a lower threshold. Low levels of impulsivity, such as moderate substance abuse or instability in intimate relationships, are not disruptive in the work environment, and will be tolerated. Compulsive traits are also bound to be valued, since individuals are expected to be in autonomous control of their environment. However, dependent traits, which involve difficulty in initiating autonomous decisions, are maladaptive in a society that values individualism. Similarly, avoidant or schizoid traits, which compromise autonomy by interfering with social networks, as well as in making contact with strangers, will also be maladaptive.

Traditional societies have an opposite response to many of the same traits. These societies value group cohesion above all, and they rein in those who are too individualistic or too narcissistic. In a traditional society, one is expected to show strong deference to elders in any decision process, and to be open with family members, but cautious with strangers. Such societies may therefore value dependence, which increases group cohesion, as well as avoidance, which makes it more likely that individuals will remain attached to their families. Even schizoid traits in traditional societies interfere less with work or with intimate relationships. As Meehl (1990) has suggested, traditional societies give schizoid individuals socially undemanding employment, and arrange their marriages. This social buffering makes it less likely that individuals with these traits will develop a personality disorder.

These considerations would not apply in quite the same way to every trait. As Chapter 9 will document, antisocial personality traits are maladaptive in any social structure, but are becoming more common in modern societies. The most likely explanation is that traditional societies have family and social structures that contain the impulsive personality traits that underlie this disorder, while modern societies lack these structures.

As long as traits remain adaptive, there is room in any society for variety. Stone (1993) has speculated that stable societies have an "ecological" balance among traits, whereas this balance of traits breaks down in rapidly changing societies. When a society undergoes a transition from tradition to modernity, the personality characteristics that had been adaptive rapidly become relatively maladaptive. Social and historical *transitions* are probably times of particular risk for the development of personality disorders.

The mechanisms proposed in this chapter are testable hypotheses, but the empirical evidence bearing on them is fragmentary. In the Epilogue, we will propose further research on social factors in the personality disorders.

7

A biopsychosocial model of the personality disorders

In the previous four chapters, we have separately considered the roles of biological, psychological, and social risk factors in the personality disorders. None of these factors are sufficient, by themselves, to explain why traits become amplified to disorders. The present chapter will therefore propose an integrated biopsychosocial theory of the etiology of personality disorders.

The proposed model will hypothesize that only the cumulative and interactive effects of many risk factors can explain how personality disorders develop. It will also consider the influence of protective factors, those biological, psychological, or social influences that make the development of disorders less likely.

Again, we must acknowledge that our data base concerning the etiology of personality disorders is preliminary. Therefore, the discussion here will necessarily be somewhat speculative. The proposed model should be considered primarily as a stimulus for further research.

Biological factors: the role of personality traits

Personality disorders are amplifications of personality traits. The relationship between traits and disorders is continuous. Trait profiles constitute the diatheses for personality disorders, and determine which specific types of disorder can develop in any individual.

Personality can be characterized by a large number of traits, some of which will be more adaptive, others less adaptive (Kagan, 1994). The biological risk factors for personality disorders would consist of an unusual intensity of less adaptive traits, unbuffered by the more adaptive traits. For example, emotional instability and impulsivity could, particularly in combination, be a risk factor for impulsive personality disorders; on the other hand, coexisting adaptive traits, such as persistence (Cloninger et al., 1993), might be protective against these disorders.

Personality traits derive from interactions between temperament and social learning. However, temperament sets limits on the influence of learning by shaping the types of experience to which individual are exposed. The early development and persistence of character traits is therefore best explained by biological factors. As an example, let us consider the dimension of extraversion-introversion. An introvert can never become an extravert, or vice versa. It is the *degree* of introversion or extraversion that is open to environmental influence.

As reviewed in Chapter 3, genetic factors account for about half the variance in traits, leaving another half for environmental influences. The influence of the environment derives from that portion that is unshared between children growing up in the same family. This explains why children develop their own personality, which is to a surprising degree, independent of parental input. It also accounts for the dramatic differences in personality characteristics between siblings raised in the same family (Dunn & Plomin, 1990). Children with different temperamental dispositions respond to the same parental behaviors in different ways. The social context outside the family also shapes personality, as shown by the well-documented effects of the media on children (Millon, 1993).

Actually, these findings will not surprise most parents. Even mental health professionals must have had the experience that, in spite of their best intentions, their children are simply not that malleable. The importance of temperament has been embodied in a witticism: "The mother of one child believes in the environment; the mother of two children believes in the genes".

Psychosocial factors: the pathways from traits to disorders

Psychosocial factors are important for the amplification of traits. However, since temperament sets limits on the behavioral repertoire of children, stressors do not usually elicit new behaviors. Rather, negative experiences of any kind amplify already existing behavioral patterns. An example is the well-established exaggeration of personality traits seen in adult patients with depression (Frances & Widiger, 1986). The process of amplification probably becomes stronger when stressors are chronic and enduring.

Many stressors could amplify traits, but the psychological risk factors for personality disorders all have in common family dysfunction and inadequate parental care. Effective parenting requires a high degree of flexibility and an accommodation of parental strategies to the individual temperaments of children, i.e., "goodness of fit". When parents apply inflexible strategies, based more on their own needs than those of their children, unwanted traits in children, far from disappearing, are likely to be exaggerated.

Social factors become particularly important when dysfunction in the family is associated with dysfunction in the community. Breakdown of extended family ties, absence of a sense of community, normlessness related to the loss of consensual values, difficulty in developing social roles, problems in choosing an occupation and a partner, and the fragility of social networks all constitute highly potent stressors. These effects are even more potent in individuals who are vulnerable by virtue of their trait profiles, and in those who also have dysfunctional families.

Let us consider, as an example, a dimension of personality that illustrates how all these factors might sufficiently amplify traits so as to cross the threshold to disorders. Extraversion is entirely adaptive under normal conditions; extraverted children are lively and social. In the presence of negative environmental factors, extraverts reach out to others for increased social contact. At some point, this trait could become exaggerated enough to become dysfunctional. For example, the child might demand to be the center of attention and show protest behaviors when attention is withdrawn. These traits, when they lead consistently to inappropriate behaviors, eventually produce negative responses. When these same behaviors are used in many contexts, and are associated with conflictual interactions, they begin to correspond to the diagnostic criteria for impulsive cluster personality disorders (such as the histrionic and narcissistic categories).

Introversion is also adaptive under normal conditions; introverted children can be quite self-sufficient. In the presence of negative environmental factors, the introverted child will tend to withdraw and seek greater protection from caretakers. When the environment is consistently negative, introversion can become pathological, and social contacts will take on the characteristics of "anxious attachment" (see Chapter 10). At a further level of amplification, these behaviors become clearly dysfunctional, and begin to approximate the criteria for personality disorders in the anxious cluster (such as the dependent and avoidant categories).

Social factors affect personality through similar mechanisms. Let us consider the fact, discussed in Chapter 6, that modern societies reward individualism. In traditional societies, where the norm is conformity to the larger social group, social anxiety and interpersonal dependence are relatively normative, and are not necessarily maladaptive, while narcissistic traits that threaten group cohesion are much more maladaptive. In modern societies, on the other hand, traits such as social anxiety and interpersonal dependence, which interfere with autonomous functioning, are relatively more maladaptive, while narcissistic traits, which tend to interfere with social networks, but not with autonomous task performance, are more adaptive.

Pathways to specific categories of personality disorders

Why do some individuals develop one category of personality disorder, while others develop a totally different category? The hypothesis of this book has been that genetically influenced personality traits determine the specificity of personality disorders. Biological variability would be the factor determining which type of disorder could develop in any individual, while psychological and social factors would affect the threshold at which these personality traits become maladaptive. This diathesis-stress model views psychological and social factors in the personality disorders as precipitating rather than causative.

Alternatively, there could be specific psychosocial risk factors related to specific disorders. Chapters 8, 9, and 10 will review the data with respect to each category. We will conclude that the evidence is suggestive but far from convincing.

There are several advantages to the first hypothesis. First, it is in accord with the overlap between the categories of personality disorder, since disorders based on similar personality dimensions could have biological factors in common. Second, it is consistent with research that demonstrates a continuous relationship between traits and disorders. Third, it provides the most parsimonious explanation of why specific etiological factors relate only weakly to any category of disorder, and why similar risk factors lead to different disorders.

Thus, personality disorders in the impulsive cluster would require the presence of preexisting impulsive personality traits. Disorders in the anxious cluster would require the presence of preexisting anxious traits. This is essentially the model proposed by Siever and Davis (1991), described in Chapters 2 and 3. The principle that disorders derive from underlying traits could apply to any other dimension of personality. For example, individuals characterized by extraversion would be more likely to develop disorders in the dramatic cluster, while those who are introverted would be less likely to develop these disorders. Conversely, disorders characterized by introversion, such as those in the odd and anxious clusters, would not develop in extraverts.

Interactions between risk factors

Let us now consider how the biological, psychological, and social factors in the personality disorders might interact. In Chapter 4, we described a number of interactions between biological and psychological risks. Some of these involve a feedback loop, in which abnormalities of temperament elicit negative parental behaviors. Others involve maladaptive personality traits that children and their parents have in common. Still others consist of the effects of personality on the quality of life experiences, and how these experiences affect the individual.

We also discussed interactions between psychological and social factors in Chapter 6. Some of these involve indirect effects, such as the failure of the social environment to buffer negative psychological experiences. Others involve direct effects, in which a disintegrated social environment presents difficulties individuals with well-functioning families can master, but which are beyond the capacity of individuals coming from dysfunctional families.

We discussed interactions between biological and social factors in Chapters 3 and 6. If personality traits are alternative evolutionary strategies, more or less adaptive, depending on environmental demands, then the same environment could be positive for some individuals, while being a risk factor for others. It is when traits are discordant with social expectations that the risk for a personality disorder is greatest.

Biological variability, by itself, leads to individual differences in traits, not to personality disorders. Psychological factors, by themselves, also do not necessarily lead to personality disorders. Social factors, by themselves, represent stressors that everyone must live with. We need a biopsychosocial model, incorporating the interactions between all three factors to explain the development of personality disorders.

A good example of these interactions is the phenomenon of resilience. One of the most striking facts in developmental psychology is that most individuals exposed to negative experiences do not develop psychopathology. Those who fail to become disordered in spite of severe risks have been described as "resilient" (Anthony & Cohler, 1987; Kaufman et al, 1979). As discussed in Chapter 6, the most likely explanations for this phenomenon are that resilience depends on adaptive personality traits, as well as on access to a buffering social environment.

How well does the model account for the clinical phenomena seen in personality disordered patients?

Chapter 1 described the essential characteristics of a personality disorder. The model presented in this chapter can account for many of these:

1. The phenomenology of personality disorders, i.e., the presence of a behavioral disturbance with a significant effect on functioning, represents the pathological amplification of traits.
2. The early onset of personality disorders is due to a combination of two factors:
    a. high intensities of personality traits associated with difficult temperamental characteristics
    b. The cumulative effects of multiple negative experiences during childhood.
3. The chronic course of personality disorders can be accounted for by a combination of two factors:
    a. The temporal stability of personality traits
    b. feedback effects, in which maladaptive behaviors lead to negative consequences, which then further amplify these traits.

In the next three chapters, we will apply this theory to specific categories of personality disorder.

8

The odd cluster

The previous chapter has proposed a general theory to account for the common factors in the development of any personality disorder, using a model that considers interactions of biological, psychological, and social factors. However, the risks for one type of disorder may not apply to another. We therefore need to examine each diagnostic category separately. Since some disorders have been researched extensively, while others have not been examined in any systematic way, we will allot more space to those about which some degree of empirical data is available.

As reviewed in Chapter 1, the categories of personality disorder described in DSM and ICD-10 have uncertain validity. They overlap with each other, probably due to shared personality dimensions. For this reason, it will be useful to consider them in groups. The next three chapters will review specific categories within the three clusters of disorders described by Axis II of DSM. In addition, we will examine each category separately, in relation to phenomenology, etiology, outcome, and treatment.

Phenomenology of the odd cluster disorders

The personality disorders in the A cluster (schizotypal, schizoid, and paranoid) are associated with unusual thoughts and behaviors, as well as with an inability to establish meaningful interpersonal relationships.

Schizotypal personality disorder

Both DSM and ICD describe a schizotypal disorder, characterized by eccentricity, social deficits, and cognitive distortions.

The DSM diagnosis of schizotypal personality disorder requires at least five of the following criteria: ideas of reference, odd beliefs or magical thinking, unusual perceptual experiences, odd thinking and speech, suspiciousness or paranoid ideation, inappropriate or constricted affect, eccentric behavior, lack of close friends, and excessive social anxiety. ICD-10 places a similarly defined condition, schizotypal disorder, among the functional psychoses. This difference in classification reflects differences in the interpretation of findings, to be discussed below, which link schizotypal disorder to schizophrenia.

Clinical example

A 37-year-old man presented to a psychiatric clinic to discuss his problems with his father's terminal illness. He was primarily interested in complaining about the medical staff looking after his father, about whom he had written copious notes, and which, in the course of the evaluation, he read from verbatim. The interviewer noted that the patient had a peculiar and eccentric manner, and that his verbal statements were both illogical and bombastic. He described feeling uncomfortable in the presence of strangers, and often thought that people in the street regarded him with hostility. He had no interest in social relationships outside his family, but had lived at home for a number of years under the protection of his parents, with whom he quarreled frequently. After the clinical evaluation, he asked for a copy of the report; when he received it, he sent back a letter explaining in some detail why it was inaccurate, accompanied by a photocopy of an article criticizing the validity of psychiatric diagnoses in general.

This patient functioned on a very low level, but did not perceive himself as in need of help. In the absence of frank delusions or hallucinations, there was no reason to recommend treatment. He continued to request further evaluations from time to time over the ensuing years.

Schizoid Personality Disorder

Both DSM and ICD differentiate schizotypal disorder from a milder condition called schizoid personality, characterized by social detachment and restricted emotions. The DSM definition requires at least four of the following criteria: no desire for close relationships, preference for solitary activities, little interest in sex, little pleasure in activities, lack of close friends, indifference to praise or criticism, and emotional coldness. ICD defines this condition similarly.

Clinical example

A 32-year-old statistician was brought to a psychiatric clinic by his brother, who was worried about his inability to have any relationships. The patient himself, although he agreed to be evaluated, did not share these concerns. He was content with his work, which involved spending long periods of time working on the computer. He had no interest in women, and his only social contacts were with his brother and sister-in-law. On examination, he was cooperative, and fully coherent in his ideas, although he made little eye contact with the interviewer. No treatment was recommended, although he was told that if he were to feel distressed in the future, the clinic was open to him.

Paranoid personality disorder

Both DSM and ICD describe paranoid personality disorder similarly, as characterized by suspiciousness in interpersonal relationships. The DSM definition requires the presence of at least four of the following criteria: suspicion of others, preoccupation with doubts about the trustworthiness of others, reluctance to confide, reading hidden meanings into benign events, bearing of grudges, tendency to feel attacked, and irrational sexual jealousy. The disorder is similarly defined in ICD.

Clinical example

A 25-year-old man was referred to a psychiatric clinic by his lawyer, in relation to an assault charge resulting from an altercation in a bar. The patient was very angry about having to be seen by psychiatrists, who he immediately stated are "more crazy than I am". He described, in great detail, how the argument had developed entirely from his being provoked. He had only been employed intermittently, due to his tendency, within a short period of time, to quarrel with his superiors. His relationships with women were also fleeting. The patient's lawyer was informed that the patient was not psychotic, and that the case should therefore be decided on its merits.

The schizophrenic spectrum

Kraepelin (1905) was one of the first to describe milder forms of the major functional psychoses, which could appear in the form of personality pathology. Schneider (1950) also thought that psychosis is one end of a spectrum of disorders, the milder forms of which could affect the personality alone. Bleuler's (1950) construct of "simple schizophrenia", i.e., the "primary symptoms" (thought disorder) without "secondary symptoms" (hallucinations and delusions), is close to the clinical picture of schizotypal disorder.

In North America the concept of a psychotic spectrum was concordant with psychodynamic theories that of which purported to account for mental disorders on psychological grounds. Menninger (1963) proposed that *all* psychopathology is on a spectrum, with psychoses being more severe forms of neuroses. Attempts to apply psychotherapy to psychotic patients were popular for a time, especially at private residential settings. This trend has since become a kind of historical curiosity. Follow-up studies of patients at one such hospital (McGlashan, 1984) found no evidence that psychotherapy influences in any way the outcome of the psychoses. These conclusions would have come as no surprise to earlier clinicians, who had defined an entity termed "pseudoneurotic schizophrenia" by its failure to respond to psychotherapy (Hoch et al., 1962). (This category, was later discarded because of its heterogeneity, and overlaps the present categories of borderline and schizotypal personality disorder.)

In the 1960s genetic research provided empirical support for the concept of a schizophrenia spectrum. These studies showed that concordance rates for schizophrenia were greater in monozygotic than in dizygotic twins, and that in those monozygotic twins who were discordant for the disorder, the unaffected twin had demonstrable "schizoid" traits (Rosenthal, 1971). Further research has shown that patients with schizotypal personality frequently have a positive family history for schizophrenia (Kendler et al., 1981; Siever et al., 1990), and that children born to schizophrenic mothers are more likely to develop either schizophrenia itself, or schizotypal disorder (Parnas et al., 1993).

A large body of literature, reviewed by Siever and Davis (1991), including genetic studies, as well as neuropsychological and neurochemical research, shows that patients with schizotypal personality disorder have biological vulnerabilities

similar to schizophrenia. Some of these common neuropsychological findings include abnormalities of attention and information processing, visual and auditory attention, and sen-
sory gating. The common neurochemical findings include
higher levels of homovanillic acid (an index of dopamine metabolism). These markers are related more strongly to the negative or deficit symptoms of schizophrenia (affective flatten-
ing, loss of volition, and illogical thinking) than to its positive
symptoms (hallucinations and delusions). In fact, the definition of schizotypal personality consists largely of negative
symptoms, but some patients also have positive symptoms
(Nestadt et al., 1994), and the category may be heterogenous
(Torgerson et al., 1993).

In view of all this evidence, the decision of ICD-10 to classify
schizotypal personality as a form of psychosis is logical. One
reason why the authors of DSM-IV did not recommend this
change may have been that *all* personality disorders have a
relationship with symptomatic diagnoses.

The status of schizoid personality disorder remains uncertain. There is a controversy about whether it belongs in the
"schizophrenic spectrum". The "schizoid" traits described by
earlier researchers really refer to schizotypal and not schizoid
personality disorder as presently defined. One recent study
(Fulton & Winokur, 1993) suggested that schizoid personality
may not be genetically related to schizophrenia at all. Moreover, there has been no evidence that schizoid patients have
either cognitive-perceptual abnormalities, or biological markers for psychosis.

The main characteristics of schizoid personality disorder
might best be understood as a severe degree of introversion
(Widiger et al., 1994). The schizoid category has been separated from another category associated with notable introversion, avoidant personality disorder, on the basis that schizoid
individuals do not really desire relationships, whereas avoidant
individuals desire intimacy but avoid contact due to their fear
of rejection (Millon, 1981). Although it is difficult to determine clinically that patients who avoid relationships do not in
fact desire them, this distinction is probably valid.

A particular problem in carrying out empirical studies of
schizoid personality disorder is its rarity in clinical settings

(Pfohl et al., 1986). The community studies quoted in Chapter 4 found in that this entity is found in between 0.5% and 1% of the population, so that there are probably more people with this disorder than clinicians see. Schizoid individuals may not suffer enough distress to seek help.

Some clinical observers (e.g., Swanson, 1970) have thought that paranoid personality disorder, characterized by suspiciousness in interpersonal relationships, has a relationship with more serious paranoid conditions, particularly delusional disorder and paranoid schizophrenia. This disorder has been shown in genetic studies to be linked to schizophrenia (Kendler et al., 1984; Fulton & Winokur, 1993) and to delusional disorder (Kendler et al., 1984). Like schizoid personality, paranoid personality is rare in clinical settings (Pfohl et al., 1986). Since these patients characteristically blame others for their troubles, they are less likely to seek treatment for themselves.

Risk factors for personality disorders in the odd cluster

Based on genetic, neurophysiological, and neuropsychological evidence, schizotypal personality disorder is the category with the strongest biological factors in its etiology. Genetic research suggests that paranoid personality disorder has a biological basis. The genetic factors involved in both these disorders might best be understood if they could potentially lead either to schizophrenia, or to a schizophrenic spectrum disorder, depending on their intensity.

The underlying genetic trait underlying schizophrenia spectrum disorders has been labeled "schizotaxia" (Meehl, 1962). According to Meehl's theory, schizotaxia would be a widely distributed trait, quite compatible with normality. Meehl used the term "schizotypy" to describe a more severe level of the same trait, which would be more likely to lead to psychopathology. Schizotypy could develop into schizophrenia itself, or into schizotypal personality, depending either on genetic loading or on environmental stressors.

We do not know the precise genetic mechanism by which the traits behind schizophrenia are transmitted. Most medical

illnesses have a pattern of inheritance consistent with polyge-
netic inheritance (Gottesman, 1991). Some combination of
genetic factors is required for clear-cut symptoms to develop,
and one would expect to see a spectrum of pathology.

The construct of a schizophrenia spectrum could also help
to explain why schizophrenia, a severe mental illness that reduces fertility, has remained common in the general population. Meehl (1990) has hypothesized that for every case of
schizophrenia there could be ten of schizotaxia. In principle,
individuals with schizotypal traits, which interfere with the ac-
quisition of social skills, should be less fertile. But traditional
societies do not expect individuals to select their own mates.
In order to protect genetic lines, families tend to make sure
that all young people reproduce. Thus, social structures in
traditional societies have developed such that the older generation chooses mates for the younger and arranged marriages are the rule. This could explain why individuals with
low social skills remain fertile, and why their genes remain in
the population. It is only when schizotypal traits are severe
enough to develop into a chronic psychosis at an early age
that reproduction becomes unlikely.

Modern societies, on the other hand, require young people
to find their own mates. As discussed in Chapter 6, this social
demand is a stressor for those who are genetically less well
endowed. We would therefore expect that schizotypy will reduce fertility in the long run, although it might take decades
to see a measurable effect.

Even for schizophrenia, genetics does not provide a full explanation of the pathways from traits to disorders. Half of MZ
twins are discordant for schizophrenia (Rosenthal, 1971), yet
we do not know what determines the emergence of positive
psychotic symptoms. Mednick et al (1988) have suggested that
there might be nongenetic biological risk factors, such as in-
trauterine viral infection and the events might also be a factor
in schizotypy (Bakan & Peterson, 1994). Thus far, there has
been no evidence for any specific psychosocial elements in the
etiology of schizophrenia (Gottesman, 1991).

Social factors in schizophrenia probably do not influence
its development, as much as play a role in its course. For example, the presence of stressful family events such as ''ex-

pressed emotion'' (negative input related to the illness) leads to more frequent relapses of the disorder, and this association has been shown to be robust in many cultures (Day et al., 1987).

There are cultural differences that affect the role functioning of schizophrenic patients. In a number of traditional societies (Murphy, 1982b; Cohen, 1992), the lifetime prevalence of schizophrenia is the same as in modern societies, but the outcome is less severe, with patients generally returning to their social roles after the acute symptoms had resolved. The illness could be less severe in traditional rural societies, where social demands are less discordant with the deficit symptoms than in an industrial or postindustrial society.

These observations on schizophrenic illness are relevant for disorders in the ''schizophrenic spectrum''. Social factors are important in determining the threshold at which, in Meehl's terms, schizotaxia becomes schizotypy. If society does not provide protective and buffering influences for those who have these traits, disorders become more common and more disabling.

In developed societies such as Japan (Nakao et al., 1992) and Canada (Paris et al., 1991), odd cluster diagnoses are associated with more impairment than other personality disorders. A likely explanation is that in modern societies, individuals do not readily find either employment or mates unless they have specific skills. These skills involve the ability to focus on a task, and the capacity to find intimate relationships. In traditional societies, nuclear and extended families would be protective for these individuals. Their families would at the very least make sure of their employment, and many of them have arranged marriages.

These hypotheses about social factors in the odd cluster disorders need to be tested by cross-cultural comparisons of their prevalence. If there are such differences, they would most likely be due to cultural factors. Social factors could determine whether individuals with these traits can find a place, however marginal, in society. Some of these individuals could require clinical attention in one society, yet not be definable as cases in another setting.

9

The impulsive cluster

Antisocial personality disorder

Phenomenology

Antisocial personality disorder (ASPD) has been an accepted category of mental illness for two centuries. The idea that there is a form of mental disorder characterized by callousness and criminality is probably universal in all cultures (Murphy, 1976). Many different terms – "moral insanity", "psychopathy", "sociopathy" – have been used in the past to describe its phenomenology. Although some writers (e.g., Blackburn, 1988) criticize the construct as a medicalization of "personal deviance", there is a broad consensus in psychiatry as to its validity.

Since the definitions of antisocial personality disorder in DSM-IV, or of dissocial personality disorder in ICD-10 are similar, we will use them interchangeably. Both systems use primarily behavioral criteria for diagnosis. The criteria in DSM require that there be a pervasive pattern of disregard and violation of the rights of others, as indicated by at least three of the following: criminal actions, deceitfulness, impulsivity, aggressiveness, recklessness, irresponsibility, and lack of remorse. This pattern must have begun before age 15, and be associated with a prior diagnosis of conduct disorder. (The symptoms of conduct disorder are essentially childhood versions of the phenomena seen in adult ASPD.) However, as shown in studies in the United States (Robins et al., 1991), in the United Kingdom (Zoccolillo et al., 1992), and in Australia (Rey et al., 1995) only one third of cases of conduct disorder go on to antisocial personality disorder. Therefore, the diagnosis of ASPD cannot be made until the patient is at least 18 years of age.

In order to diagnose ASPD in adults, consistent criminal behavior is a crucial criterion. It is therefore not surprising that from two thirds to three quarters of male prison populations meet the present definition (Hare, 1983; Côté & Hodgins, 1990). Since delinquency and criminality can readily be measured, they have been used as markers for ASPD in epidemiological research. Yet less than half of these patients in community samples have a criminal record; the most common features are violence, traffic offenses, and instability in work and marriage (Robins et al., 1991).

The older and broader construct of "psychopathy" placed more emphasis on personality characteristics that may accompany criminality, particularly manipulativeness and interpersonal exploitativeness (Cleckley, 1964). A group of researchers in Canada (Hare, 1993; Harpur et al., 1994) have argued that there are two factors in psychopathy, one describing criminality, and the other describing pathological interpersonal behavior. They criticize the present definition of ASPD for describing only the first of these two dimensions. When both factors are considered, only a minority of criminals meet diagnostic criteria for the disorder (Harpur et al., 1994). The present definition of ASPD has the advantage of being grounded in behavioral markers, but may be based too much on overt evidence of criminality.

Clinical example

A 22-year-old man presented to a psychiatric clinic on the advice of his lawyer. The charge against him was fraud. Since the evidence was unequivocal, the defense was prepared to account for his behavior on the basis of a mental disorder. Although he had been previously convicted in juvenile court, this was the first time he had been threatened with imprisonment. Records from a child psychiatric clinic, 10 years previously, indicated that he had been frequently truant from school, as well as unmanageable at home. During his adolescence, he had been involved in several forms of crime, beginning with burglaries and progressing to credit card theft. Over the last several years, he had been involved with a series of women. One of them bore him a child, after which he soon abandoned her. His evaluation interview was notable for a charming manner, and a lack of concern about his "life style", which he described by saying "these are the things you have to do to get by in the world".

Epidemiology

Its clear-cut behavioral criteria make it practical to examine ASPD in epidemiological research (Cadoret, 1986). It was the only personality disorder included in the well-known Epidemiological Catchment Area (ECA) study (Robins & Regier, 1991), which determined the prevalence of psychiatric disorders in a number of sites in America, as well as in a more recent large-scale epidemiological study (Kessler et al., 1994), using a sample from 48 American states. An instrument developed in the ECA study, the Diagnostic Interview Schedule (DIS), measures the presence of ASPD, and has also been used in populations in other parts of the world: Canada, Europe, New Zealand, Japan, Korea, and Taiwan.

The prevalence of ASPD is similar in several English-speaking countries: in two American studies, the ECA and the Kessler et al. study, it was, respectively, 2.4% and 3.5%; in a Canadian study (Bland et al., 1988), it was 3.7%; in a New Zealand study (Oakley-Browne et al., 1989), it was 3.1%.

The prevalence of ASPD is strongly correlated with demographic variables, such as age, gender, and socioeconomic status. North American studies (Robins et al., 1991; Kessler et al., 1994) found that antisocial behavior is far more common in youth, in males, and in lower socioeconomic classes. Studies that show that the symptoms of ASPD tend to "burn out" over time confirm this association with youth (see Chapter 11). The association with male gender is very consistent, the disorder being five to seven times more common in men than in women. The association with lower socioeconomic status is also consistent, and there is a strong negative relationship to education.

ASPD does not show differential prevalence by race, nor have researchers found differences between ethnic groups living in the same city. The ECA study reported an increased prevalence in urban as opposed to rural sites, and one city (St. Louis) had a particularly high rate of ASPD. Kessler's group did not confirm urban-rural differences, but found that ASPD was more common in the Western states, regional differences that might be due to the migration of antisocial individuals, or to the effects of social factors.

Although ASPD is recognized and found in all societies (Murphy, 1976; Robins, 1978), there are important cross-cultural differences in its prevalence. These differences are sufficiently striking that they are unlikely to be due to problems in the translation of instruments. These differences provide strong evidence for the role of social factors in ASPD.

The most important evidence comes from East Asia. Samples from urban and rural areas of Taiwan (Hwu et al., 1989; Compton et al., 1991) found an unusually *low* prevalence of ASPD, ranging from 0.03% to 0.14%. There are some reasons to believe that these low rates might also apply to mainland China (Cheung, 1991), although no systematic studies have been carried out there. In a primary care setting in Japan (Sato & Takeichi, 1993), ASPD was also very rare.

A low prevalence of ASPD is not, however, universal in East Asian societies. In South Korea, where alcoholism is also frequent, there is a high prevalence of ASPD (Lee et al., 1987). The prevalence of ASPD is not low in the less socially integrated setting of Hong Kong (Chen et al., 1993). The disorder may have a different prevalence in societies with seemingly similar cultures. For example, Cooke (1994) reported low rates of psychopathy in forensic populations in Scotland.

The second important line of epidemiological evidence pointing to social factors in ASPD is that the disorder is increasing in prevalence in North America. The ECA study estimated that the lifetime prevalence of ASPD in the United States has nearly doubled among young people in 15 years, results later confirmed by Kessler's group. Rapid increases in prevalence of mental disorders over short periods of time can, with few exceptions, only be accounted for by changes in the social environment.

Etiology

Biological factors

There is consistent evidence that biological factors are involved in criminality. Criminal behavior runs in families (Rutter & Madge, 1976), which could be due to either genetic or environmental effects. However, twin studies have shown MZ-DZ differences in concordance for criminality (Cloninger et al., 1978). Adoption studies show that criminality in a biological parent is a risk factor for criminality in a child (Mednick et al., 1984; Crowe, 1974). Biological markers may also be associated with criminality (Raine et al., 1995)

There are problems with these findings. Criminality can be confounded with the effects of alcoholism, which has a stronger genetic component (Bohman et al., 1982). In addition, criminality itself is heterogeneous. For example, in a study of Swedish adoptees (Cloninger et al., 1982), which focused on "petty criminality" (more characteristic of ASPD than of violent crime), there was a small genetic effect, with substantial environmental risk factors.

We do not know whether biological factors carry great weight in antisocial personality disorder. There have been no twin studies determining concordances for this diagnosis. There have been, however, reports suggesting the presence of biological markers in patients with ASPD. The most consistent findings are neuropsychological differences (Sutker et al., 1993). Antisocial individuals fail to develop conditioned responses to stimuli related to fear (Hare, 1983; Mednick & Moffit, 1985). These systematic observations concord with clinical reports that antisocial patients have a lack of normal fearfulness, and an inability to learn from negative experiences (Cleckley, 1964). These findings are consistent with a theory developed by Eysenck (1977), that reduced conditionability is the diathesis for antisocial behavior. There are conditions under which fearlessness can be adaptive, and antisocial individuals in the military may function well in combat, but not in peacetime (Yochelson & Samenow, 1976).

Kagan (1994) has labeled the constitutional factor in antisocial personality as "uninhibited temperament", in contrast to the behavioral inhibition seen in individuals with anxious traits. Farrington (1991) concluded that an inhibited temperament is a protective factor *against* criminality. This temperamental variation would not be sufficient by itself to cause criminality, but might be a necessary precondition for its development. In Chapter 10 we will examine the implications of the converse trait, an inhibited temperament. In contrast, uninhibited temperament, with inordinate lack of fear in social situations, is associated with a decreased fear of punishment (Kagan, 1994).

Studies of the personality dimensions of antisocial patients have demonstrated high scores on "psychoticism" and extraversion in Eysenck's schema (Eysenck, 1977); low neuroticism, low agreeableness, and low conscientiousness in the five-factor model (Widiger et al., 1994); as well as high scores on novelty seeking, low scores on reward dependence, and low scores on harm avoidance in Cloninger's schema (Cloninger, 1987). Since all these dimensions of personality have a genetic component, these findings may reflect, indirectly, temperamental factors behind ASPD.

Siever and Davis (1991), whose neurobiological theory of the personality disorder was reviewed in Chapters 2 and 3, have proposed that ASPD could be associated with a combination of impulsivity (modulated by low levels of serotonin) and increased behavioral activation (modulated by high levels of monoamines). Although there have been no specific studies to support this hypothesis, men with a trait defined as "impulsive aggression" have unusually sluggish central serotonin activity (Coccaro et al., 1989).

Another possible biological factor might involve comorbidity between ASPD and attention deficit hyperactive disorder (ADHD). Long-term follow-ups of hyperactive children show that about a third of ADHD cases develop significant criminality (Weiss & Hechtman, 1992; West & Farrington, 1973). However, hyperactivity is only a risk for ASPD when combined with conduct disorder (Rutter, 1993a).

The strong gender difference in the prevalence of ASPD also implicates biological factors. There are several possible explanations for this difference. One is that the genetic factors in antisocial personality have different effects in males and females (Sigvardsson et al., 1982). The higher rate in males might be due to greater aggressivity, since levels of physical aggression are the most consistent gender difference between male and female children (Maccoby & Jacklin, 1974). Female patients with the same temperament might develop either a different personality disorder in the impulsive cluster, or other symptoms entirely. Pedigree studies (Winokur et al., 1969) have found that the female relatives of probands with ASPD have a higher rate of either depression or "hysteria".

Psychological factors
The classical study describing the risk factors for ASPD is a large-scale prospective study carried out in St. Louis, Missouri,

by Lee Robins (1966). The research tested the hypothesis that specific symptoms in childhood are the precursors of ASPD. Over 500 children seen at a child guidance clinic were followed as adults. One of the principal findings was that *only* those children whose delinquency had begun prior to adolescence could be diagnosed later as "sociopathic". This observation has been confirmed in a British study (West & Farrington, 1973).

We do not understand why some children with conduct disorder go on to develop ASPD, and others do not. However, Robins has provided us with important information about the risk factors.

In two thirds of the families of children who later developed sociopathy, both parents had psychiatric or behavioral problems. The most frequent and most important of these problems, and the one that also accounted for most of other risks, was antisocial behavior in the *father*. There was also a higher frequency of antisocial behavior in the mother, and more parental alcoholism.

These findings might reflect genetic factors common to antisocial parents and their antisocial offspring. However, given the uncertain degree of heritability in ASPD, it is probable that having an antisocial parent is a strong environmental risk factor for children. One should not be surprised, for example, to find that family dysfunction is associated with being raised by an antisocial parent. Traumatic experiences might be more common in children growing up in such families. Although physical abuse from parents was not a risk factor for ASPD in the Robins study, in research conducted in Scandinavia, Pollock et al. (1990) found that, in conjunction with parental alcoholism, it was the strongest antecedent of adult antisocial behavior.

Another important finding in the Robins study was that the family structure of children who developed ASPD leads to the failure of parents to discipline and supervise their children. Again, this was later confirmed in a British study (West & Farrington, 1973). Parental discord made no independent contribution to the risk when pathology in the father was taken into account. However, separation or loss of a parent was an independent risk factor. Only one third of ASPD cases were raised by two parents, an unusual rate at the time when the children were originally assessed (70 years ago). There was also a positive relationship between sociopathy and large family size.

Other studies examining risks for delinquency and crime present a similar picture. For example, in a prospective study conducted in the Boston area (McCord, 1978), the most powerful predictor of delinquency was parental instability, while the presence of a relationship to a stable and affectionate parent was a strong protective factor. In a British prospective study (West & Farrington, 1973), the risk factors were low family income, large family size, parental criminality, low intelligence, and lack of discipline and control from parents.

These findings again point to family dysfunction as the most important psychological risk factor for ASPD. The most likely mechanism by which dysfunctional families promote psychopathy is through a decreased frequency or inconsistency of punishment, with an absence of clear consequences and limits for children's behavior (Kagan, 1994)

Social factors

Cross-cultural differences in prevalence, as well as the recent increase in the prevalence of ASPD in North America, point to a crucial role for social pathology in this disorder. What is the mechanism for the effects of social factors? Chapter 6 suggested that social structures affect prevalence by lowering or raising the threshold at which other risks influence the development of disorders. The East Asian cultures with low prevalence must be strongly protective *against* antisocial personality, probably through interfaces between culture and family structure. The low rates in Taiwan could be due to high levels of cohesion in traditional Chinese families. Such families have characteristics that present a veritable mirror image of the risk factors for ASPD: fathers are strong and authoritative, expectations of children are high, and family loyalty is prized. (In the Robins study, there was a particularly low rate of ASPD found in Jewish subjects, which she attributed to their strong family structures.) Of course, highly traditional families have their own difficulties, and their repressive style could make children susceptible to other forms of personality disorder (see Chapter 10). However, children raised with clear boundaries and limits are at low risk for ASPD.

Contrary to popular opinion, poverty does *not* explain the prevalence of antisocial personality disorder. Robins found no relationship between lower socioeconomic status and sociopathy, independent of criminality in the father. Poverty is not related to crime when families are functioning well. As Vaillant and Vaillant (1981) found in a long-term follow-up of an inner-city sample, most people raised in poverty work hard to make their lives better, and *never* turn to crime. This conclusion is supported by another finding from the Robins study, that membership in gangs was only a risk factor for children who already came from dysfunctional families.

The greatest increase in the prevalence of both criminality and ASPD in the West since the Second World War has taken place in the face of unprecedented prosperity (Rutter & Rutter, 1993). It is probably family dysfunction, acting as a mediating factor for social influences, that is most responsible for the increasing prevalence of ASPD.

The vulnerability to ASPD is probably much more widely distributed than antisocial behavior itself. Underlying impulsive traits do not attain dysfunctional proportions if they are "contained" by a strong family and by social structures. Overt antisocial behavior will only emerge in the presence of family dysfunction and social disintegration.

Outcome and treatment

Antisocial patients usually improve over time and are less likely to show criminal behavior past middle age (Chapter 11 will review this research). Longitudinal research on defense styles during adulthood documents reductions in impulsivity in many types of character structures (Vaillant, 1977). The explanation could be, in part, biological, since there is continuous brain maturation during adulthood, which might also be associated with changes in levels of specific neurotransmitters. Improvements in neurochemical balances, particularly related to the serotonergic system, might decrease impulsivity. A second explanation of the "burnout" of ASPD could be psychological. However slow they are to learn from experience, antisocial individuals can gradually undergo some degree of social learning.

Of any personality disorder, the treatment of ASPD offers the most pessimistic prospects for success. Attempts to treat antisocial patients have generally involved either individual and group psychotherapies, or the creation of artificial environments in the form of "therapeutic communities". However, there is no evidence that any of these methods has any lasting effects.

Writing 20 years ago, Yochelson and Samenow (1976) reviewed a wide literature on the treatment of these patients. These authors had become involved with the treatment of these cases at a time when large numbers of psychopaths were being admitted to a Washington, DC psychiatric hospital, under a widened insanity defense. Combining their own discouraging experiences in therapy with those of more formal clinical trials, they concluded that ASPD is, in the majority of cases, untreatable.

No convincing data have emerged since then to modify this judgment (Robins et al., 1991). Although devoted clinicians in forensic settings continue to apply clinical skills to psychopathic inmates, there have been no convincing clinical trials showing that any method of therapy is consistently effective for this population (Dolan & Coid, 1993). There might, however, be exceptions among certain subgroups. Woody et al. (1985) found that antisocial patients who *also* meet criteria for a clinical diagnosis of depression can be approachable in outpatient therapy. These results define a small subpopulation at the less severe end of the antisocial continuum, but are not generalizable to typical cases of ASPD. Although 5% of patients with ASPD eventually complete suicide (Robins, 1966), often in prison, when their ability to carry out impulse actions is blocked, major depression is not generally comorbid with psychopathy.

Antisocial individuals rarely ask to change their behavior. If anything, they usually demand that society change. This is the main reason why the treatment prospects for these patients are bleak.

Borderline personality disorder

Phenomenology

Borderline personality disorder (BPD) has suffered from a misleading name, as well as from its reputation as an obscure derivative of psychoanalytic theory. Stern (1938) was the first to describe borderline patients, thought to be functioning on a "border" between neurosis and psychosis. "Borderline" was a poorly chosen name. If one does not subscribe to the idea that all mental illness is on a continuum, the label is meaningless. An alternative and more descriptive term, "unstable personality disorder", had been suggested for use in DSM-III. This label, similar to that presently used in ICD-10, would most certainly have been an improvement. However, the editors of DSM concluded that it was best to keep a term recognizable to American psychiatrists (Spitzer et al., 1979). The borderline diagnosis remains more popular in America than in Europe. Its usefulness has not been apparent to most British psychiatrists (Tyrer & Stein, 1993), and its popularity across the Atlantic is largely viewed with "bemusement" in the United Kingdom (Tyrer, 1988).

In order to be a researchable diagnosis, borderline personality disorder had to be operationally defined. A group at McLean Hospital in Massachusetts (Gunderson & Singer, 1975) pioneered this approach, and in the ensuing years, BPD became the subject of an extensive empirical literature (Paris, 1994). For example, the Diagnostic Interview for Borderlines, either in its original form (Gunderson & Kolb, 1978), or in a revised version (Zanarini et al., 1989b), uses observable criteria, which yield a reliable diagnosis, distinct from either depression, schizophrenia, or the other personality disorders. Diagnoses of BPD can also be made using structured interviews based on DSM diagnostic criteria, such as the SCID-II (Spitzer and Williams, 1986), or by interviews that have cross-cultural validity, such as the International Personality Disorder Examination (Loranger et al., 1994).

Although borderline personality has not generally found favor outside North America and Scandinavia, Kroll et al. (1982) found that patients who meet research criteria for the diag-

nosis are quite common in British hospitals. They are identified by other diagnostic labels, such as "explosive", "hysterical", "immature", and "inadequate" personality disorders.
BPD was also the most frequent personality disorder diagnosis
made among clinical populations in the international study by
Loranger et al. (1994). Research on BPD in Japan (Moriya et
al., 1993; Ikuta et al., 1994) showed that the essential features
of the disorder are present in Japanese patients, but, because
of Japanese culture, relationships demonstrate more dependency than in comparison groups of borderline patients in
America.

The definition of borderline personality in DSM-IV requires
the presence of at least five of the following nine criteria: fran-
tic efforts to avoid abandonment, intense but unstable relationships, identity disturbance, impulsivity, recurrent suicidal
behavior, affective instability, chronic emptiness, inappropriate
anger, and transient paranoid ideation or dissociative symptoms. (The ICD definition of emotionally unstable personality
disorder, borderline subtype, is quite similar.)

Clinical example

An 18-year-old high school student presented for treatment after the
death by suicide of her best friend. The friend, who had been treated
for borderline personality disorder at the same clinic, had suggested a
suicide pact with the patient. After she refused, the friend proceeded to
jump off a bridge. The relationship between these two women was
intense to the point of "symbiosis". The patient was also suicidal, with
recurrent episodes of wrist slashing and several nonfatal overdoses of
medication. She also had significant micropsychotic symptoms, in
particular, the intense fantasy that her life was a dream, and that she
was living on another planet, where she had another existence and a
real family. She would hear the voices of individual characters in this
fantasy speaking to her and asking her to join them. In spite of these
symptoms, she was a lively, bright, and articulate young woman who
had many friends and who was obtaining high marks in her studies.

Critics of the construct of borderline personality (e.g., Clarkin et al., 1983) have pointed out that patients with this diagnosis are heterogeneous. Some have suggested alternate
ways of categorizing them. In Chapter 4, we examined and
rejected one such proposal, that BPD be reclassified as a

chronic form of post-traumatic stress disorder. Akiskal et al. (1983) suggested that borderline personality is related to mood disorders, and should be called "subaffective dysthymia". Gunderson and Phillips (1991) rejected this interpretation, pointing out that all the personality disorders are comorbid with depression, that there are no biological markers associated with personality disorders independent of this comorbidity, and that the treatment of patients with personality disorders with antidepressants has not been successful. Another suggestion, put forward by advocates of the five-factor model of personality, is that BPD is best characterized by extreme levels of "neuroticism" (Costa & Widiger, 1994). The problem with this interpretation is that there are also high levels of neuroticism present in other, phenomenologically distinct, personality disorders (Zweig-Frank & Paris, in press).

Siever and Davis (1991) hypothesize that the clinical dimensions that underlie BPD are impulsivity and affective instability. These core dimensions describe readily observable phenomena: impulsivity, characterized by parasuicidal behavior, self-mutilation, substance abuse, and unstable interpersonal relationships; affective instability, characterized by rapid mood changes.

The most typical symptom of BPD is probably recurrent parasuicide. Psychiatrists in emergency rooms are familiar with patients who present with either overdoses, or wrist slashing, usually after a disappointment in a relationship. These patients may often be diagnosed as depressed. However, the abnormal mood in BPD is unlike the stable depression seen in classical mood disorders. On the contrary, the mood is highly reactive and responsive to environmental factors (Gunderson & Phillips, 1991). Another important aspect of the comorbidity of BPD is that borderline patients (as well as antisocial patients) are frequently found among clinical populations treated for substance abuse (Krantzler et al., 1994).

The gender distribution of BPD is a mirror image of ASPD, with about 80% of cases occurring in females. Borderline and antisocial patients differ phenomenologically, in that the antisocial patient has low emotional responsiveness and a lack of concern or ruthlessness in interpersonal relationships; while the borderline patient is impulsive but emotionally hyperreactive, with an overconcern about the reactions of other people, and a tendency to turn against the self (Benjamin, 1993).

These clinical presentations might reflect differential effects of the same traits in men and women. If these two disorders share a common biological vulnerability, their different behavioral expressions could be due to gender, involving hormonal factors, as well as differences in socialization. Alternatively, phenomenological differences could reflect two biologically distinct disorders. Siever and Davis (1991) have suggested that these ASPD and BPD differ in levels of neurotransmitter activity, particularly in relation to the greater affective instability seen in borderline patients.

Borderline psychopathology is too complex to be accounted for by our present state of knowledge in the neurosciences. An additional complication is that BPD is also associated with cognitive-perceptual disturbances, such as pseudohallucinations, transitory paranoid ideation, and dissociation. These symptoms can differentiate BPD from the other personality disorders (Zanarini et al., 1989b, 1893c, 1990), and have therefore been included in the revised criteria for the disorder in DSM-IV.

There have been several reasons for the strong interest of researchers in BPD. First, the disorder is associated with a high degree of morbidity and functional impairment (Nakao et al., 1992; Paris et al., 1991). Second, these patients present particularly difficult clinical problems (Gunderson, 1984). Third, as Chapter 11 will discuss, BPD carries a high risk of suicide (Paris, 1993). In order to develop treatment strategies for these patients, we need to know more about the etiology of the disorder.

Etiology

Biological factors

The biological factors in BPD remain essentially unknown. There is no evidence for a specific genetic factor linked to the disorder. Twin studies, albeit in small samples, have found that most monozygotes with BPD are nonconcordant (Torgersen, 1984). There have been no adoption studies of borderline pathology. There are no biological markers specific to the disorder. Although borderline patients with traits of impulsive aggression have sluggish serotonin metabolism (Coccaro et al., 1989), there is no specific correlate for affective or behavioral instability. Nevertheless, it seems unlikely that, in the absence of underlying trait vulnerabilities, environmental influences alone could produce a disorder as disabling as BPD.

Psychological factors

As reviewed in Chapter 4, cross-sectional retrospective studies point to a number of psychological factors in BPD. The risks most specific to the disorder are traumatic experiences, such as childhood sexual and physical abuse (Links et al., 1988a; Herman et al., 1989; Zanarini et al., 1989a; Ogata et al., 1990a; Paris et al., 1994a, 1994b). These factors are nonetheless frequent, albeit less so, in other personality disorders. Other risks, including early separation or loss from parents, parental psychopathology, parental neglect, and low family cohesion are equally prevalent in other categories of disorder (Paris, 1994).

Clinical theories have attempted to account for borderline pathology on the basis of one or another of these factors, particularly child abuse (Herman & van der Kolk, 1987) or emotional neglect (Adler, 1985). As discussed in Chapter 4, our own study of risk factors in BPD (Paris et al., 1994a, 1994b) led to much more conservative conclusions. Only a subgroup of borderline patients had childhood sexual abuse with parameters indicating severe trauma. Since many patients with the same risk factors do not have BPD, and since many borderline patients lack these risk factors, no psychological factor by itself seems to account for the development of the disorder.

It is noteworthy that several of the risk factors for BPD (physical abuse, early separation or loss from parents, parental psychopathology, parental neglect, and low family cohesion) are also common in ASPD. This provides further support for the hypothesis that ASPD and BPD represent gender-linked variants of the same biological vulnerability and/or of the same psychological risk factors.

Social factors

The social risk factors in BPD have not been the subject of specific research studies, nor has the prevalence of this disorder been precisely determined. Data drawn from North American studies, one using an adaptation of the interview used in the ECA study, the Diagnostic Interview Schedule (Swartz et al., 1990), and one using a self-report instrument, the Personality Disorder Questionnaire (Reich, 1989), suggest that the community prevalence of borderline personality is probably around 2%. Unlike ASPD, the prevalence of BPD does not seem to vary with social class (Swartz et al., 1990).

Loranger et al. (1994) found that clinicians can diagnose BPD in patient populations in cultures around the world. However, since these studies involved tertiary care settings in large urban centers, they are probably not representative of community prevalence. It would not be surprising if, as has been found for ASPD, there are wide variations from one society to another. One line of evidence that supports this conjecture is that some of the characteristic behaviors associated with this diagnosis, most particularly repetitive parasuicide, are much more common in modern than in traditional societies (Paris, 1992).

Indirect but converging evidence suggests that BPD is increasing in prevalence in North America. This conclusion is not based on studies of this diagnosis, but on increases in its most common behavioral symptoms. One line of evidence involves completed suicide among young people. There has been a dramatic increase in the youth suicide rate in North America over the last 30 years (Sudak et al., 1984). Using a method called "psychological autopsy", about a third of these suicides can be retrospectively diagnosed as BPD (Rich & Runeson, 1992; Lesage et al., 1994). Since substance abuse among the young is associated with parasuicide and suicide (Rich et al., 1988), cohort changes in the prevalence of substance abuse (Robins & Regier, 1991) might also be accompanied by increases in the prevalence of BPD.

Both completed suicide and serious substance abuse are more common in males, while BPD is most common in females. There is evidence that parasuicide, a symptom seen most frequently in females, began to increase in prevalence around the same time as rates of youth suicide and substance abuse (Weissman, 1967). (This finding is nearly 30 years old, and needs to be updated.)

In Chapter 6 we addressed the question as to whether any of the psychological risk factors for the personality disorders are becoming more prevalent. The evidence showed that the risk factor most strongly associated with BPD, child abuse, is not becoming more frequent. The two factors that *are* becoming more common, separation or loss of parents, and psychopathology in parents, are not specific to any particular personality disorder.

Nonetheless, BPD could reflect, in some respects, the problems of modernity. Borderline personality primarily affects young people and involves serious problems in identity formation. Its risk factors implicate dysfunctional families, and modern social structures may not adequately buffer the negative effects of growing up in such families.

Millon (1987, 1993) has developed the most comprehensive model of the role of social factors in borderline psychopathology. Applying social learning theory, Millon argues that the anomie that characterizes contemporary society is having a particularly negative effect on youth. In his view, the breakdown of social norms is creating an increased risk for borderline psychopathology. He further hypothesizes that rapid social change interferes with the intergenerational transmission of values and reduces the influence of the extended family and community. (Millon's model is very similar to ideas presented in Chapter 6.)

Outcome and treatment

The outcome of BPD resembles that of ASPD. The symptoms of the disorder tend to "burn out" in middle age (McGlashan, 1986a; Paris et al., 1987, 1988, 1989; Stone, 1990). (Chapter 11 will review this research in more detail.) The mechanisms for change over time might be similar to those hypothesized above for ASPD: biological maturation and gradual social learning.

Like antisocial personality disorder, BPD tends to be resistant to usual forms of psychiatric treatment (Paris, 1993,

1994). As Chapter 11 will discuss in greater detail, the results for pharmacotherapy in these patients have been thus far rather unimpressive, while traditional psychotherapies are also largely unsuccessful. Recent clinical trials of cognitive-behavioral therapy are more encouraging, but offer only partial relief for these challenging patients (Linehan, 1993).

Histrionic personality disorder

Histrionic personality disorder (HPD) is a personality pattern characterized by dramatic communication, an impressionistic cognitive style, and the sexualization of relationships. The DSM definition requires at least five of the following criteria: a need to be the center of attention, inappropriate sexualization, shallow emotions, use of physical appearance to draw attention, impressionistic speech, theatricality, suggestibility, and a tendency to exaggerate the quality of intimacy in relationships. (The ICD definition is similar.)

Clinical example
A 20-year-old university student presented to a psychiatric clinic after the breakup of a relationship with a boyfriend. She described a flamboyant life style, and made it clear she could attract any man she pleased. However severe her distress, she would always be "dressed to the nines". Her demeanor in reporting her problems involved describing her encounters with men in a humorous, contemptuous way. Although she experienced distress, associated with the instability of her intimate relationships, she attributed her difficulties to the inadequacy of her partners, rather than to her own behavior.

The histrionic category has been neither as precisely defined nor as systematically researched as have been ASPD and BPD. In the most careful epidemiological study of HPD, Nestadt et al. (1990) found that this disorder affects about 2% of the population; is, contrary to common belief, equally common in males and females; is most frequent before age 25; and is associated with a frequent history of separation or divorce.

In contrast to the community, in clinical populations, this diagnosis is most frequently made in women (Chodoff, 1982).

Halleck (1967) suggested that gender shapes this behavior, in that histrionic personality patterns can develop in women who are not able to directly express aggression, and who utilize a dependent role to create bonds that ultimately control others. Lerner (1974) hypothesized that histrionic personality is a caricature of the classical image of femininity, and may reflect the social reinforcement of childlike behavior in women.

There is some evidence that histrionic traits are heritable, at least in females (Torgersen, 1980). However, psychosocial factors are probably much more important for the development of a diagnosable disorder (Blacker & Tupin, 1991). Given the increased influence of feminism, one might expect that as women are encouraged to express their feelings in different ways, there will be a decrease in its prevalence. (There has been a waning in the frequency of conversion symptoms in some Third World societies (Nandi et al., 1992), but there is no correspondence between "hysterical" symptoms and HPD.)

HPD is associated with a relatively higher level of functioning than either ASPD or BPD (Nakao et al., 1992). There have been no studies that have examined cohort effects or the influence of social class and culture on the prevalence of histrionic personality disorder. There has been no systematic research on the risk factors associated with this diagnosis. There has been no research on the outcome of the disorder, or on the specific efficacy of treatment methods for histrionic patients.

Narcissistic personality disorder

Narcissistic personality disorder (NPD) is characterized by a grandiose concept of the self and by an exploitative relationship to others. The construct resembles Hare's (1980) second factor in psychopathy. Psychoanalysts (e.g., Kohut, 1970, 1977; Kernberg, 1976) have written a great deal about NPD. There are probably two reasons for this interest. First, patients seeking analysis often present with these kinds of problems. Second, narcissistic patients are, paradoxically, resistant to change in dynamic psychotherapy.

The DSM definition requires the presence of at least five of the following criteria: grandiosity, preoccupation with fantasies of success, feeling of being special, requirement for admiration. (NPD is not listed in ICD-10.)

Clinical example

A 30-year-old professional man presented for treatment because of his inability to establish an intimate relationship. Although he had many love affairs, he found that every woman in his life was inadequate. He spent a good deal of time fantasizing about the "perfect woman", and in many ways he preferred pornography to encounters with real partners. He was successful in his field, but obsessed with attaining great wealth, whatever the personal cost. When his strategies, whether in love or in work, failed to obtain success, he responded with rage or withdrawal. It was not readily apparent to him that his expectations of life were unreasonable.

Narcissism is a recognizable personality trait. Livesley et al. (1993) found that it reflects genetic influence. However, it is not clear that extreme levels on this dimension comprise a recognizable disorder. In epidemiological studies reviewed by Weissman (1993), narcissistic personality disorder had a low prevalence ($< 0.5\%$). Reports of the long-term functional outcome of NPD (McGlashan & Heinssen, 1989; Plakun, 1991) have described hospitalized cases and are hardly representative of the narcissistic patient in outpatient therapy. One short-term study (Ronningstam et al., 1995) suggests that grandiosity is not always a stable feature of this disorder. It remains unclear to what extent NPD is a useful diagnosis, since its clinical tradition has been restricted to the psychoanalytic literature, and since it lacks a research base.

Gunderson et al. (1990) have attempted to make NPD more valid by developing a semistructured diagnostic interview for this diagnosis, similar to the one developed by his group for BPD. Raskin and Terry (1988) have also developed a self-report instrument for the same purpose. In spite of these efforts, the definition of NPD remains fuzzy. This may explain why it has not been accepted into ICD. At present, although lacking in validity, it seems to be of some clinical value in describing patients, and an example of its therapy will be presented in Chapter 12. However, the problems with this diagnosis need to be resolved before we can study its risk factors.

As with ASPD and BPD, histrionic and narcissistic personality disorders have certain characteristics in common. Clinicians make the diagnosis of histrionic personality more often in females and narcissistic personality more often in males (Golomn et al., 1995). Yet these categories describe similar behaviors: attention-seeking, and dependence on environmental reinforcers.

The phenomenon of narcissism has been an object of concern for social theorists. Some writers (e.g., Lasch, 1979b) have even suggested that pathological narcissism characterizes the modern era. Kohut (1977) hypothesized that narcissistic traits were becoming more common in the modern world due to changes in family structure, such that children undergo less repression of their emotions, and feel more "entitled". Millon (1981) offered a related theory, hypothesizing that narcissism is related to the modern trend for parents to overvalue children, as opposed to criticizing their behavior.

Family structure and impulsive personality disorders

Impulsivity could be associated with specific forms of family dysfunction. The research findings reviewed above indicate that the family structures associated with both ASPD and BPD involve low cohesion and a failure to establish clear boundaries and limits. Such families are more likely to expose children to both trauma and neglect. A reversed pattern, in which families are excessively cohesive and suppress either conflicts or negative emotions in their children, may be associated with anxious personality traits.

Beavers (1977) has classified these contrasting family styles into a "centrifugal" type, in which parents push children into premature autonomy, and a "centripetal" type, in which parents resist separation and encourage dependency. In empirical research designed to test these hypotheses (Beavers & Hampson, 1990), it was found that family style, in interaction with measures of family competence, was a powerful predictor of psychopathology in children. The "centrifugal" type is associated with both impulsivity and with lower family competence. Chapter 10 will address the pathology found in centripetal families.

As discussed in Chapter 6, "centrifugal" family structures are becoming more common in modern society. These trends might be even stronger among subcultures characterized by high levels of social disintegration. Differences in family structure, if further amplified by social factors outside the family, might help account for the reported cross-cultural differences in the prevalence of antisocial personality.

Social factors in impulsive personality disorders

As proposed in Chapter 6, differences in social expectations between traditional and modern societies selectively reinforce the development of personality traits. Social learning within the family, associated with certain structural characteristics, can help shape personality. Some forms of family structure are more prevalent in some cultures than in others. The highly cohesive families of Taiwan and Japan stand in dramatic contrast to the less cohesive families of North America.

It is a researchable question as to whether these differences have affected the prevalence of impulsive cluster personality disorders. Cohesive families appear to be protective against antisocial personality and are more common in parts of the world where antisocial personality has a low prevalence, whereas less cohesive families, which are a risk factor for antisocial personality, are much more common in those parts of the world where the prevalence of ASPD is increasing. Even though East Asian cultures, like most other societies, are also undergoing rapid changes, high family cohesion is a protective factor against the effects of rapid social change.

A second factor is social learning outside the family. Highly cohesive families should be more common in societies characterized by high cohesion. This appears to be the case in both Taiwan (Hwu et al., 1989) and Japan (Doi, 1973). The transmission of norms and values, strongly reinforced in many different social settings, is an important protective factor against impulsive personality disorders. On the other hand, a culture with few agreed norms would not provide such protection.

A third factor is social disintegration itself, which is associated with the breakdown of structures in the family and in the community. In the absence of these structures, the effects of family breakdown are not buffered, and their negative effects are amplified.

None of these social factors would lead to impulsivity on their own. They would have their most potent effects on individuals who are temperamentally inclined to act on their impulses. It is worth noting that the findings of the Robins study applied to children who *already* had impulsive behaviors. None of the risk factors she identified need lead to antisocial personality in populations not otherwise at risk.

Similarly, Linehan (1993) has hypothesized that children who later develop borderline personality disorder have a constitutionally determined emotional instability, characterized by a stronger reaction to negative events, and a longer period needed to return to an emotional baseline. This affective lability requires more buffering from parents, who are needed to help modulate and control dysphoric emotions. In this view, BPD could not develop unless both a temperamental factor and a relative lack of parental responsiveness were present.

Linehan (1993) has further hypothesized that the modern world, which demands greater individual autonomy and which allows less dependence on or attachment to others, interferes with the ability of children with greater emotional needs to obtain sufficient care from their families. This principle might be equally applicable to narcissistic traits. Narcissism, even thought it is encouraged in the modern world, can be understood, in part, as an attempt by children to deal with inadequate parental responsiveness (Kohut, 1970), and in part as a compensation for social attachments.

It is of interest that among the indicators of social disintegration described by Leighton (1959), two of the items (broken homes and criminality) are among the risk factors for antisocial personality disorder. The model of social integration-disintegration implies that those factors that bind together individuals in a community and which provide access to social roles are protective, whereas those factors that isolate individuals, and require them to create their own roles, are risks for psychopathology.

The factors that describe social disintegration describe many of the known risks for ASPD, and the breakdown of social norms may also relate to the development of other impulsive personality disorders. Impulsive traits might be particularly sensitive to amplification by social disintegration, since they require structures and limits. Decreases in social integration in North America, accompanied by changes in family structure, might therefore provide the best explanation for the recent cohort effects on the prevalence of ASPD. Conversely, high levels of social integration, associated with cohesive family structures, could account for the low prevalence of ASPD in certain East Asian societies.

The increase in the prevalence of ASPD in North America has been the crucial data for all the arguments developed in this chapter. It remains possible that *all* forms of personality disorder are on the increase. It might simply be that the phenomena associated with impulsivity are more noticeable. If other personality disorders had been studied in the same systematic way as ASPD has been, we could answer this question.

If more than one group of personality disorders is increasing in prevalence, this finding would support the hypothesis that the same social risk factors apply to all categories of disorder. If, on the other hand, it is *only* the impulsive personality disorders that are increasing in prevalence, this would support the hypothesis that the demands of contemporary society places individuals with impulsive temperaments at risk.

10

The anxious cluster

This cluster of disorders is characterized by traits associated with anxiety. When these traits interfere either with the capacity to work or the ability to develop intimate relationships, we can diagnose a personality disorder.

Avoidant personality disorder

Avoidant personality disorder (APD), or its equivalent in ICD, anxious personality disorder, is characterized by a hypersensitivity to rejection that leads to avoidance of intimate relationships. This diagnosis was one of the most commonly made in the international study of personality disorders (Loranger et al., 1994).

The DSM-IV definition of APD requires the presence at least four of the following seven criteria (somewhat paraphrased): avoidance of interpersonal contacts at work; unwillingness to get involved with people unless certain of being liked; restraint in intimate relationships; preoccupation with criticism and rejection; inhibition in new interpersonal situations; view of self as inept, unappealing, or inferior; reluctance to take risks or engage in new activities.

Clinical example

A 32-year-old woman presented at a clinic for evaluation of lifelong social anxiety. Once she felt secure in any interpersonal situation, these difficulties would remit. For example, she was an effective secretary, having worked in the same office for over 10 years. She had also lived with the same female roommate for the last 4 years, and was quite comfortable either at home, or with her family. The patient had not, however, been able to sustain a significant relationship with a man. She had attempted to develop such relationships in her 20s, but had given up after several disappointments. She sought help because she had begun to realize that she might never be able to have a family of her own.

Dependent personality disorder

Dependent personality disorder (DPD) is a common diagnosis (Hirschfeld et al., 1991). It is characterized by a subordination of personal needs, making others assume responsibility for decisions, and a lack of self-confidence (Bornstein, 1992). The DSM-IV definition of DPD requires the presence of at least five of the following criteria (again, somewhat paraphrased): difficulty making decisions, need for others to assume responsibility, difficulty expressing disagreement, difficulty in initiation of projects, going to excessive lengths to obtain nurturance and support, feeling uncomfortable when alone, urgent need for replacement when close relationships end, preoccupation with fears of being left alone.

Clinical example

A 35-year-old man obtained a psychiatric evaluation on the advice of his mother. Since childhood, he had needed others to care for him and to make important decisions. His immediate problems were his inability to hold a job, and the threat of a marital breakdown. He had previously worked as a baker, had been laid off, and then quickly went bankrupt after trying to open his own shop. His wife, who had been financially supporting him, was threatening to leave him. He was unable to account for any of these difficulties, in each case describing how employers, partners, and his wife had all let him down.

Dependent personality seems to lack a clear delineation from the other categories in the anxious cluster. From the point of view of phenomenology, APD and DPD have some obvious points of overlap. Studies that have examined demographics, comorbidity, family history, diagnostic sensitivity, and the specificity of traits to diagnoses also show only minor differences between these two categories (Reich, 1990a, 1990b, 1991; Oldham et al., 1992). Although DSM-IV states that DPD is more common in women, other evidence (Bornstein, 1992) suggests that it is equally common in men.

Compulsive personality disorder

Compulsive personality disorder (CPD) is characterized by emotional constriction, stubbornness, and rigidity. The main features of CPD are a need for control in work and in interpersonal relationships.

The DSM-IV definition of CPD requires the presence of at least four of the following criteria: preoccupation with detail, perfectionism, excessive devotion to work, overconscientiousness, hoarding, reluctance to delegate tasks, miserliness, rigidity, and stubbornness.

Clinical example

A 35-year-old man presented to a clinic after losing his job. He had functioned successfully at a lower level of the hierarchy, but, following a promotion, was unable to cope with his workload. His perfectionism had led to procrastination, and he was unable to meet his own standards or to delegate tasks to others. He felt lonely in life, never having been able to choose a wife, but stated that his contemporaries had "settled" for unsatisfactory relationships only because they needed to have a family.

CPD is a common disorder, affecting 1.7% of the population, and is more common in males, as well as in married and employed individuals (Nestadt et al., 1991). Some factor analytic studies of symptoms seen in personality disordered patients (Livesley et al., 1992) suggest that compulsive personality does not share many traits with the avoidant and dependent categories, so that compulsive personality might be better placed outside the three clusters.

Biological risk factors for anxious cluster disorders

The biological factors common to the anxious cluster have been described by several related terms: anxious temperament, trait anxiety, or behavioral inhibition. Anxious cluster disorders are comorbid with symptomatic anxiety disorders (Stein et al., 1993). Thus, APD and DPD are comorbid with generalized anxiety disorder, with panic and agoraphobia, with social phobia, and with obsessive-compulsive disorder

(Brooks et al., 1991; Reich, 1991; Mavissakalian et al., 1993; Skodol, 1993; Hoffart et al., 1994; Oldham et al., 1995). CPD is also comorbid with the anxiety disorders (Brooks et al., 1991), although it has no particular association with obsessive-compulsive symptoms (Pollack, 1987). Conversely, the symptomatic disorder that is most comorbid with personality disorders is generalized anxiety disorder (Blashfield et al., 1994), a DSM category that approximates trait anxiety. These findings all point to a common diathesis, which could lead either to anxious symptoms, anxious personality characteristics, or both.

In an Australian twin study, Carey and DiLalla (1994) found that anxious temperament is strongly heritable and correlates with the broad dimension of neuroticism. Reich (1991) argues, based on family history studies, that anxious cluster disorders are more strongly familial than disorders in the impulsive cluster. Evidence from twin studies suggests that symptomatic anxiety disorders are heritable (Reich, 1991), but the heritability of anxious cluster disorders is unknown. There could be separate heritability for compulsive traits (Torgersen, 1980; Nigg & Goldsmith, 1994).

Most of these findings can be understood on the basis of inborn differences in the intensity of social anxiety in children. In a classic series of studies, Kagan (1988, 1994) described a specific form of anxious temperament, which he labeled "behavioral inhibition". The operational definition of behavioral inhibition involves unusual levels of shyness in infancy, as demonstrated by anxiety and withdrawal when faced with unfamiliar social stimuli. Kagan found that this trait shows a strong genetic influence, with a heritability of about 50%. Behavioral inhibition is associated with high levels of physiological arousal, which Eysenck had hypothesized to be associated with the broader dimension of neuroticism.

Kagan studied cohorts of infants with behavioral inhibition, and then followed them up, first at age 7, and then at age 13. In three quarters of the cases, they continued to have this trait. We await further follow-up of Kagan's cohort to know whether behavioral inhibition continues into adulthood. If so, it would be of great interest to determine whether, as adults, these individuals become vulnerable either to anxiety disorders or to anxious cluster personality disorders.

Most children eventually manage to "grow out" of shyness. If there is a subgroup in which behavioral inhibition persists into adulthood, there could be two explanations. One is that high levels of trait anxiety are the least likely to remit spontaneously. The other possibility is that anxious temperament is most likely to improve when parents expose their children to anxiety-provoking social situations. Behavioral inhibition is more common in younger than in older siblings, which could reflect the tendency of parents to be more protective with younger children. Kagan believes that children are more likely to overcome behavioral inhibition if their families encourage and help them to do so. This involves naturalistic exposure and deconditioning, which could explain why 25% of Kagan's cohort no longer showed behavioral inhibition at age 7.

The implications of this research are that anxious cluster disorders develop due to interactions between temperament and experience. If families do not encourage a shy child, either because of lack of interest or because they share the child's fears, then these personality traits will become more stable and more dysfunctional. We will present evidence below that the families of patients with anxious cluster disorders are, in fact, more likely to be both overprotective and unsupportive.

Psychological risk factors for anxious cluster disorders

Compared with the large amount of research on antisocial and borderline personality, there have been few empirical studies on the psychological risk factors for disorders in the anxious cluster. The existing research suggests that risks for avoidant and dependent personality overlap. There have been no systematic studies on the risks for compulsive personality.

In a retrospective study of patients with avoidant personality disorder, Arbel and Stravynski (1991) described an unencouraging home climate, as well as few demonstrations of parental love and pride. These characteristics resemble a style of parenting that Parker (1983) has termed "affectionless control". These perceptions of family environment could also reflect temperament. Nevertheless, it seems reasonable that patients with APD begin with a biological diathesis, and a lack of parental support for autonomy amplifies an anxious temperament.

Bornstein et al. (1992) have reviewed the psychological risk factors for dependent personality disorder. The attachment problem in the patients (Livesley et al., 1990), are commonly associated with overprotective parenting. For example, in a study using the Family Environment Scale (Head et al., 1991), DPD was associated with abnormalities of family structure, in particular low expressiveness and high control.

These studies on APD and DPD tend to support a theory discussed in the previous chapter (Beavers, 1977; Beavers & Hampson, 1990), that families whose children develop anxious personality disorders have a "centripetal" structure, i.e., with parents who keep their children within the family circle, interfere with their autonomy, and create patterns of abnormal dependence.

Attachment theory and the anxious cluster

Attachment theory (Bowlby, 1969, 1973, 1980) is an ambitious attempt to create an integration between two other models: psychoanalysis and ethology. The theory aims to explain normal and abnormal bonding, in both children and adults. The basic premise is that attachment between children and their caretakers is a biological program adapted for survival. Anxiety is the response to the threat of separation from a caretaker, and depression the response to the loss of a caretaker.

Bowlby (1973) described "anxious attachment" in children, characterized by an abnormal fear of separation. He hypothesized that this phenomenon reflects either the communication of anxious attachment in parents to their children, or direct parental threats of abandonment. Bowlby further proposed that abnormalities in the attachment system during childhood are risk factors for psychopathology in adulthood, particularly anxiety disorders.

Attachment theory has stimulated a great deal of empirical research (Hinde & Stevenson-Hinde, 1991). One method of assessing abnormal attachment behavior is by observing children in the "Strange Situation" (Ainsworth et al., 1978). This measure involves a structured assessment of a child's response to separation from the mother, followed by an exposure to a stranger, and then by the return of the mother. Using this instrument, attachment patterns can be classified into several types: secure, avoidant, or anxious-resistant. Secure children deal easily with the Strange Situation, avoidant children avoid the mother when she returns, while anxious-resistant children cling to her with overt anxiety.

A semistructured interview (Main & Hesse, 1991) can measure these attachment patterns in adults. In parallel with the patterns in children, adult attachment styles can be described as autonomous (or secure), detached (or avoidant), or enmeshed (or anxious-resistant). Different patterns of adult attachment may be characteristic of different personality disorders. For example, the presence of enmeshed or detached attachment styles in adults distinguish between avoidant and schizoid personality (West et al., 1994).

Bowlby assumed that the source of individual differences in attachment behavior, whether in childhood or adulthood, was caretaker behaviors during childhood. However, recent findings indicate that temperamental factors influence the attachment system. For example, anxious temperament has a relationship to distress behavior in the Strange Situation (Thompson et al., 1988).

The stability of attachment patterns, as well as their relationship to child-rearing practices, is the subject of controversy. Some children with avoidant or anxious patterns have entirely normal parenting (Kagan, 1989), which could be explained if attachment patterns derive from temperamental variations, and not necessarily from parental behaviors.

There is evidence for cultural differences in attachment patterns (Kagan, 1994). A "secure" style of attachment has been considered normative, but may not be the only type associated with good functioning. Kagan (1989) has criticized attachment theory for its culturally based assumption that "love" is the most important element of normal development and mental health. For example, an avoidant attachment style (in which the child shows little reaction to the absence or return of the mother) is associated with good functioning in Scandinavia, where the culture gives greater value to control of one's emotions (Kagan, 1989).

Nonetheless, anxious patterns of attachment, when sufficiently amplified, lead to pathology. The clinical effects of anxious attachment in adults strongly resemble anxious cluster disorders, with detached patterns approximating avoidant personality, and enmeshed patterns approximating dependent personality. (Detached attachment styles can also resemble schizoid personality.)

Adult attachment styles probably derive from temperamental variations. These styles become amplified to pathological levels when parents fail to respond appropriately to anxiety by providing both adequate care and appropriate support for the child's autonomy.

Social risk factors for anxious cluster disorders

Bowlby (1969) based attachment theory on the principle that anxiety about attachment, and dependence on significant others, are evolutionary necessities. Human infants are born in a state of "neoteny", i.e., they have many fetal characteristics, and they are totally dependent on their caretakers for survival. In what Bowlby calls "the environment of evolutionary adaptiveness", strong attachments to caretakers were essential to avoid predation. In addition, early human groups developed as small communities surrounded by hostile outsiders, so that the avoidance of strangers was necessary. Even in modern societies there are many real dangers, for both children and adults, from contact with strangers!

An anxious temperament will be more adaptive in some social structures than in others. The structures of traditional societies promote high levels of cohesion, both in the family and in the larger community. The values of traditional societies that shape personality tend to reinforce these strong attachments. Cohesive family structures and cohesive social structures both reward dependent traits, and punish excessive individualism. In these settings, individuals with dependent and avoidant traits more readily fit in to the expectations of the community, and might not be considered pathological.

The evidence reviewed in Chapter 6 on cross-cultural differences in personality supports this hypothesis. Let us consider the example of Japan. The Japanese are higher as a group on dimensions of introversion and neuroticism (Iwawaki et al., 1977), and also are more likely to have social phobias (Kirmayer, 1991). We would therefore expect to find that they have more personality traits associated with the anxious cluster disorders, i.e., social avoidance and dependence. Although neither the clinical dimensions nor the categories of personality disorder have been studied systematically in East Asian societies, we do have evidence, reviewed in Chapter 9, that antisocial personality is less common in Japan, as well as in Taiwan. It would not be surprising if anxious cluster disorders are more common in both these societies.

Psychotherapists in Japan have described a much more normative role for dependency in that culture (Doi, 1973). This pattern would apply to any society with high social cohesion. Japan, although a developed country, is a very cohesive society, as are traditional societies in developing countries. As discussed in Chapter 6, children in these societies have fewer overt behavioral problems.

On the other hand, modern societies require individualism and autonomy. Successful individuals must manage frequent interactions with strangers. In these societies, unless families help children with behavioral inhibition overcome their difficulties, they will become socially maladaptive, since as adults they will not be able to find employment or a mate on their own. Discordance between dependent or avoidant traits and social expectations can also create a vicious cycle: the more the individual is unable to cope with social demands, the more their traits are amplified.

The above model would not apply to compulsive personality. If anything, a need for control in interpersonal relationships fits in rather well with the expectations of modern societies, which value achievement more highly than attachment. Compulsive traits may, in any case, derive from different temperamental factors than anxious temperament. The general mechanism for amplification of traits to disorders proposed in Chapter 7, if applied to compulsive personality, would involve interactions between increased levels of social demand and decreased levels of social support.

The social factors in the anxious cluster personality disorders may not be qualitatively different from those in other clusters. Social disintegration and rapid social change, by increasing requirements for individual autonomy, create demands that are most likely to make anxious traits maladaptive. Moreover, the conditions of modernity undermine the protective factors in the family and community, i.e., the presence of securely available social networks, which can help individuals with these traits to adapt.

It is not known whether there are any cross-cultural differences in the prevalence of anxious cluster disorders. Another unknown is whether there are any cohort effects on the prevalence of these disorders. These data could help to determine whether there are specific risk factors for specific clusters, or whether the same risk factors apply to all personality disorders. The theoretical model developed here is consistent with either of these possibilities.

11

Treatment

This chapter will evaluate present methods of treatment for patients with personality disorders. First we will examine the outcome of these disorders, since any claims for successful treatment must be measured against their natural course. Second, we will consider what empirical research can tell us about the effectiveness, or the ineffectiveness, of the most common modalities of therapy. Third, we will attempt to determine which patients are most likely to benefit from treatment. Finally, we will describe certain pitfalls in the therapy of personality disordered patients.

Outcome of the personality disorders

We cannot fully understand the effects of treatment in psychiatric disorders unless we know their outcome. Chronic disorders remit only slowly over time. A gradual improvement in the course of treatment may therefore only reflect natural history.

Personality disorders are, by definition, chronic. We need to examine the empirical literature as to their outcome. But before doing so, we must address three methodological problems. First, outcome research in North America prior to 1980 suffered from an absence of well-defined criteria for diagnosis. Second, not all studies assess patients from multiple points of view; to be comprehensive, research needs to take into account symptoms, levels of functioning in different sectors, as well as whether the criteria for the original personality disorder diagnosis are still present. Third, many outcome studies have been relatively short term (<5 years), while fewer have been truly long term (≥15).

The largest number of studies have followed patients with borderline personality disorder. There are four published large-scale follow-ups of borderline patients 15 years after their initial assessment (McGlashan, 1986; Plakun et al., 1986; Paris et al., 1987, 1988, 1989; Stone, 1990). The author, who led one of these investigations, has also published two literature reviews on this subject (Paris, 1988, 1993). The conclusions can be briefly summarized:

1. In the short term, there is relatively little change in borderline patients.
2. Recovery begins to become apparent after an average of 10 years.
3. After 15 years, the majority of cases no longer meet diagnostic criteria for the disorder.
4. Improvement is apparent in all aspects of the disorder, but is most striking for impulsivity.
5. Many patients, even when they no longer meet criteria for BPD, continue to have serious problems later in life, and remain at risk for relapse.
6. A minority establish successful intimate relationships, but in most cases, improvement is associated with a withdrawal from intimacy.
7. About 10% of borderline patients eventually commit suicide.
8. There are no clear-cut predictors of the outcome of BPD at baseline, either for level of functioning, or for suicide.
9. There is no evidence that treatment has an effect on long-term outcome.

These findings are sobering, albeit in line with the chronicity of this disorder. The data put into context the claims by some clinicians (e.g., Boyer & Giovacchini, 1990; Kernberg, 1987) that these patients can be successfully treated only if seen for many years. Over long periods, naturalistic recovery intervenes, and improvement will occur with or without therapy. Nevertheless, we can provide follow-up until patients *do* recover.

There have been few empirical outcome studies of the other categories of disorder (Perry, 1993). By and large, the most improvement over time occurs in the impulsive cluster. As discussed in Chapter 9, impulsivity becomes less intense as we age. (This is an exception to the general principle that personality traits are stable.) Studies of antisocial personality show a gradual remission of symptoms, similar to changes documented for borderline personality (Maddocks, 1970; Guze, 1976). The most striking improvements are in criminal behavior, but, as with BPD, "recovered" patients continue to have personality pathology (Black et al., 1995).

Schizotypal personality disorder is associated with a poor long-term outcome (McGlashan, 1986c). This is to be expected in a disorder that lies in the schizophrenic spectrum.

There are, thus far, no data on the long-term outcome of anxious cluster personality disorders.

Another, more indirect approach to studying the effects of time on the personality disorders is to conduct cross-sectional studies to determine whether specific categories are more common in different age groups. In general, the results confirm the findings of longitudinal research. Two studies (Zimmerman & Coryell, 1989; Cohen et al., 1994) found that older patients have a lower overall prevalence of personality disorders, indicating that many types of disorder remit with time. Reich et al. (1988) examined the three DSM clusters, and found that it is impulsive and anxious traits that decline with age, while odd cluster traits do not. Cohen et al. (1994) have also found that impulsive cluster personality disorders are more prevalent in younger subjects.

In summary, the main implication of outcome research is that many categories of personality disorder demonstrate naturalistic recovery, so that the results of treatment must be better than time alone.

Why are personality disorders resistant to treatment?

Patients with personality disorders have a reputation for presenting insoluble clinical problems. Some years ago, Tyrer

(1988) concluded that there was a lack of documentation for the effectiveness of *any* treatment modality in this group. Since then, although a few studies have documented positive results, these disorders remain, by and large, characterized by chronicity and treatment resistance.

Empirical studies help to elucidate the problems in the treatment of patients with personality disorders. When a patient presents for symptomatic treatment, the presence of any "comorbid" personality disorder makes improvement less likely. Depressed patients who have a personality disorder respond more poorly to both psychopharmacology and psychotherapy (Pilkonis & Frank, 1988; Shea et al., 1990, 1992; Andreoli et al., 1993). (On the other hand, the presence of a personality disorder is not an absolute contraindication for symptomatic treatment; clinicians may find it useful, without expecting dramatic results, to offer patients trials of medication.)

There are few effective or specific treatments for the symptoms of the personality disorders themselves. Most of the research on the use of drugs concerns patients with borderline personality. As summarized in two recent reviews (Soloff, 1993; Coccaro, 1993), borderline patients show mild degrees of improvement with many drugs, but fail to respond definitively to any of them. The agents studied include low-dose neuroleptics, antidepressants (including monoamine oxidase inhibitors and specific serotonin reuptake inhibitors), and mood stabilizers such as lithium and carbamazepine. Some of these drugs, such as low-dose neuroleptics and antidepressants, yield improvements that are statistically significant but clinically insignificant. Moreover, clinical trials indicate that the positive effects are short term, so that there appears to be no value to keeping patients on maintenance dosages. At present, it seems safe to say that patients with BPD who are managed without drugs suffer no serious disadvantage.

It is noteworthy, nonetheless, that many patients with personality disorders, most particularly those falling in the borderline category, are treated in practice with a large number of pharmacological agents. The reasons are either that clinicians do not recognize the personality pathology, or if they do, that the patient still merits symptomatic therapy.

Trials of medication in these patients have become more common with the availability of specific serotonin reuptake inhibitors (SSRIs), which have low side-effect profiles, but which may not be more effective than older antidepressants.

The problem for clinical practice is distinguishing between pharmacological effects and placebo responses. Although some cases respond to medication, there are too many personality disordered patients receiving polypharmacy. Management sometimes reflects the frustration of treating these patients, rather than a rational therapeutic plan.

There have been hardly any systematic clinical trials of psychopharmacological agents for nonborderline personality disorders. Neuroleptics have some value for patients with schizotypal personality (Serban & Siegel, 1984; Goldberg et al., 1986), but these drugs are much less effective against "negative" symptoms than for the positive symptoms of schizophrenia. There have been no studies of drugs in schizoid or paranoid personality. In the impulsive cluster, there has been no research on antisocial personality, and one would not expect clinical trials to be possible in that population. In the anxious cluster, although some clinicians (e.g., Kramer, 1993) have proposed that SSRIs decrease social anxiety and increase assertiveness, there has been no solid evidence supporting this hypothesis.

Recent progress in neurochemistry raises the possibility that there might be drugs in the future that will be able to modify personality traits (Masters & McGuire, 1994). If such drugs were available, they could become crucial in the treatment of patients.

At present, the backbone of therapy for the personality disorders consists of psychosocial interventions. The major recommendation for treatment in this book will therefore involve psychotherapy. However, this prescription applies only to some, not all, patients with personality disorders. In view of the evidence that these patients do relatively poorly in therapy, any prescription must be made with caution.

Two principles can help clinicians work around these limitations. The first is to devise treatment methods that take into consideration why personality disorders are chronic. Many of the problems in the treatability of the personality disorders can be accounted for by the stability of traits. This stability is probably due to a combination of strong genetic influences (Plomin et al., 1990), the effects of social learning early in life (Bandura, 1977), and the cyclic and self-reinforcing nature of interpersonal behavior (Wachtel, 1977, 1994). The next chapter will propose therapeutic methods to take traits into account.

The second principle is that psychotherapy should be prescribed only to those personality disordered patients who can benefit from it. In the next section, we will examine methods by which suitable patients can be identified, so as to target those who are more treatable, and to avoid applying scarce resources to less treatable cases. This will be the subject of the rest of this chapter.

Assessing treatability in personality disordered patients

The problems in the psychotherapy of personality disordered patients are intrinsic to the nature of their psychopathology. The general definition of a personality disorder states that these patients must have significant problems in both their work and in their relationships. Psychotherapy, which is both work *and* a relationship, is therefore bound to be difficult.

Therapeutic alliance

Every patient in psychotherapy must be allied with the therapist to work towards mutually agreed goals. The construct of a "therapeutic alliance" describes this process. Measures of the alliance are robust predictors of the outcome of psychotherapy (Luborsky et al., 1988).

Contrary to what some might expect, there is much stronger evidence for the importance of patient factors in developing an alliance, and for the outcome of therapy itself, than there is for therapist factors (Garfield, 1994). Although a minimal level of competence is an obvious prerequisite for conducting therapy, there is thus far weak evidence that either therapist experience or skill has a strong impact on the effectiveness of treatment (Beutler et al., 1994).

Maladaptive interpersonal behavior patterns outside therapy could interfere with the capacity to develop an alliance inside therapy. For example, the alliances of patients with borderline personality disorder are unusually fragile (Frank, 1992), and over half of these patients become early dropouts from psychotherapy (Skodol et al., 1983; Gunderson et al., 1989). Although the strength of the therapeutic alliance may be the best predictor of outcome, it can only be reliably measured after patients have already had a few sessions of treatment. This is a rather impractical way to practice differential therapeutics!

Defense styles

Another construct that describes the normal and abnormal ways that individuals manage their interpersonal relations is "defense styles". Defenses are the characteristic ways by which individuals cope with life problems. They can be assessed empirically, either through self-report inventories (Bond et al., 1983), or through the scoring of vignettes from psychiatric interviews (Perry & Cooper, 1989). The different categories of defenses can also be ranked, from the most to the least adaptive.

Levels of defense maturity are correlated with functional levels in personality disordered patients (Bond et al., 1983). The most severe personality disorders, such as BPD, have the least adaptive defenses (Bond et al., 1994). If defense styles were predictive of treatment response, it could be useful to separate personality disordered patients into those with more mature defense styles, who would form stronger treatment alliances, and be more likely to respond to treatment; and those with less mature defense styles, who would form weaker treatment alliances, and would be less likely to respond to treatment.

Functional level

Researchers have consistently demonstrated a significant correlation between pretreatment functional levels and therapy outcome (Kernberg et al., 1972; Luborsky et al., 1988; Propst et al., 1994). On the whole, those patients who were doing better before treatment get more out of therapy. Horwitz (1974) wryly described this phenomenon as "the rich get richer, and the poor get poorer". However, a more charitable interpretation is that patients who have previous areas of success in their life are in a better position to resolve problems in other areas where they are having difficulties.

Diagnosis could also be, to some extent, a guideline to treatability. Thus, odd cluster patients are less treatable. Clinical experience also shows that patients with antisocial personality disorder are resistant to *any* form of intervention (Gabbard & Coyne, 1987; Stone, 1993). In fact, in work with a large number of patients committed to hospital under a broadened insanity defense, Yochelson and Samenow (1976) obtained their only good clinical results, achieved in a very small minority of cases, with interventions designed to *lower* self-esteem and make their patients feel more guilty. (One is reminded here of anecdotes that hardened criminals can only be reformed through religious conversion!) On the other hand, patients with any of the other personality disorders falling in the impulsive cluster, as well as with disorders in the anxious cluster, are quite commonly offered psychotherapy.

Certain categories of personality disorder tend to be associated with lower levels of functioning (Nakao et al., 1992; Paris et al., 1991). However, there remain wide individual differences in functional level between patients with the same diagnosis. Luborsky (1963) pioneered the measurement of functional level by developing the Health Sickness Rating Scale (HSRS). DSM later adopted this measure as its Global Assessment of Functioning (GAF), or Axis V. GAF scores measure what clinicians have called "ego strength". Functional level might help predict treatability in personality disordered patients, since, in contrast to the alliance, it can be measured prior to therapy.

The DSM system operationally defines functional level as a composite of three factors: the severity of symptoms, the ability to form relationships, and the capacity to work. It could be useful in practice to break down the overall construct into these three facets. In relation to symptom severity in personality disorders, it is possible that either the presence of certain specific features, or the presence of all, and not just some, of the criteria for a disorder, might predict treatability. Concerning the ability to form relationships, patients with personality disorders have their most severe problems in this sector of their lives, and these difficulties generally become the focus of treatment. That the severity of relationship problems might also be useful in predicting treatability.

The hypothesis of this chapter, however, is that work history is the best predictor of treatability in personality disordered patients. Psychotherapy is hard work and requires a great deal of persistence. Patients need to come regularly and apply themselves to the task. Patients who have not maintained any employment for more than a few months at a time will react badly to the frustrations inherent in treatment. On the other hand, as Chapter 12 will illustrate, patients with severe interpersonal problems, but with relatively good work histories, can be surprisingly responsive to psychotherapy.

Wide variance between patients in their treatability might account for the absence of consistent effects of treatment in personality disordered patients. In order to apply our resources rationally, every patient considered for therapy needs careful evaluation before we initiate therapy. The aim would be to carry out a triage among those who are untreatable, those who require primarily support and crisis intervention, and those who can benefit from more extensive treatment methods.

The effectiveness of psychotherapy in the personality disorders

Some clinicians (e.g., Langs, 1982) have recommended psychotherapy as the treatment of choice for a wide range of patients with personality pathology. The presence of a personality disorder has also been considered to be the primary indication for long-term psychotherapy (Gunderson, 1985). We need to know whether there is empirical evidence to show that these methods are effective.

Eysenck (1969) was the first to challenge therapists to demonstrate empirically that psychological treatment is more efficacious than naturalistic recovery. For many clinical problems, this challenge has since been successfully met. There is now a vast literature (Smith et al., 1980; Lambert & Bergin, 1994) which shows that psychotherapy is more effective than placebo for many of the symptomatic disorders seen in outpatient settings. For example, in patients with mild to moderate depression, psychotherapy is just as effective as pharmacotherapy (Beck, et al., 1983; Elkin et al., 1989).

We can only generalize these findings, derived from research on briefer courses of therapy, to patients receiving short-term treatment. Long-term psychotherapies have the broader aim of changing personality structure. Psychoanalysts have assumed that by increasing the length of therapy, one can reverse the effects of long periods of social learning in the patient's past. A longer treatment might intuitively seem to be more indicated for patients with long-term problems. However, there have been no empirical studies of the effectiveness of long-term therapy in personality disordered patients.

Some patients with personality disorders improve symptomatically with shorter courses of therapy. For example, in a study from our own center, using short-term therapy of up to 12 sessions (Propst et al., 1994), personality disordered patients, by the end of treatment, and at a 6 month follow-up, showed as much increase in GAF scores or in scores on a symptom checklist as did patients with adjustment disorders, mood disorders, or anxiety disorders. In a study examining the effects of therapy lasting up to 40 sessions (Winston et al., 1994), patients with anxious cluster or histrionic personality disorders showed significantly greater improvements in functioning than a waiting list control group. But we can hardly generalize these studies to *all* patients with personality disorders, since the subjects had already been prescreened as suitable for psychotherapy.

Research in general clinic populations has not shown that patients necessarily get better as treatment becomes longer. Howard et al. (1986), in a study of patients seen in weekly therapy, found that improvement occurs within the first few sessions for most patients, that the majority of cases are as improved as they will ever be after 10 to 12 sessions, and that there are few benefits, in respect to symptomatic relief, of going beyond a course of 25 weeks. Nevertheless, a recent study (Kopta et al., 1994; Howard et al., in press), showed that if changes in self-esteem are the target, results take longer, with therapeutic effects peaking at 40 to 50 weeks. Although improvements in interpersonal problems required at least 25 sessions, there were differential effects depending on which personality traits were involved, so that behaviors associated with overcontrol benefited most readily from therapy, while traits such as detachment or self-effacement showed less change after 40 sessions. Another study that did use clinical diagnoses found that among a group of outpatients receiving brief therapy, patients with personality disorders attained more gains with longer treatments of up to 50 sessions (Høglend, 1993).

Even 50 sessions might be considered "brief therapy" for some patients. However, only one study has examined the effectiveness of psychodynamic therapy over longer periods, a project conducted at the Menninger Clinic in Kansas (Kernberg et al., 1972). From a group of patients who had been admitted to a private psychiatric hospital, 42 received long-term follow-up. Although no formal diagnoses were made, the case histories (Wallerstein, 1986) indicate that these patients all suffered from severe personality disorders.

The therapeutic results were rather humbling. In spite of many years of treatment by experienced therapists, most of the patients showed only moderate levels of improvement (Kernberg et al., 1972). Higher initial ego strength predicted that patients would do somewhat better, but was not a strong predictor of outcome. The Menninger study had many methodological limitations. Since there was no control group for the cohort in treatment, those improvements that did occur might have been due to time, or to other life experiences, rather than to therapy.

There have been, unfortunately, few other clinical trials in the last 20 years to examine whether psychotherapy is effective for patients with personality disorders. One explanation is that clinicians who undertake therapy are not necessarily research oriented. Economic factors also play a role, since such studies would be labor intensive and require years of careful follow-up. However, in the absence of the evidence that only research can provide, claims by clinicians that patients with personality disorders *always* require lengthy courses of psychotherapy must be regarded with skepticism.

The practitioners of cognitive-behavioral therapy (CBT) are much more oriented to research, and have shown consistent interest in evaluating the effectiveness of their methods. Beck (1983) originally developed techniques to treat depression, but Beck and Freeman (1990) later suggested expanding cognitive therapy to the treatment of personality disorders, in which abnormal cognitions are characteristic. Young (1990) has proposed a similar method.

Beck and Freeman have described a cognitive approach for each of the categories listed in DSM. Unfortunately, they did not carry out any clinical trials to determine whether their methods are actually effective. Some of their suggestions were also rather naive, such as prescribing cognitive therapy for patients with antisocial personality disorder.

Linehan (1993) carried out the only controlled clinical trial of cognitive-behavioral therapy in personality disordered patients. She specifically designed a method, called "dialectical behavior therapy" (DBT), for patients with borderline personality. After 1 year of therapy, parasuicidal episodes became less frequent, and improvement was stable at 1 year follow-up. Nevertheless, in spite of having fewer behavioral symptoms, such as suicide attempts, patients remained highly dysphoric and chronically impaired in their functioning.

Linehan's findings are groundbreaking, in that they show that psychotherapy *can* reverse some of the pathology associated with a severe personality disorder. An unanswered question is to what extent these positive results are attributable to specific techniques. Linehan compared patients in DBT to a control group of patients receiving "treatment as usual in the community", i.e., receiving a heterogeneous group of therapies, mostly of a supportive nature. This could suggest that DBT has specifically effective techniques. However, another possible explanation of Linehan's good results might be that the usual approach to these patients involves a great deal of muddle and improvisation, and that impulsive cluster patients are better managed using precise, well-structured, and manualized therapy.

Dialectical-behavior therapy for borderline patients is a complex technique. It is difficult to know whether its results require the application of the entire package, or whether particular elements account for its effectiveness. To answer this question, one would have to carry out a "dismantling" strategy, i.e., pulling apart techniques, and offering them separately, to determine which are most therapeutic.

In an uncontrolled trial, Stevenson and Meares (1992) found that borderline patients improve after 2 years of psychodynamic therapy. However, the patients who stay in this form of therapy are probably not representative of the larger population with BPD. In fact, more than half of borderline patients drop out early when offered this form of treatment (Skodol et al., 1983; Gunderson et al., 1989). Linehan's method, on the other hand, had an extraordinarily low drop-out rate (16%). If cognitive therapy should turn out to be applicable to lower-functioning personality disordered patients, who are less suitable for psychodynamic psychotherapy, then it would indeed represent a major breakthrough!

Clinical trials are needed on the effectiveness of cognitive therapy for other categories of personality disorder. Thus far, one uncontrolled study suggested using social skills training for patients with avoidant personality disorder (Stravynski et al., 1994), but in a second study (Alden et al., 1989), similar methods were ineffective.

In summary, the evidence thus far shows that psychotherapy can be a valuable treatment for *some* patients with personality disorders. The evidence does not support claims by clinicians that psychotherapy is the definitive method of treatment for most personality disordered patients.

Two conclusions seem justified at this point: (1) The effectiveness of psychotherapy varies with functional level, as well as with diagnosis; and (2) the most positive results thus far have involved cognitive-behavioral therapy for borderline personality.

Since there have been too few data to support any final opinion, our conclusions must remain provisional. In the first place, the research reviewed in this chapter largely concerns symptoms. Symptom control is a reasonable measure of improvement in depression and anxiety, but not in patients with personality disorders who require broader improvements in functioning, i.e., being able to work effectively and to have satisfying intimate relationships. Second, most research involves psychotherapy lasting from a few months to a year. Hardly any studies have assessed the effects of therapy over long periods, a sine qua non for evaluating the treatment of any chronic illness.

Pitfalls in the treatment of patients with personality disorders

The review in the present chapter has attempted to place the treatment of the personality disorders on a reasonably firm empirical footing. At this juncture, we will offer a critique of approaches, all too common in practice, that lack an empirical basis. We will address three pitfalls facing clinicians: failure to select suitable patients, unnecessary length of therapy, and inappropriate use of trauma theory.

Failure to select suitable patients

Psychotherapy research supports a philosophy of treatment based on triage. We need to discriminate between those for whom our resources might be wasted, and those for whom they might make a real difference. As discussed above, this decision depends on functional level as well as on categorical diagnosis.

Some therapists seem to believe, nevertheless, that sufficient levels of therapeutic skill can override any and all of the difficulties of severe psychopathology. The recommendations of clinical authorities claiming to have an effective method are applied, and then used to counter inevitable reverses in the course of practice. Clinicians may respond to severe levels of disability in patients by believing that they need *more*, not less treatment. Theorists who recommend "heroic" treatments (e.g., Boyer & Giovacchini, 1990) present case histories describing surprising and heartening improvements in recalcitrant cases. Their methods are never subjected to systematic clinical trials, but are presented "on faith".

These ideas have led well-meaning therapists to spend years treating difficult patients, waiting for a moment of truth that never comes. Clinical authorities should be honest about the difficulties of treating patients with personality disorders. For example, Kernberg (1976) has acknowledged that there are untreatable patients, and points out that if one is to invest years of time on a case, one should have some prior indication that success is possible.

Unnecessary length of therapy

There are two reasons why the treatment of personality disordered patients tends to be unnecessarily long. The first relates to patient selection. On the one hand, if the patient is treatable, then it may be worthwhile to take the time necessary to reshape maladaptive behavior patterns. On the other hand, when unrealistic goals are set for patients who receive little substantial benefit but who continue to require the support of seeing the therapist, the result is interminable treatment. It was Freud (1937) who first noted that the psychoanalytic method has an intrinsic tendency toward interminability. In fact, quite a few of the patients in the Menninger study eventually became "lifers" (Horwitz, 1974).

The second reason for unnecessary length is the belief that longer treatments have more effect on personality structure than shorter ones. As already discussed, there is no evidence either for or against this idea. But since long-term therapy is hardly a cost-effective procedure, it must be shown to have predictable results. At our present state of knowledge, it would make more sense to accept the chronicity of the personality disorders, and to keep the goals of treatment modest. Rather than take on patients "for life", we can follow them intermittently, with adequate provision for crisis intervention when needed (McGlashan, 1993).

Inappropriate use of trauma theories

The first two pitfalls are associated with the most grandiose assumptions of psychodynamic therapy: that therapy can succeed with any patient if it is "deep" enough and long enough. Trauma theory derives from another assumption rooted in psychoanalysis: the primacy of early experience. In Chapter 4, we criticized this assumption at some length, as well as challenging the idea that histories of trauma in childhood account for personality pathology in adulthood.

In the present chapter, it is worth reemphasizing that treating patients with personality disorders on the basis of these ideas has little basis in empirical research. Therapies that focus on trauma are colorful, and have sometimes obtained media coverage, but have not received any serious clinical trials. Until such trials are carried out, we must remain cautious.

This is not to say that childhood trauma plays *no* role in the therapy of patients with personality disorders. One may validate the reliability of these memories by interviewing other family members (Paris, 1995). If traumatic histories appear to be reliable, it is, of course, important to address their impact. In such cases, one can follow the recommendations of Linehan (1993) to address their historical context as "invalidating", to reduce the later shame and stigma attached to them, and to examine current maladaptive behavior patterns linked to these experiences.

Childhood trauma should rarely, however, be the primary focus of treatment. As the next chapter will suggest, what is most important in psychotherapy is resolving problems in the present. The importance of past difficulties lies in putting present difficulties in context. In contrast, treatment methods based on the search for "repressed" memories of trauma focus on the past. This approach has led, in some cases, to negative consequences (McHugh, 1994). The most serious outcomes involve suggestible patients who dramatically produce traumas on demand, accusing family members of unspeakable atrocities (Loftus & Ketcham, 1994; Ofshe & Watters, 1994; Wright, 1994).

The approach to psychopathology favored in this book is intended to be undramatic! If personality disorders are products of interactions between genes, experience, and social context, then there may be no childhood events to "work through", and there may be no one to blame.

Clinical guidelines

The following guidelines for clinical management of patients with personality disorders are consistent with the empirical research reviewed in this chapter:

1. Most patients with personality disorders remain chronically impaired, and require intermittent follow-up.
2. The limiting factor for change is the stability of personality traits.
3. The goals of treatment should be kept modest.
4. Patients with personality disorders are different from each other and we can achieve more in subgroups with higher levels of functioning.

The next chapter will present a treatment model in line with these guidelines.

12

Clinical practice

We will now apply the guidelines proposed in the previous chapter, and offer a set of recommendations for clinical practice to help patients make better use of their personality traits. The primary goal of this method is improved adaptations.

Before proceeding, two disclaimers must be registered. First, it is not the intention of the author to describe a new type of psychotherapy. Over the last 50 years, many such proposals have appeared, leading to the creation of innumerable "schools" of therapy. Unfortunately, even when these schools bear new labels, when scrutinized, they usually turn out to be variants of existing therapeutic approaches. The model of therapy being proposed here is in no way meant to be unique!

Second, the ideas to be presented in this chapter reflect the author's clinical experience and his theoretical perspective, but remain unsupported by data. At best, they are *consistent* with the findings of empirical research. No approach to psychotherapy can be considered as valid without systematic research: we need to manualize methods, and then submit them to rigorous clinical trials.

Unfortunately, as reviewed in the previous chapter, there have been no large-scale studies of the efficacy of psychotherapy for personality disorders. Because of the practical difficulties and expense involved in conducting such research, the data at our disposal derive from brief therapies, which may or may not be applicable to the chronic problems presented by personality disordered patients. Clinical guidelines, including the ones to be presented here, can only be provisional. The ideas in this chapter are guidelines to future research, but do not describe a definitive method of treatment.

The stability of personality traits: clinical implications

As reviewed in Chapter 3, personality traits are highly stable. This consistency is a limiting factor in the treatment of personality disorders, but can also be the basis for setting reasonable goals.

The broad structure of personality is a given, and should not be expected to undergo radical change. Some clinicians have claimed that psychopharmacology can modify personality (Kramer, 1993), while others have made the same claim for psychotherapy (Langs, 1982). There is, in fact, no evidence to support these ideas.

On the other hand, treatment might reverse the process by which traits are amplified to disorders. If disorders are exaggerations of normal traits, and if psychosocial factors largely mediate the amplification process, then psychotherapy, which focuses on these factors, should be of some use. Instead of trying to change personality, we can teach patients how to make more adaptive use of traits. Psychotherapy could focus on redirecting behavioral characteristics, so as to maximize the patient's social adaptation. We should work *with* traits, and not *against* them.

This approach is derived from a biopsychosocial model of the personality disorders. If etiology is multidimensional, then treatment must be equally multidimensional. Psychotherapy takes account of biological factors by working within the limits set by traits, of psychological factors by helping patients to understand their life history and to modify their maladaptive cognitions, and of social factors by encouraging patients to develop social roles compatible with their personality.

The author was trained as a psychodynamically oriented psychotherapist. In the previous chapter, claims that psychoanalytic methods are uniquely applicable to the personality disorders were subjected to strong criticism. Nonetheless, the ideas in the present chapter fall under the broadest definition of a psychodynamic approach. Reviewing the patient's personal history is an important element of any psychotherapy. This is *not* because understanding the past automatically leads to behavioral change. Rather, the historical context associated with the development of maladaptive behaviors provides a perspective on the present. When patients see that maladaptive behaviors are anachronisms, they may more readily replace them with adaptive behaviors.

The problem with a *purely* dynamic perspective, particularly for patients with personality disorders, is its focus on "interpretation". These are statements linking past and present, which derive historical reconstructions from developmental theory. Links between past and present are a useful first step in identifying maladaptive patterns. But interpretations, by themselves, rarely produce change (Wachtel, 1977).

The idea that change in psychotherapy depends on "accurate" interpretation has been an article of faith for psychodynamic therapists. Unfortunately, there is almost no empirical evidence to support this belief. All forms of psychotherapy, whether they make use of psychoanalytic, behavioral, cognitive, or interpersonal models, produce roughly equivalent results (Smith et al., 1980; Luborsky et al., 1988; Frank & Frank, 1991). This suggests that the operative mechanisms of change in therapy are not specific to *any* technique. There is evidence that the results of treatment are better when therapists accurately identify the main themes in the patient's associations, and then make use of these issues in their comments (Luborsky & Crits-Christoph, 1990). But this does not mean that making links between past and present is essential for behavioral change.

All therapies work through common mechanisms. The most basic mechanism involves the use of a therapeutic relationship to help patients solve their problems. The aspects of therapy that are independent of either theory or technique have been called "nonspecific" effects but they could also be considered as "specific" since by reducing demoralization and increasing hope, therapists activate adaptive behaviors (Frank & Frank, 1991). In a review of research on process variables in psychotherapy, Orlinksy et al. (1994) conclude that therapy requires a good working alliance, as well as a focus on the patient's emotions. But, these factors are facilitative and enabling rather than sufficient for change.

Behavioral change takes place primarily in the *present* life of the patient. The mechanisms of change for patients with personality pathology involve the learning of new behaviors. Social learning theory (Bandura, 1977) best describes this process. As reviewed in Chapter 2, this theory describes two ways by which children learn new behaviors: reinforcement, and modeling. These same principles are applicable to how patients learn in psychotherapy. Reinforcements takes place when patients try out new behaviors, and then find that they are more successful in achieving their goals. Modeling takes place in that the patient observes that the therapist conducts the treatment in an effective manner, providing an example of adaptive functioning.

In order to teach new behaviors, the therapist must first establish the maladaptive nature of old behaviors, and the inappropriateness of the patient's cognitive schemata. This is the main task of the early stages of treatment. Once patients recognize that behaviors are not working for them, the therapist can move on to suggesting alternatives. At the same time, the therapist works to help the patient to develop more adaptive cognitive schemata. In this stage, treatment largely consists of the patient reporting whether or not they were able to stop maladaptive behavior patterns, and how successful they were in replacing them with more adaptive responses. Basically, change involves a trial-and-error process, in which the buffer of a therapeutic relationship supports the practicing of new behaviors, using the therapist as an expert consultant. The primary mode of psychotherapy is therefore one of problem solving.

There is some empirical evidence that this approach is effective in the personality disorders, at least for borderline personality (Linehan, 1993). In the future, parallel models will be developed for patients suffering from other categories of disorder.

These ideas are parallel to the practice of cognitive behavioral therapy. Its practitioners were, in fact, the first to propose that the understanding of personality traits is essential in psychotherapy (Beck & Freeman, 1990). The aims of cognitive-behavioral interventions in the personality disorders are to make these traits more adaptive. In borderline personality, for example, the goals are to modulate emotions to optimal intensities, to limit rigid and inappropriate behaviors, and to expand behavioral repertoires (Linehan, 1993).

In comparison with the approach of formal cognitive-behavioral therapy, the clinical approach described in this chapter might seem relatively unsystematic. However, as pointed out in Chapter 11, we do not know precisely which elements in these treatments are most effective. Moreover, clinicians, who are already treating personality disordered patients in psychotherapy with some degree of success, may not wish to jettison their present methods in favor of a systematic and manualized technique. More likely, they will prefer to apply the most useful ideas from many forms of therapy, and create a personal synthesis.

The principles advocated here are an integration of the psychodynamic and behavioral models. In a book published nearly 20 years ago, and still relevant today, Wachtel (1977) proposed that therapeutic methods that focus on individual history, and those that focus on the obstacles to change in the present, are essentially complementary. Wachtel argued that effective therapy must combine psychological insight, as emphasized by the psychodynamic approach, with the rigorous approach to change emphasized by the traditions of behavior therapy.

Differential therapeutics

"Differential therapeutics" (Frances et al., 1984) is the art of prescribing the right treatment for an individual patient. This principle is of particular importance in the personality disorders, in that some patients are treatable, some partially treatable, and some not treatable at all.

The same treatment methods are not applicable to all categories of disorder. In part, this is because some personality traits are relatively easier to modify than others. As discussed in Chapter 2, some dimensions of personality are less heritable, and are more susceptible to environmental influences; these include the capacity for social intimacy (Livesley et al., 1993; Tellegen et al., 1988), as well as agreeableness (Bergeman et al., 1993). Related traits, such as positive emotionality and social closeness, are among the few influenced by factors in the shared environment. Findings that all the traits that are less influenced by genetic factors relate to problems in intimacy should be encouraging to therapists, since difficulties with intimacy are common in practice, and may be more amenable to psychological interventions.

Treatment for the categories of personality disorder reflect differences as to whether traits can be readily modified.

Odd cluster

These patients will be the least treatable. It is possible that certain schizoid patients might be helped, by encouraging them to avoid those situations, such as intimate relationships, which they find most difficult, and to focus on those, such as work, which they may manage with less difficulty.

Impulsive cluster

With the exception of antisocial personality, the overall approach to these patients is to help patients develop better control of impulses and emotions. Linehan's dialectical behavior therapy, designed on these principles, teaches borderline patients to identify feeling states, to avoid acting on them, and to find alternate, more adaptive approaches to interpersonal problems. Similar methods might be helpful for patients with histrionic and narcissistic personality disorders.

Anxious cluster

A key clinical problem with these patients is that they deal with dysphoria by withdrawal or procrastination. They need to learn to take more risks, so as to become more, not less, "impulsive". Parents successfully overcome behavioral inhibition in their children by exposing them to situations that produce anxiety (Kagan, 1994); this is the inverse of overprotection, seen in the families of patients with avoidant and dependent personalities (see Chapter 10).

The relevance of social context for the treatment of patients with personality disorders

The social factors in personality disorders are structurally rooted in modern society. They cannot therefore readily be changed by clinicians. Thirty years ago some clinicians in the community psychiatry movement recommended specific social reforms in the name of mental health. These efforts were remarkably unsuccessful. As pointed out by a critic at the time (Grinker, 1964), such grandiose programs only distracted psychiatry from focusing on those conditions for which it has specific forms of treatment. To attempt to change the contemporary social fabric would be to repeat these past errors.

Patients with personality disorders have difficulty in finding social roles, but are more likely to recover if they establish such roles. There is no way, however, by which clinicians can provide a full range of social roles for their patients. In the past, the family and the community made sure that every individual had access to employment, and had the option of living in a family. We cannot return to the structures of traditional societies, even though they provided protection against personality pathology.

Personality disordered patients benefit from establishing social networks and supports. Clinicians can therefore encourage them to develop more connections with community organizations. Support groups in the community, often based on the model of Alcoholics Anonymous (AA), target individuals suffering from social isolation. Helping patients to join such groups is undoubtedly helpful in individual cases. However, many patients will be either unwilling or unable to follow through on these suggestions.

In spite of our best efforts, anomie continues to characterize contemporary society. We do not have sufficient human resources or money to make more than a dent in this problem. As discussed in Chapter 6, social isolation is the "side effect" of modernity.

Therapists working with personality disordered patients have no choice but doing clinical work, rather than attempting the impossible. Nevertheless, the more personality disordered patients can find some way, no matter how limited, to "plug in" to society, the more likely they are to improve. This is an essential element of a therapy oriented towards social adaptation. Let us consider how these principles might be applied in each cluster of personality disorder.

Odd cluster

These patients, who are not generally capable of sustained relationships, have a need for steady employment, preferably in work settings that are interpersonally undemanding. The job market is therefore a crucial factor for their mental health. The problem is that postindustrial society has fewer and fewer positions available that require repetitive attention to a task. Many jobs demand the very cognitive and interpersonal skills that these patients lack. As a result, schizoid and schizotypal patients are increasingly becoming the discards of modern society.

Impulsive cluster

Psychotherapy is not appropriate for patients with antisocial personality disorder, who are best managed in the criminal justice system. That conclusion could change dramatically in the future if we were to develop effective pharmacological agents to control severe impulsivity, a scenario in which the entire legal system would require a major input from psychiatry (Masters & McGuire, 1994).

Psychotherapy is the mainstay of present management for the other patients in the impulsive cluster. However, problems in the application to these patients of models of a purely psychological approach to impulsivity can be counterproductive. There are two reasons for this. One is that when therapy focuses excessively on childhood experiences, it may reinforce the status of patients as victims, failing to help them take control of their life in the present. The second reason is that psychotherapy tends to reinforce the excessive narcissism that characterizes patients in the impulsive cluster.

With its focus on internal emotional states and needs, treatment may encourage self-regard rather than an adequate concern for others. Psychodynamic psychotherapy is part of the problem, and not part of the solution, for many impulsive patients.

Therapy oriented to the social context could address some of these difficulties. For example, many patients have had insufficient structures in their family life and in their social milieu and need structured interventions in therapy (Paris, 1994). Impulsive patients also have a better outcome when they find external structures in life (Bardenstein & McGlashan, 1990).

The personality traits that are most troublesome in impulsive cluster patients are emotional lability, impulsivity, and narcissism. It follows that they need to learn to examine emotions more critically, to act less on impulse, and to take greater account of the needs of other people. External social structures that encourage persistence, competence, and achievement in work, as well as secure attachments in intimate relationships, help these patients become less dependent on ephemeral reinforcers, such as sexual attractiveness or power.

Narcissistic personality disorder raises problems of particular interest for social psychiatry. Therapists need to combat the excessive self-concern in narcissistic patients, and to increase their commitments to work and relationships. These external structures act as buffers for excessive individualism.

The problem is that psychotherapists as a group are often just as influenced as anyone else, if not more so, by the individualistic values of modern society (Henry, 1971). The entire psychotherapeutic enterprise is oriented to encouraging assertiveness in patients, and to validating perceived needs. There is, therefore, an implicit bias in therapy that favors the needs of the individual over the family or the larger group. It may be no accident that psychotherapy as a method appeared at the very moment in history when traditional social structures were rapidly breaking down. This individualistic bias is particularly strong in North America, where it reflects the value system of the culture as a whole (Frank & Frank, 1991; Torrey, 1992).

Anxious cluster

In this group, a bias in favor of individualism and emotional expressiveness might be more appropriate. These individuals are overcompliant, and may therefore benefit most from "classical" approaches, such as getting in touch with their inner selves and escaping the domination of others. Since these patients lack normal entitlements, they are *insufficiently* narcissistic. The problem in this group is how to prevent these patients from using defenses of avoidance, dependence, and procrastination, and from using psychotherapy as one more place to hide from life.

Certain general principles apply to patients in any category of personality disorder. First, personality pathology requires more than the traditional elements of therapy, i.e., interpretation and support. As Reich (1933) first pointed out, "character analysis" demands *confrontation* to make ego-syntonic behaviors ego-dystonic. (It goes without saying that one has to confront patients tactfully, and only after carefully convincing them that their behaviors are indeed maladaptive.)

Second, as Wachtel (1977) has emphasized, the process of learning more adaptive behaviors is more than a phase of treatment; it is the essence of therapy. Social learning in personality disordered patients takes a long time because maladaptive behaviors must first be unlearned and then replaced with a repertoire of new and more adaptive behaviors.

Third, every patient's social networks must be taken into account. Most people meet their attachment needs within well-functioning families. If psychotherapy encourages patients to be excessively individualistic, these networks break down further (Glantz & Pearce, 1989).

Awareness of the family system is an ethical issue. The therapist's interventions have a powerful impact on people other than the individual patient. For example, if psychotherapists routinely favor marital dissolution, either implicitly or explicitly, as the most appropriate response to conflicts in intimate relationships, such interventions may (or may not) benefit individual patients, but will in many cases have a negative impact on their spouses and their children.

In contemporary society, fewer and fewer individuals live in nuclear families (Westen, 1985). Modern social structures do not ensure that everyone can marry and have children. As a result, more individuals remain alone in life. Some will be content, and may even value and make creative use of their solitude (Storr, 1991). Others will be far from content, and may feel lonely and emotionally deprived.

Not all lonely people, with or without diagnosable personality disorders, will be capable of establishing stable intimacy in modern society. For this reason, it is particularly important for them to have other satisfactions in life. They require first, stable and reasonably satisfying employment, and second, a social network consisting of less intimate extrafamilial attachments. For example, in a long-term outcome study of borderline personality disorder (McGlashan, 1993), the ability to work was most strongly associated with stable recovery, whereas a greater investment in intimate relationships led to relative instability, since patients became dysfunctional if those relationships broke down.

Individual variability in personality traits implies that there is a good degree of variation in what people need to feel fulfilled in their lives. Some patients may attain the ultimate mental health goals ("love and work"), but others will not. When faced with patients with a diagnosis of personality disorder, treatment goals should be realistic and modest. It might even be useful to think about personality disordered patients in the same way as we view patients with other chronic disorders. If there are biological factors that prevent adaptation, treatment methods might be framed in terms of rehabilitation (van Reekum et al., 1993), i.e., helping those who lack adaptive skills to conform to social expectations. Clinicians may need to take account of the depth of pathology in the personality disorders, and consider partial recoveries as successes.

Clinical examples

We will now consider how the principles recommended in this chapter apply in practice to patients with personality disorders. The case examples presented below correspond to some of the diagnostic categories of personality disorder described by DSM-IV, Axis II. Not all categories will be considered: schizotypal, paranoid, and antisocial personality disorders will be excluded because they are untreatable at present with psychotherapy. (In each patient, although the criteria for a DSM diagnosis will be examined in detail, they would also have met ICD criteria for a corresponding disorder).

Since clinical trials of therapy for personality disordered patients have been rare, the "data base" for this chapter will, by necessity, be the clinical experience of the author. The brief examples presented here are intended to be illustrative of a psychotherapeutic approach, not as definitive answers to the complex clinical problems inherent in the personality disorders. We will need many more decades of research before we have solid guidelines to treatment.

Furthermore, the examples to be presented here do not contradict in any way the cautions in the previous chapter about the use of psychotherapy in the personality disorders: *The approach described here is not applicable to the majority of patients.*

The cases will be examples of a more treatable subgroup, drawn from a larger and less treatable population. All of the patients, in spite of their difficulties, had relatively high levels of functioning, particularly at work. Their areas of strength allowed them, to some extent, to deal with their weaknesses.

What options are there then for the majority of personality disordered patients, who function at much lower levels, and who cannot benefit from the methods recommended here? In most cases, the best model involves multiple crisis intervention. When patients are in difficulty, we can offer them short-term therapy and/or medication for symptoms. When they are out of crisis, we can leave the door open for them to return. Although some patients may want, or seem to need, continuous follow-up, it is often sufficient to maintain availability.

There will always be a few cases where even this minimalist approach will fail. As Frances et al. (1984) have recommended, for patients who do not benefit from any intervention, no treatment may be the "treatment of choice".

Three general principles will be demonstrated in each of the case examples: treatability, the adaptive use of traits, and the social context of psychotherapy.

Treatability

Before undertaking therapy, we must assess treatability. This evaluation depends on the principle that patients with major areas of competence in their functioning are more likely to be able to make use of psychotherapeutic interventions. The most important measure of this competence is the ability to work. Even when interpersonal problems are moderate or severe, patients who are able to fulfill some productive social role are more approachable in therapy.

The adaptive use of traits

The treatment of personality disordered patients involves making better use of their traits; in most cases, this will involve helping patients to work more effectively and more competently. Where therapy deals with problems in intimacy, particularly in individuals with somewhat lower levels of functioning, the goals will be more limited. The presence of a reasonably satisfying work environment can buffer difficulties in interpersonal relationships. Moreover, many patients who cannot manage intimacy obtain meaningful satisfactions from their social network. Each of the therapies to be described below did focus to some extent on problems in intimacy, with the aim of helping patients who could achieve stable relationships to do so, and of helping patients who could not to find alternate solutions. In each case, the therapist implicitly accepted the major limitations that patients had in this sphere. Not accepting them might have led either to an interminable treatment, or to a frustrating therapeutic impasse, leaving both patient and therapist with a sense of failure.

The social context of psychotherapy

The cases will demonstrate how social factors are involved in the development of personality disorders, and how adaptation to the social environment plays a role in planning treatment. In some instances, taking into account the interests of persons other than the patient was relevant.

Schizoid personality disorder

This is the one category in the odd cluster for which psychotherapy might conceivably be useful. As discussed in Chapter 8, schizoid personality disorder differs from schizotypal and paranoid personality in that it need not be genetically linked to schizophrenia. Therefore, these patients, characterized by extreme degrees of introversion, benefit from psychotherapeutic strategies designed to develop more adaptive uses for this trait.

Case history

Clinical presentation   A 30-year-old pediatric nurse was referred by her supervisor because she was unable to manage the psychosocial aspects of her work. She was having particular difficulty with the needs of the parents of hospitalized children.

Her past history was that she had been an unusually shy child who had never formed meaningful friendships with her peers. Her family was large, and her parents were too preoccupied to provide her with much individual attention. Since she was unusually bright, she devoted herself to her studies.

As an adult, she had no experience at all with the opposite sex. She did not feel deprived by her life choices. She was entirely devoted to her profession, in which she was highly knowledgeable.

Diagnosis   Her personality pattern reflected detachment from social situations and a restricted range of emotion. She met all seven criteria for schizoid personality disorder in DSM-IV.

Treatment   A weekly series of psychotherapy sessions were instituted, and lasted for 6 months. Overtly the treatment seemed to lack any degree of content. The patient made little eye contact, and was silent for long periods. However, although she was always uncomfortably anxious in the therapeutic situation, these meetings offered her an opportunity to desensitize herself to an interpersonal encounter. Over time, she began to talk about her difficulties. In particular, she was able to discuss how frightened she felt that the parents of the children she was treating would judge her harshly.

On 1-year follow-up, she was functioning much better at work. She had begun to work in the Arctic, where there was a great need for her services. She was more comfortable working in this alien culture, into which she would not in any case expect to fit. She launched a successful career by developing services for the native populations there. She continued neither to desire nor to seek close relationships.

Treatability

In this example of a schizoid patient, the ability to benefit from therapy was suggested by her occupational competence. Had she not been able to work productively in a structured setting, and gain self-esteem from that work, she would probably have not been able to deal effectively with her interpersonal difficulties.

The adaptive use of traits

Her personality traits, characterized by high interpersonal anxiety and social withdrawal, presented at a disabling level, and threatened her ability to work. These traits were a limitation, but she also had important strengths, including hard work and persistence. Finding a social environment in which introverted traits are more adaptive was crucial for her improvement. Her interpersonal needs were met in part through her work, since in this sector of her life there was a structured setting in which she could interact relatively comfortably with other people.

The social context of psychotherapy

This patient might have had less difficulty in another type of work, since she could not readily meet the interpersonal demands of nursing practice. However, she was ultimately able to work in a less demanding environment that was more suitable for an introvert.

Borderline personality disorder

This category is associated with disabilities in many areas of functioning. Borderline patients have wide variations in treat-

ability. Some can only be managed with multiple crisis interventions, but others, who have sectors of high functioning,
may obtain real benefit from psychotherapy (Paris, 1994).
However, even when patients recover from BPD, they retain
major difficulties in relationships and are vulnerable to further decompensations. These limitations affect the success of
treatment, even in the more manageable cases.

Case history

Clinical presentation   A 22-year-old architecture student sought treatment for recurrent suicidal ideas. She was highly creative and had even
been rated as the best student in her class. Her interpersonal relationships, on the other hand, were highly troubled. She had few friendships,
and her social life consisted of a series of short-lived and impulsive love
affairs. The patient had unsuccessful relationships with several men,
some of whom she had initially encountered in public places. She was
a poor judge of character; none of these men were suitable in either
age and background. She approached relationships from a point of
view of romanticism and fantasy, rather than making decisions on facts.

Some of her most disturbing symptoms involved extended periods
spent in dissociative states. She claimed that she spent many of her
evening hours in "astral travel", making contact with spirits from another
world. When asked about her earliest memories, she replied, "do you
want to hear about this life or my previous ones?" She then went on to
describe a series of earlier incarnations, ranging from being a com-
poser during the eighteenth century, to having been a refugee who was
killed at the end of the Second World War. She often felt that suicide
would be her best solution, since her next incarnation might give her a
better life than this one.

Her early life history was marked by emotional neglect. Her father had
been a petroleum geologist, and her family had frequently moved from
one country to another. The parents provided little personal attention for
the children. Over the years, the patient had found she could retreat
into a rich fantasy world. Although she became quickly involved with
other people, she rarely became intimate with them.

Diagnosis   This patient's personality pattern reflected instability in relationships, self-image, and affects, as well as impulsivity. She met eight
of the nine DSM-IV criteria for BPD (the exception being criterion 8, describing inappropriate intense anger).

Treatment   The initial plan was to provide her with a safe haven,
through an alliance with a therapist on whom she could comfortably de-

pend. She attended therapy over the last 2 years of her university course, and over this time gradually became less suicidal. In the course of these sessions, she tended initially to talk about her fantasies. Instead, the therapist actively encouraged her to focus on events in her everyday life. In doing so, he also confronted her about her maladaptive attachments to men, which were largely responsible for her suicidality. The treatment concluded at the time of her graduation. On 5-year follow-up, she had continued to be successful in her field. She was living a lonely existence, but was no longer considering suicide as an option.

Treatability

In this example of borderline personality, the patient had unusually florid cognitive symptoms. However, she was never psychotic, nor did the quasi-psychotic phenomena interfere with her functioning. Her ability to work successfully in spite of her subjective distress suggested that she would be treatable, and allowed the therapist to focus on her problems with self-esteem and her destructive interpersonal patterns.

The adaptive use of traits

The goal of the therapy was to allow her to continue to use imagination and intuition in her work, but to block the maladaptive use of these same traits in her relationships. Although she did give up her most dysfunctional behaviors, her traits set limits on the outcome. It was difficult for her to enter relationships on any other basis than fantasies based on her unmet needs. In the end, she learned from experience that she could not manage close relationships, gave up on her search for them, and did not establish any stable intimacy. This long-term outcome is not unusual in BPD (McGlashan, 1993).

The social context of psychotherapy

There were a number of social factors implicated in the development of this patient's psychopathology. She came from a background in which high geographical mobility was associated with both family dysfunction and isolation from the larger community. Her story reflects in many ways difficulties in identity formation for young people who lack models (see Chapter 5). In a more traditional and socially integrated environment, which would have structured relationships for her, she might have suffered a good deal less.

Narcissistic personality disorder

Case history

Narcissistic personality disorder (NPD) has been the subject of a large volume of clinical literature. The main contributions, published 20 years ago (Kohut, 1970, 1977; Kernberg, 1976), emphasized the strong needs these patients have for external recognition. For this reason, narcissistic patients often make better use of their talents at work, where recognition depends on one's abilities, than in interpersonal relationships, which require empathy and concern for others. Their difficulties in managing intimacy usually become the focus of treatment.

Clinical presentation   A 30-year-old physician came for therapy after a divorce. The marriage, which had lasted 3 years, was marked by his chronic infidelity, substance abuse, and verbal attacks on his spouse. Nonetheless, he felt grieved by the loss of his wife.

Diagnosis   This patient's personality pattern reflected grandiosity, a need for admiration, and a lack of empathy. He met eight of the nine criteria for NPD in DSM-IV (the exception being criterion 8, concerning envy).

Treatment   The therapy addressed some of the reasons for this man's maladaptive personality traits. In childhood, his parents had not re-sponded to his needs. Although his mother was a clergywoman, she was entirely preoccupied with her career. The patient was clever and physically attractive, and had discovered early in life that he could com-pensate for this neglect through charm and sexual flirtation, and was al-ways surrounded by women.

This patient's self-blame and depressive feelings made him somewhat more accessible to therapy. He continued to be successful in his work, where difficulties with intimacy did not arise. Much of the therapy con-sisted of confrontations concerning his inability to understand or take into account the needs of other people, and considering alternate strat-egies for managing interpersonal conflict. These difficulties were also placed in the historical frame of the failure of his parents to empathize with his feelings when he was a child.

When he began a new intimate relationship with a woman 1 year after his divorce, the treatment focused on his difficulty in being open with her and asking for help. The outcome was that he was able to maintain this relationship, and to remain faithful. However, his improvement was fragile, as demonstrated by the fact that he continued to fantasize about new sexual conquests. He was only able to control his tendency to act on his fantasies by telephoning members of his AA group. With the help of regular attendance at AA meetings, he was also able to stop using substances.

Treatability

In this example of a narcissistic patient, success at work was a measure of his ability to benefit from treatment. The therapy was able to focus on his problems in intimate relationships, and to help the patient develop a better sense of responsibility for his difficulties with other people.

The adaptive use of traits

His traits were characterized by a dependence on external rewards, and a need for continuous novelty and stimulation. The patient was therefore encouraged to seek recognition, not through the domination and seduction of women, but through productivity in work. As a physician, he could be reasonably successful if he were persistent. He had to accept that this mode would not provide him with the "high" he obtained from flirting or plotting a seduction. Another element that helped him to moderate his traits involved expanding his social network. Because of his shame, he was at first able to relate to people only inside AA. Later on he made contact with people who were not in the organization. He was further encouraged to meet his needs for stimulation through his developing career, and not through a series of "fantasy women".

The social context of psychotherapy

The social factors in this patient's personality disorder are of interest. He came from a traditional and religious family in a small town. However, his impulsive personality traits demanded more structure from his upbringing than he actually received. By failing to guide him and to be responsive to his emotional needs, his parents could not help him develop a secure identity. Although he was able to develop a professional role, society did not provide him with a structure for developing intimate relationships. As a result, he was able to develop socially desirable skills associated with autonomy and individualism, but at great personal cost.

The destructiveness of this patient towards others demonstrates the social impact of narcissistic personality. Nonetheless, his feelings of inner isolation and depression led him to seek treatment and motivated him to moderate his traits, so that he eventually became capable of developing some degree of intimacy.

Histrionic personality disorder

Histrionic patients resemble those with NPD, in that they are over-invested in external recognition. However, on the whole, they are better candidates for psychotherapy, since they tend to be less grandiose, less entitled, and less impulsive. The therapeutic strategy is to redirect their emotional needs into more adaptive channels.

Case history

Clinical presentation A 28-year-old special education teacher asked for therapy because she was in danger of destroying her marriage. Her relationship with her husband had been stable until fairly recently, when she felt strongly tempted to start an extramarital affair with a colleague. The crisis arose when her husband became less emotionally available, as he attempted to start his own business. She found herself even more labile than usual, responding with anger or tears to minor stressors. In addition, she found the demands of her 4-year-old daughter trying, and was unnecessarily irritable with her.

The patient had a particular reason to be concerned about family breakdown. Her daughter might be deprived of a father, as she herself had been at age 13. Her relationship with her own father had been intense and idealizing until he had died suddenly and unexpectedly after surgery. As a child, her family had valued her physical attractiveness. She had been the apple of her father's eye; her mother told her that she must never leave the house without makeup. As an adolescent, she always had admiring men surrounding her. A superior level of intelligence allowed her to become the first person in her family to complete university and develop a professional career.

Diagnosis This patient's personality pattern reflected excessive emotionality and attention seeking. She met all eight criteria for HPD in DSM-IV.

Treatment The treatment strategy was to modify her needs for external confirmation from men, and to help her to gain more satisfaction from both her job and her role as a mother. On 5-year follow-up, she was able to maintain her marriage, take advanced training in her field, and go on to have a second child.

Treatability

The treatability of this patient was suggested by a positive work history. As compared to the other cases presented from the impulsive cluster, this patient had much less disturbed inter-personal relationships. She had been able to manage marriage and motherhood up to the time of her clinical presentation, and had loyal attachments to a wide circle of friends.

The adaptive use of traits

The therapist encouraged the patient to use her personality traits, such as a lively temperament, a quick wit, and a need for external recognition, in her work as a teacher, where they were definite assets. These traits were not so adaptive in her family, where she needed to scale down her demands, partic-ularly at times when her husband and daughter were them-selves needy.

The social context of psychotherapy

The social factors in this patient's difficulties reflect some of the transitions that affect the lives of contemporary women. She had been brought up in a family where self-esteem de-rived from physical attractiveness. However, she later entered a world of professional accomplishment in which her parents would have been unable to guide her. There was also an im-portant social dimension inherent in the course of this ther-apy. With a different therapeutic approach, e.g., a greater fo-cus on validating the patient's needs for recognition, her marriage might well have ended in divorce. Such an outcome would have most likely been negative for the patient and for the other members of her family.

Avoidant personality disorder

Disorders in the anxious cluster, although commonly seen in clinical practice, present special difficulties. Anxiously attached individuals tend to develop anxious attachments in treatment. They may use therapy as a place where they can continually be protected from a threatening world, rather than as a necessary but temporary haven while learning to become more autonomous. Thus, the avoidant patient may continue to avoid entering intimate attachments outside the treatment, and the dependent patient may wish to depend unnecessarily on the therapist. Change in these patients can be slow, and they tend to require an active approach.

Case history

Clinical presentation   A 50-year-old physiotherapist had seen many other therapists in the past. None of these treatments had any lasting results. Her strengths included success in work, and loyal friends of the same sex. Her chief complaint was an inability to form any permanent heterosexual attachments. This problem was associated with difficulties in tolerating either separation from or demands by another person for intimacy. She seemed to have an inordinate need to be in control of the boundaries of any relationship.

She remembered herself as a shy child, always close to tears, who was highly sensitive to any changes in her environment. Her early life had been marked by multiple losses. She was the last-born of a large family, and had been given away at birth to her aunt and uncle for raising. Her aunt then died, and she was returned to her family, where she felt, quite justifiably, that she was an outsider.

Diagnosis   Her personality pattern was marked by social inhibition, feelings of inadequacy, and hypersensitivity to negative evaluation. She met six out of the seven criteria for APD in DSM-IV (the exception being criterion 1, describing the avoidance of occupational activities involving interpersonal contact).

Treatment   As an adult, although she had no difficulty sharing or examining her feelings, she felt unable to take risks with her life. Several attempts at change through psychotherapy had been fruitless. It was only in late middle age that her problems began to remit. For the first time, she was able to develop a stable and meaningful attachment to a man. Both parties to this relationship needed their boundaries, and when they had briefly attempted to live together, they quarreled disastrously. She was most comfortable when she was able to see him regularly but could retain her own residence. The therapist encouraged this choice, communicating to the patient that avoiding this level of intimacy was simply a way of acknowledging her needs as an individual, and was not a personal failure. At the same time, he helped her to feel that her decision not have a family did not indicate any deficit in her, but reflected a rational appraisal of her needs, based on her personality traits.

This chronic but eventually remitting course could admit of different explanations. One possibility is that her anxious temperament ameliorated over time. Alternatively, it became possible for her to form an intimate attachment only at a time in her life cycle when the ensuing commitments would be more manageable, and in circumstances where she would not be expected to live with another person, or raise a child.

Treatability

As with all the cases presented here, the capacity to work indicated treatability. Another encouraging sign was that all the patient's relationships, other than intimate ones, had been successful.

The adaptive use of traits

The treatment strategy was to capitalize on her most positive trait, that of persistence, and to minimize her most negative trait, that of avoidance. There was a basic limitation as to what therapy could accomplish, given the consistent problems she had with boundaries.

The social context of psychotherapy

The social dimension of her psychopathology involved an upbringing that failed to provide her with sufficient structure. If she had been raised in a traditional society, she might have had the choice of entering family structures that place less demands on its members for intimacy, or of finding another structure outside marriage. As it was, she entered a professional world where the social expectations for exclusive intimacy with a partner were unreachable for her, and made her feel like a failure. Unlike the schizoid patient described above, she desired intimacy in some form. Her solution involved an unconventional but ultimately workable compromise between closeness and separateness.

Dependent personality disorder

Case history

Clinical presentation A 30-year-old accountant presented because of difficulties in his work and his marriage. At his job, he functioned well within a hierarchy, but he became excessively anxious whenever he had to make decisions on his own. In his marriage, he felt dominated by his wife, yet terrified that she might leave him.

He described himself as having been a clingy child, and often felt he was a burden to his mother, who seemed to be chronically depressed. His father, a former prisoner in the Second World War, was often irritable, and took little interest in his children. The patient's most vivid childhood memory involved having been seriously ill, and then sent away by his parents for treatment in a distant hospital for several months, where they rarely visited him.

Although he had been able to obtain a university education, he did not leave home until he married at age 28. His wife, introduced to him by a relative, was an authoritative woman who made most of the decisions in the home.

Diagnosis His personality pattern was characterized by a lack of autonomy and an excessive need for nurturance. He met all eight criteria for DPD in DSM-IV.

Treatment In psychotherapy, emphasis was placed on expanding those areas in which he functioned with some degree of autonomy. Thus, there was a good deal of discussion about how he could manage better at work: asking advice from others in his firm, but accepting the anxiety that came with taking responsibility for his own decisions. He also frequently asked for advice from the therapist, who would then ask him to recall instances in which he had been able to reach useful decisions in the past. He was able to make more progress at his job than in resolving his conflicts at home, where he continued to feel victimized by but ultimately dependent on his wife. The couple decided not to have children, which probably helped them to maintain a stable relationship.

Treatability

In spite of conflict in both sectors, his ability to hold a responsible job and to maintain a relationship with his wife were indicators of a good prognosis.

The adaptive use of traits

The therapy aimed to make use of his more adaptive traits, such as persistence. For example, his dependence was more adaptive in the work situation if he could consult with his colleagues. Given his personality traits, and his choice of a mate, the treatment focused on helping him to find a way around his conflicts with his wife, rather than attempting to develop what might have been, for him, an uncomfortable level of assertiveness.

The social context of psychotherapy

This patient had been alternately overprotected and under-protected as a child, and was not taught or modeled how to develop autonomy. His adaptations reflected his ability to function successfully within a social structure, his difficulties reflected the points at which those adaptations broke down.

Compulsive personality disorder

Patients with strong compulsive traits can be unexciting for psychotherapists. Nonetheless, they are in many ways easier to treat. Compulsive individuals are hard working, persistent, and goal directed. These are qualities that tend to predict success in treatment. Therapy itself is a "compulsive" procedure, in that it is tightly scheduled, requires persistent effort, and is characterized by slow progress. Although compulsive patients may lack the spontaneity and creativity required for good ther-apeutic work, therapy is a modality that is consistent with their personality. The main danger is that they may use treatment to justify further procrastination, and avoid life decisions while ostensibly waiting for the perfect situation, or the "decisive moment" to take action.

Case history

Clinical presentation A 30-year-old businessman consulted for an in-ability to make decisions in life. Although he had been able to begin a professional career, he made very little money because of continued procrastination. He had experienced a series of love affairs with rather flamboyant women, all of which had ended indecisively.

As a child he had always been serious and cautious. At age 13, these traits became exaggerated when his father became bankrupt due to unwise investments. As a result, they had to move out of their house for a more modest accommodation. As the eldest son, he had greater responsibility for his family and did not move out until he was 25. His plodding but persistent approach, with the aid of generous scholarships, helped him to finish university and to obtain employment.

Diagnosis The patient's personality was characterized by orderliness, perfectionism, and control. He met seven of the eight criteria for CPD in DSM-IV (the exception being criterion 3, describing an excessive devotion to work).

Treatment The strategy of the psychotherapy was to confront him with his use of procrastination as an avoidance mechanism. He saw every career move as fraught with unseen dangers, and feared "settling" for any woman, and incurring a burden of unbearable compromises.

This treatment was lengthy (3 years), but the ultimate outcome was favorable. The patient became more assertive at work, and was able to make a sufficient income. He married a professional woman who in many ways shared his compulsivity, and who provided him with a stable and reliable partnership. On 5-year follow-up, they had one child and had managed to fit parenting into their demanding schedule.

Treatability

This patient was a notable underachiever at work, but had enough investment and success at his job to benefit from a treatment that was focused on his interpersonal relationships.

The adaptive use of traits

This patient's compulsive traits were malleable, in that he could apply persistence and goal-directedness where it was appropriate, on his job, and not apply them where they were inappropriate, in his search for the "perfect woman".

The social context of psychotherapy

Psychologically, many of his difficulties were a reaction to his disappointment with his father. However, there were also social dimensions to his difficulties. He lived in a society in which individual choice is overvalued, so that the fear of making wrong choices can become paralyzing. As with several of the other patients described here, he suffered from a lack of modeling and guidance, either from his family, or from the larger society.

Conclusions

All the case examples presented here reflect, to some extent, the tensions created by contemporary society. It is interesting to speculate how all these patients might have functioned in a more traditional social structure. One possibility is that some of them would not have developed in the same way, since they would have had more consistent socialization and stronger role models. These protective factors have been shown to be of particular importance for young men (Werner & Smith, 1992), but they are probably becoming more important for women, who society also expects to develop high levels of autonomy.

There are personality traits that could be troublesome in any social setting, and some of these patients would probably have had difficulty in a traditional society. For example, both the schizoid and avoidant women might have had arranged marriages, and this contingency could have reduced their social isolation. However, such marriages would also have deprived them of useful careers, and they might have felt excluded and uncomfortable inside the extended family structure. There are, in fact, alternate roles to marriage available in traditional societies, such as religious vocations, which allow individuals to avoid the problems of intimacy, and to have a sense of dedication and purpose through service.

In summary, these clinical vignettes demonstrate principles developed earlier in the chapter:

1. The treatment of personality disordered patients involves reversing the amplification of traits to disorders.
2. Psychotherapeutic interventions have the primary goal of correcting the maladaptive use of traits in the patient's present life.
3. For patients at somewhat lower levels of functioning, most of the therapeutic work focuses on helping them to work,

while for those at higher levels, the work can focus more on resolving problems in interpersonal relationships.

4. The most effective strategy for these patients involves working with traits, and not against them; patients who recover from personality disorders continue to show the same traits applied more flexibly and adaptively.

5. Patients with personality disorders are more likely to recover if they can find a productive place in society.

6. Patients with personality disorders can do psychological harm to those with whom they are intimate and this is a legitimate concern for clinicians.

Epilogue: summary and research implications

At this point, it would be useful to summarize the major ideas presented in this book:

1. Personality disorders have only recently been recognized as categories of psychiatric illness. Yet, these conditions are responsible for disturbances in functioning as great as in other mental disorders.
2. Personality disorders can best be conceptualized as amplifications of underlying personality traits. The biological factors in their etiology are temperamental variations, which strongly influence traits. The psychological risk factors for personality disorders concern family dysfunction. Social risk factors have their greatest impact on those who are already at biological and/or psychological risk.
3. Epidemiological research can examine the effects of social factors on the personality disorders by demonstrating differential prevalence of these disorders under different social conditions.
4. Social factors affect personality structure. One mechanism involves the influence of the social context on family functioning. There have been recent increases in the frequency of breakdown of nuclear families, as well as an increased prevalence of mental disorders affecting parenting capacity. Rapid social change has led to the breakdown of social networks and structures.
4. A biopsychosocial model of the personality disorders should take into account all the interactions between these factors.
5. The treatment of personality disorders has had limited results. The persistence of traits is the limiting factor in ther-

apy. However, psychotherapy of the personality disorders might be able to manage these patients better by working *with* traits, and by focusing on social adaptation and competence.

The present book has proposed a general theoretical model of the personality disorders. The arguments in support of this model have inevitably had to be somewhat speculative. But in principle, the hypotheses of this book are open to empirical testing. There are a number of possible future directions for research:

1. There is no point in researching entities that are likely to be discarded as invalid. We need to better define the individual categories of personality disorder. In the present classification, only antisocial personality disorder has been well validated, and even this entity has its controversial aspects. Two other categories, schizotypal and borderline, have a reasonable level of validity. The other categories describe entities based on very few data. Each personality disorder diagnosis therefore needs to approach more closely the criteria for the validity of any psychiatric disorder (Robins & Guze, 1970): specific etiological factors, specific outcome, and specific treatment response.

2. Personality disorders can be studied in two separate but complementary ways. A categorical approach describes the qualitative difference between psychopathology and normality, while a dimensional approach acknowledges the continuity of traits and disorders. Biological factors seem to be more specific to the dimensions of personality, but psychosocial factors have been studied in relationship to categories.

3. We need research to identify the biological factors in personality disorders: to determine their heritability, whether they are accompanied by biological markers, and whether children who later develop personality disorders begin life with extreme temperaments.

4. We need much more research concerning the influence of psychological factors on the development of personality disorders. In order to overcome the inevitable distortions of

retrospective studies, future studies should use prospective designs.

5. We need to determine the community prevalence of the personality disorders. These studies could begin in Western societies, and then be repeated in cross-cultural research around the globe. Once we know the basic prevalence of any personality disorder, the next step would be to examine the relationship of that prevalence to social class, culture, and cohort effects. Studies of the prevalence of personality disorders should compare those societies that are more "traditional" and those that are more "modern". In this way, we could empirically test the hypothesis offered in this book that the social risk factors for the personality disorders involve social disintegration and rapid social change.

6. If the personality disorders have a multidimensional etiology, multivariate studies are needed to examine biological, psychological, and social factors in the same patient populations.

7. While waiting for breakthroughs on the biological front, we can study interactions between the psychological and social risk factors for the personality disorders. For example, we might attempt to determine the mechanisms behind the variations in the prevalence of antisocial personality disorder in different societies, and examine the association of such variations with family structures. Other hypotheses that could be tested are whether the presence of different social risk and protective factors in various societies determines whether "schizotaxia" leads to odd cluster personality disorders, whether trait impulsivity leads to impulsive personality disorders, and whether behavioral inhibition leads to anxious cluster personality disorders.

8. We need to know more about the natural course of the personality disorders. We cannot conclude that any of the present methods for treating these patients are effective without systematic, clinical trials. Studies of outcome might also compare the long-term course of the same disorders in different societies, or in different cultural groups within the same society. Such studies could test the hypothesis that the presence of social structures and supports makes recovery from personality disorders more likely.

9. We badly need systematic clinical trials to determine whether there are effective ways of treating patients with personality disorders. These trials would have to examine treatment over longer periods than in previous psychotherapy research. In addition, research should aim to determine more precisely which populations of patients benefit from which forms of therapy, as well to define the mechanisms of change for personality disordered patients.

This book has taken pains to underline that no single factor can account for the development of psychopathology. The message is that the real world is immensely complex, and that the importance of any factor cannot be understood unless examined in interaction with a multitude of other influences. It is this complexity that makes the study of personality disorders fascinating and rewarding.

References

Adler G. (1985) *Borderline psychopathology and its treatment.* New York, Jason Aronson.

Ainsworth M. D., Blehar M. C., Waters E., & Wall S. (1978) *Patterns of attachment.* Hillsdale, NJ, Erlbaum.

Akiskal H. S., Hirschfeld R. M. A., & Yervanian B. I. (1983) The relationship of personality to affective disorders: a critical review. *Archives of General Psychiatry,* **40**, 801–10.

Al-Issa I. (1982) Sex differences in psychopathology. In I. Al-Issa (Ed.) *Culture and psychopathology.* Baltimore, University Park Press, pp. 3–32.

Alden L. (1989) Short-term structured treatment for avoidant personality disorder. *Journal of Consulting and Clinical Psychology,* **56**, 756–64.

American Psychiatric Association. (1952) *Diagnostic and statistical manual of mental disorders.* Washington, DC, American Psychiatric Press.

American Psychiatric Association. (1968) *Diagnostic and statistical manual of mental disorders.* 2nd edition. Washington, DC, American Psychiatric Press.

American Psychiatric Association. (1980) *Diagnostic and statistical manual of mental disorders,* 3rd edition. Washington, DC, American Psychiatric Press.

American Psychiatric Association. (1994). *Diagnostic and statistical manual of mental disorders,* 4th edition. Washington, DC, American Psychiatric Press.

Andreoli A., Frances A., Gex-Fabry M., Aapro N., Gerin P., & Dazord M. (1993) Crisis intervention in depressed patients with and without DSM-III-R personality disorders. *Journal of Nervous and Mental Disease,* **181**, 732–6.

Anthony E. J. & Cohler B. J. (Eds.) (1987) *The invulnerable child.* New York, Guilford.

Arbel N. & Stravynski A. (1991) A retrospective study of separation in the development of adult avoidant personality disorder. *Acta Psychiatrica Scandinavica,* **83**, 174–8.

Badgley R. F. (1984) *Committee on sexual offenses against children and youth, Canada: sexual offense against children.* Ottawa, Supply and Services Canada.

Bagby R. M., Joffe R. T., Parker J. D. A., & Schuller D. R. (1993) Re-examination of the evidence for the DSM-III personality disorder clusters. *Journal of Personality Disorders,* **7**, 320–8.

Bakan P. & Peterson K. (1994) Pregnancy and birth complications: a risk factor for schizotypy. *Journal of Personality Disorders,* **8**, 299–306.

Baker R. A. (1990) *Hidden memories.* Buffalo, NY, Prometheus.

Bandura A. (1977) *Social learning theory.* Englewood Cliffs, NJ, Prentice Hall.

Barkow J. H., Cosmides L., & Tooby J. (1992) *The adapted mind: evolutionary psychology and the generation of culture.* New York, Oxford University Press.

Barnier A. J. & McConkey K. M. (1992) Reports of real and false memories: the relevance of hypnosis, hypnotizability, and the context of memory test. *Journal of Abnormal Psychology,* **101**, 512–27.

Bartlett F. C. (1932) *Remembering: a study in experimental and social psychology.* New York, Cambridge University Press.

Beavers R. W. (1977): *Psychotherapy and growth: a family systems perspective.* New York, Brunner Mazel.

Beavers R. W. & Hampson R. B. (1990) *Successful families.* New York, Norton.

Beck A. T. (1983) *Cognitive therapy of depression.* In P. J. Clayton & J. E. Barrett (Eds.) *Treatment of depression,* New York, Raven, pp. 265–90.

Beck A. T. & Freeman A. (1990) *Cognitive therapy of personality disorders.* New York, Guilford.

Benedict R. (1938, reprinted 1961) *Patterns of culture.* New York, Houghton Mifflin.

Benjamin L. (1993) *Interpersonal diagnosis and treatment of personality disorders: a structural approach.* New York, Guilford.

Bergeman C. S., Chipuer H. M., Plomin R., Pedersen, N. L., McClearn G. E., Nesselroade J. R., Costa P. T., & McCrae R. R. (1993) Genetic and environmental effects on openness to experience, agreeableness, and conscientiousness: an adoption/twin study. *Journal of Personality,* **61**, 158–179.

Berrios G. S. (1993) European views on personality disorders: a conceptual history. *Comprehensive Psychiatry,* **34**, 14–30.

Berry J. W., Poortinga Y. H., Segall M. H., & Dasen P. R. (1992) *Cross-cultural psychology: research and applications.* Cambridge, Cambridge University Press.

Beutler L. E., Machado P. P., & Neufeldt S. A. (1994) Research on therapist variables in psychotherapy, In S. L. Garfield, & A. E. Bergin (Eds.) *Handbook of psychotherapy and behavior change,* 4th edition. New York, Wiley, pp. 229–69.

Black D. W., Baumgord C. H., & Bell S. E. (1995) A 16–45 year follow-up of 71 men with antisocial personality disorder. *Comprehensive Psychiatry*, **36**, 130–40.

Blackburn R. (1988) On moral judgments and personality disorders. *British Journal of Psychiatry*, **153**, 505–512.

Blacker K. H. & Tupin J. P. (1991) Hysteria and hysterical structure: developmental and social issues. In M. J. Horowitz (Ed.) *Hysterical personality style and the histrionic personality disorder*, revised edition. Northvale, NJ, Jason Aronson, pp. 17–66.

Bland R. C., Newman S. C., & Orn H. (1988) Lifetime prevalence of psychiatric disorders in Edmonton. *Acta Psychiatrica Scandinavica*, **77** (Suppl. 338) 24–32.

Blashfield R. K. (1990) An American view of the ICD-10 personality disorders. *Acta Psychiatrica Scandinavica*, **82**, 250–6.

Blashfield R., Noyes R., Reich J., Woodman C., Cook B. L., & Garvey M. J. (1994) Personality disorder traits in generalized anxiety and panic disorder patients. *Comprehensive Psychiatry*, **35**, 329–34.

Bleuler E. (1950) *Dementia praecox or the group of schizophrenias*. New York, International Universities Press.

Bohman M., Sigvardsson S., Cloninger R., & von Knorring, A.-L. (1982) Predisposition to petty criminality in Swedish adoptees: I: genetic and environmental heterogeneity. *Archives of General Psychiatry*, **39**, 1233–41.

Bolgar R., Zweig-Frank H., & Paris J. (1995) Childhood antecedents of interpersonal problems in young adult children of divorce. *Journal of the American Academy of Child and Adolescent Psychiatry*, **34**, 143–50.

Bond M. P., Gardner S., Christian J., & Sigal J. J. (1983) Empirical study of self-rated defense styles. *Archives of General Psychiatry*, **40**, 333–8.

Bond M., Paris J., & Zweig-Frank H. (1994) Defense styles and borderline personality disorder. *Journal of Personality Disorders*, **8**, 28–31.

Bornstein R. F. (1992) The dependent personality: developmental, social, and clinical perspectives. *Psychological Bulletin*, **112**, 3–23.

Bouchard T. J., Lykken D. T., McGue M., Segal N. L., & Tellegen A. (1990) Sources of human psychological differences: the Minnesota study of twins reared apart. *Science*, **250**, 223–8.

Bower G. H. (1990) Awareness, the unconcious, and repression. In J. Singer (Ed.) *Repression and dissociation*. Chicago, University of Chicago Press, pp. 209–31.

Bowlby J. (1969, 1973, 1980) *Attachment and loss*, 3 volumes. London, Hogarth Press.

Boyd R. & Richerson, P. J. (1986) *Culture and the evolutionary process*. Chicago, University of Chicago Press.

Boyer L. & Giovacchini P. L. (Eds.) (1990) *Master clinicians on treating the regressed patient.* Northvale, NJ, Jason Aronson.

Brewin C. R., Andrews B., & Gotlib I. H. (1993) Psychopathology and early experience: a reappraisal of retrospective reports. *Psychological Bulletin,* **113**, 82–98.

Brier J. & Zadli L. L. (1989) Sexual abuse histories and sequelae in female psychiatric room patients. *American Journal of Psychiatry,* **146**, 1602–6.

Bronfenbrenner U. (1970) *The ecology of human development.* Cambridge, MA, Harvard University Press.

Brooks R. B., Baltazar P. L., McDowell D. E., Munjack D. J., & Bruns J. R. (1991) Personality disorders co-occuring with panic disorder with agoraphobia. *Journal of Personality Disorders,* **5**, 328–36.

Brown G. W. & Harris, T. (1978) *Social origins of depression.* New York, Free Press.

Brown G. W. & Harris, T. (1982) Social class and affective disorder. In I. Al-Issa (Ed.) *Culture and psychopathology.* Baltimore, University Park Press, pp. 125–56.

Browne A. & Finkelhor D. (1986) Impact of child sexual abuse: a review of the literature. *Psychological Bulletin,* **99**, 66–77.

Buss D. M. & Plomin R. (1984) *Temperament: early developing personality traits.* Hillsdale, NJ, Erlbaum.

Byrne C. P., Cernovsky A., & Velamoor V. R. (1990) A comparison of borderline and schizophrenic patients for childhood life events and parent-child relationships. *Canadian Journal of Psychiatry,* **35**, 590–5.

Cadoret R. J. (1986) Epidemiology of antisocial personality. In W. H. Reid, D. Dorr, J. I. Walker, & J. W. Bonner (Eds.) *Unmasking the psychopath.* New York, Norton, pp. 28–44.

Carey G. & DiLalla D. L. (1994) Personality and psychopathology: genetic perspectives. *Journal of Abnormal Psychology,* **103**, 32–43.

Carpenter W. T., Kirkpatrick B., & Buchanan R. W. (1990) Conceptual approaches to the study of schizophrenia. In A. Kales, C. N. Stefanis, & J. A. Talbott (Eds.) *Recent advances in schizophrenia.* New York, Springer Verlag, pp. 95–116.

Carson R. C. & Sanislow C. A. (1993) The schizophrenias. In P. B. Sutker & H. E. Adams (Eds.) *Comprehensive textbook of psychopathology,* New York, Plenum, pp. 295–336.

Casey P. R., Tyrer P. J., & Dillon S. (1986) The diagnostic status of patients with conspicuous psychatric morbidity in primary care. *Psychological Medicine,* **14**, 673–81.

Casey P. R. & Tyrer P. R. (1986) Personality, functioning, and symptomatology. *Journal of Psychiatric Research,* **20**, 363–74.

Caspi A. & Silva P. A. (1995) Temperamental qualities at age three predict adult personality traits. *Child Development,* **66**, 486–98.

Charron M. F. (1981) *Le suicide au Québec.* Québec, Ministère des Affaires Sociales, Gouvernement du Québec.

Chen C., Wong J., Lee N., Chan-Ho M., Lau J. F., & Fung M. (1993) The Shatin Community mental health survey in Hong Kong. *Archives of General Psychiatry,* **50,** 125–33.

Chess S. & Thomas A. (1990) The New York Longitudinal Study: the young adult periods. *Canadian Journal of Psychiatry,* **35,** 557–61.

Cheung P. (1991) Adult psychiatric epidemiology in China in the 1980's. *Culture, Medicine and Psychiatry,* **15,** 479–96.

Chodoff P. (1982) Hysteria and women. *American Journal of Psychiatry,* **139,** 545–51.

Chu J. A. & Dill, D. L. (1990) Dissociative symptoms in relation to childhood physical and sexual abuse. *American Journal of Psychiatry,* **147,** 887–92.

Clarke A. & Clarke A. (1979) *Early experience and behavior.* New York, Free Press.

Clarkin J. F., Hull J. W., Cantor J., & Sanderson C. (1993) Borderline personality disorder and personality traits: a comparison of SCID-II BPD and NEO-PI. *Psychological Assessment,* **5,** 472–6.

Clarkin J. F., Widiger T. A., Frances A., Hurt S. W., & Gilmore M. (1983) Propotypic typology and the borderline personality disorder. *Journal of Abnormal Psychology,* **92,** 263–75.

Clayton P. J. & Barrett J. E. (Eds.) (1983) *Treatment of depression.* New York, Raven, pp. 265–90.

Cleckley H. (1964) *The mask of sanity.* 4th edition. St. Louis, Mosby.

Cloninger C. R. (1987) A systematic method for clinical description and classification of personality variants. *Archives of General Psychiatry,* **44,** 579–88.

Cloninger C. R. (1991) *Structure and inheritance of personality dimensions.* Presented to the Second International Congress on the disorders of the personality, Oslo, Norway.

Cloninger C. R., Martin R. L., Guze S. B., & Clayton P. J. (1990) The empirical structure of psychiatric comorbidity and its theoretical significance. In J. D. Maser & C. R. Cloninger, (Eds.) *Comorbidity of anxiety and depression.* Washington, DC, American Psychiatric Press, pp. 439–62.

Cloninger C. R., Reich T., & Guze S. B. (1978) Genetic-environmental interactions and antisocial behavior. In R. Hare & D. Schalling (Eds.) *Psychopathic behavior: approaches to research,* New York, Wiley.

Cloninger C. R., Sigvardsson S., & Bohman M. (1982) Predisposition to petty criminality in Swedish adoptees II: cross-fostering analysis of gene-environment interaction. *Archives of General Psychiatry,* **39,** 1242–53.

Cloninger C. R., Svrakic D. M., & Pryzbeck T. R. (1993) A psychobiological model of temperament and characters. *Archives of General Psychiatry*, **50**, 975–90.

Coccaro E. F. (1993) Psychopharmacological studies in patients with personality disorders: review and perspective. *Journal of Personality Disorders*, (Suppl.), **7**, 181–92.

Coccaro E. F. & Murphy D. S., (Eds.) (1990) *Serotonin in major psychiatric disorders*. Washington, DC, American Psychiatric Press.

Coccaro E. F., Siever L. J., Klar H. M., Maurer G., Cochrane K., Cooper T. B., Mohs, R. C., & Davis K. L. (1989) Serotonergic studies in patients with affective and personality disorders. *Archives of General Psychiatry*, **46**, 587–99.

Cohen A. (1992) Prognosis for schizophrenia in the third world: a re-evaluation of cross-cultural research. *Culture, Medicine and Psychiatry*, **16**, 53–75.

Cohen B. J., Nestadt G., Samuels J. F., Romanovski A. J., McHugh P. R., & Rabins P. V. (1994) Personality disorder in later life: a community study. *British Journal of Psychiatry*, **165**, 493–9.

Coid J. W. (1989) Psychopathic disorders. *Current Opinion in Psychiatry*, **2**, 750–6.

Compton W. W., Helzer J. E., Hwu, H.-G., Yeh E.-K., McEvoy L., Tipp J. E., & Spitznagel E. L. (1991) New methods in cross-cultural psychiatry: psychiatric illness in Taiwan and the United States. *American Journal of Psychiatry*, **148**, 1697–704.

Conte J. R., Wolf S., & Smith T. (1989) What sexual offenders tell us about prevention strategies. *Child Abuse and Neglect*, **13**, 293–301.

Cooke D. J. (in press) Psychopathic disturbance in the Scottish prison population: the cross-cultural generalizability of the Hare psychopathy checklist. *Psychology, Crime and Law*.

Costa P. T. & McRae R. R. (1988) From catalog to Murray's needs and the five factor model. *Journal of Personality and Social Psychology*, **55**, 258–65.

Costa P. T., & McCrae R. R. (1992) *NEO-PI-R professional manual*. Psychological Assessment Resources, Inc.

Costa P. T. & Widiger T. A. (Eds.) (1994) *Personality disorders and the five-factor model of personality*. Washington, DC, American Psychological Association.

Côté G. & Hodgins S. (1990) Co-occurring mental disorders among criminal offenders. *Bulletin of the American Academy of Psychiatry and the Law*, **18**, 271–81.

Cross-National Collaborative Group. (1992) The changing rate of major depression. *Journal of the American Medical Association*, **268**, 3098–3105.

Crowe R. R. (1974) An adoption study of antisocial personality. *Archives of General Psychiatry*, **31**, 785–91.

Dahl A. A. (1993) The personality disorders: a critical review of family, twin, and adoption studies. *Journal of Personality Disorders* (Suppl.), **7**, 86–99.

Dawkins R. (1976) *The selfish gene.* New York, Oxford University Press.

Day R., Neilse J. A., & Korten A. (1987) Stressful life events preceding the acute onset of schizophrenia. *Culture, Medicine and Psychiatry*, **11**, 123–205.

DeJong C. A., van den Brink M., Harteveld F. M., & van der Wielen E. G. (1993) Personality disorders in alcoholics and drug addicts. *Comprehensive Psychiatry*, **34**, 87–94.

DeMause L. (Ed.) (1974) *The history of childhood.* New York, Psychohistory Press.

DiNicola V. F. (1990) Anorexia multiforme: self-starvation in historical and cultural context. *Transcultural Psychiatric Research Review*, **27**, 165-96

Doi T. (1973) *The anatomy of dependence.* Tokyo, Kodansha International

Dolan B. & Coid J. (1993) *Psychopathic and antisocial personality disorders.* London, Royal College of Psychiatrists.

Dohrenwend B. P. & Dohrenwend B. S. (1969) *Social status and psychological disorder: a causal inquiry.* New York, Wiley.

Downey G. & Coyne J. C. (1990) Children of depressed parents: an integrative review. *Psychological Bulletin*, **108**, 50-76.

Dunn J. & Plomin R. (1990) *Separate lives: why siblings are so different.* New York, Basic Books.

Durham W. H. (1992) *Co-evolution: genes, culture, and human diversity.* Stanford, CA, Stanford University Press.

Durkheim E. (1951) *On suicide.* New York, Free Press.

Eaton W. W. (1986) *The sociology of mental disorders*, 2nd edition, New York, Praeger.

Edgerton R. B. (1992) *Sick societies: challenging the myth of primitive harmony.* New York, Free Press.

Eisenberg L. (1986) When is a case a case? In M. Rutter, C. E. Izard & P. B. Reard (Eds.) *Depression in young people.* New York, Guilford, pp. 469-78.

Elkin I., Shea T., Watkins J. T., Imber S. D., et al. (1989) National Institute of Mental Health Treatment of Depression Collaborative Research Program: general effectiveness of treatments. *Archives of General Psychiatry*, **46**, 971-82.

Ellenberger H. F. (1970) *The discovery of the unconscious.* New York, Basic Books.

Emerson J., Pankrantz L., Joos S., & Smith S. (1994) Personality disorders in problematical medical patients. *Psychosomatics*, **35**, 469-73.

Engel G. L. (1980) The clinical application of the biopsychosocial model. *American Journal of Psychiatry*, **137**, 535-44.

Engelsmann F. (1982) Culture and depression. In I. Al-Issa (Ed.) *Culture and psychopathology.* Baltimore, University Park Press, pp. 251-74.

Erikson E. (1950) *Childhood and society.* New York, Norton.

Evidence-Based Medicine Working Group. (1992) Evidence-based medicine: a new approach to teaching the practice of medicine. *Journal of the American Medical Association,* **268**, 2420–5.

Eysenck H. (1969) *The effects of psychotherapy.* New York, Science House.

Eysenck H. J. (1977) *Crime and personality.* London, Paladin.

Eysenck H. J. (1982) *Culture and personality abnormalities.* In I. Al-Issa (Ed.) *Culture and psychopathology.* Baltimore, University Park Press, pp. 277-308.

Eysenck H. J. (1987) The definition of personality disorders and the criteria apropriate to their defintion. *Journal of Personality Disorders,* **1**, 211-19.

Eysenck H. J. (1991) Genetic and environmental contributions to individual differences: the three major dimensions of personality. *Journal of Personality,* **58**, 245–61.

Fabrega H. (1994) Personality disorders as medical entities: a cultural interpretation. *Journal Personality Disorders,* **8**, 149–65.

Farrington D. (1991) Antisocial personality from childhood to adulthood. *The Psychologist,* **4**, 389–94.

Feldman R. B., Zelkowitz P., Weiss M., Heyman M., Vogel J., & Paris J. (1995) A comparison of the families of borderline personality disorder mothers and the families of other personality disorder mothers. *Comprehensive Psychiatry,* **36**, 1–8.

Finkelhor D., Hotaling G., Lewis I. A., & Smith C. (1990) Sexual abuse in a national survey of adult men and women: prevalence characteristics and risk factors. *Child Abuse and Neglect,* **14**, 19–28.

Fisher H. (1992) *The anatomy of love.* New York, Fawcett Columbine.

Flach F. (1990) The resilience hypothesis and post-traumatic stress disorder. In M. E. Wolf & A. D. Mosnaim (Eds.) (1990) *Post-traumatic stress disorder: etiology, phenomenology, and treatment.* Washington, DC, American Psychiatric Press, pp. 37–45.

Fontana A. & Rosenheck R. (1994) Posttraumatic stress disorder among Vietnam theatre veterans: a causal model of etiology in a community sample. *Journal of Nervous Mental Disease,* **182**, 677–84.

Frances A., Clarkin J., & Perry S. (1984) *Differential therapeutics in psychiatry.* New York, Brunner/Mazel.

Frances A. & Widiger T. (1986) The classification of personality disorders: an overview of problems and solutions. In A.

Frances & R. Hales (Eds.) *Review of Psychiatry*, **5**:240–57. Washington, DC, American Psychiatric Press.

Frank A. F. (1992) The therapeutic alliances of borderline patients. In J. F. Clarkin, E. Marziali & H. Munroe-Blum (Eds.) *Borderline personality disorder: clinical and empirical perspectives.* New York, Guilford, pp. 220–47.

Frank J. D. & Frank J. B. (1991) *Persuasion and healing,* 3rd edition, Baltimore, Johns Hopkins.

Frankel F. H. (1993) Adult reconstructions of childhood events in the multiple personality literature. *American Journal of Psychiatry*, **150**, 954–8.

Freeman D. (1983) *Margaret Mead and Samoa.* Cambridge, MA, Harvard University Press.

Freud S. (1937, reprinted 1964) *Analysis terminable and interminable. SE: XXIII*, 216–254, London, Hogarth.

Fromm E. (1955) *The sane society.* New York, Holt, Rinehardt, Winston.

Fulton M. & Winokur G. F. (1993) A comparative study of paranoid and schizoid personality disorders. *American Journal of Psychiatry*, **150**, 1363–7.

Gabbard G. O. & Coyne L. (1987) Predictors of response of antisocial patients to hospital treatment. *Hospital and Community Psychiatry*, **38**, 1181–5.

Garfield S. L. (1994) Research on client variables in psychotherapy. In S. L. Garfield & A. E. Bergin (Eds.) *Handbook of psychotherapy and behavior change,* 4th edition, New York, Wiley, pp. 190–228.

Geertz C. (1983); *Local knowledge.* New York, Basic Books.

Glantz K. & Pearce J. K. (1989) *Exiles from Eden: psychotherapy from an evolutionary perspective.* New York, Norton.

Goldberg E. M. & Morrison S. L. (1963) Schizophrenia and social class. *British Journal of Psychiatry*, **109**, 785–802.

Goldberg S. C., Schulz C., & Schulz P. M. (1986) Borderline and schizotypal patients treated with low-dose thiothixene and placebo. *Archives of General Psychiatry*, **43**, 680–6.

Golomn M., Fava M., Abraham M., & Rosenbaum J. F. (1995) Gender differences in personality disorders. *American Journal of Psychiatry*, **152**, 579–82.

Gordon R. A. (1990) *Anorexia and bulemia.* Cambridge MA, Blackwell.

Gottesman I. (1991) *Schizophrenia genesis.* New York, Freeman.

Grinker R. R. (1964) Psychiatry rushes madly in all directions. *Archives of General Psychiatry*, **10**, 228–37.

Grunbaum A. (1984) *The foundations of psychoanalysis.* Berkeley, CA, University of California Press.

Gunderson J. G. (1984) *Borderline personality disorder.* Washington, DC, American Psychiatric Press.

Gunderson J. G. (1985) Conceptual risks of the -II division. In H. Klar & L. J. Siever (Eds.) *Biological response styles: clinical implications.* Washington, DC, American Psychiatric Press, pp. 81–95.

Gunderson J. G., Frank A. F., Ronningstam E. F., Wahter S., Lynch V. J. & and Wolf P. J. (1989) Early discontinuance of borderline patients from psychotherapy. *Journal of Nervous Mental Disease,* **177**, 38–42.

Gunderson J. G. & Kolb J. E. (1978) Discriminating features of borderline patients. *American Journal of Psychiatry,* **135**, 792–6.

Gunderson J. G. & Phillips K. A. (1991) A current view of the interface between borderline personality disorder and depression. *American Journal of Psychiatry,* **148**, 967–75.

Gunderson J. G., Ronningstam E. & Bodkin A. (1990) The diagnostic interview for narcissistic patients. *Archives of General Psychiatry,* **47**, 676–80.

Gunderson J. G. & Singer M. T. (1975) Defining borderline patients: an overview. *American Journal of Psychiatry,* **132**, 1–9.

Gunderson J. G., Zanarini M. C.& Kisiel C. L. (1991) Borderline personality disorder: a review of data on DSM-III-R descriptions. *Journal of Personality Disorders,* **5**, 340–52.

Guze S.B. (1976) *Criminality and psychiatric disorders.* New York, Oxford University Press.

Halleck S. L. (1967) Hysterical personality – psychological, social and iatrogenic determinants. *Archives of General Psychiatry,* **16**, 750–7.

Hare R. D. (1980) Psychopathy. In H. Van Praag, M. Lader, O. Rafaelson, & E. Sacher (Eds.) *Handbook of biological psychiatry.* New York, Dekker.

Hare R. D. (1983) Diagnosis of antisocial personality in two prison populations. *American Journal of Psychiatry,* **140**, 887–90.

Harpur T. J., Hart S. D., & Hare, R. D. (1994) Personality of the psychopath. In P. T. Costa and T. A. Widiger (Eds.) *Personality disorders and the five-factor model.* Washington, DC, American Psychological Association, pp. 149–74.

Head S. B., Baker J. D., & Williamson D. A. (1991) Family environment characteristics and dependent personality disorder. *Journal of Personality Disorders,* **5**, 256–63.

Helzer J. E. & Canino, G. J. (Eds.) (1992) *Alcoholism in North America, Europe, and Asia.* New York, Oxford University Press.

Henry W. E. (1971) *The fifth profession.* San Francisco, Jossey-Bass.

Herman J. (1992) *Trauma and recovery.* New York, Basic Books.

Herman J. & Schatzow E. (1987) Recovery and verification of memories of childhood sexual trauma. *Psychoanalytical Psychology* **4**, 11–4.

Herman J. & van der Kolk B. (1987) Traumatic antecedents of borderline personality disorder. In B. van der Kolk (Ed.) *Psychological trauma.* Washington, DC, American Psychiatric Press, pp. II – 126.

Herman J. L., Perry J. C., & van der Kolk B. A. (1989) Childhood trauma in borderline personality disorder. *American Journal of Psychiatry*, **146**, 490–5.

Hetherington E. M., Cox M., & Cox R. (1985) Long-term effects of divorce and remarriage on the adjustment of children. *Journal of the American Academy of Child Psychiatry*, **24**, 518–30.

Hinde R. A. & Stevenson-Hinde J. (1991) Perspectives on attachment. In C. M. Parkes, J. Stevenson-Hinde, & P. Marris (Eds.) *Attachment across the life cycle.* London, Tavistock.

Hirschfeld R. M. A. (1993) Personality disorders: definition and diagnosis. *Journal of Personality Disorders*, **7**(Suppl.), 9–18.

Hirschfeld R. M. A., Shea M. T., & Weise R. (1991) Dependent personality disorder: perspectives for DSM-IV. *Journal of Personality Disorders*, **5**, 135–49.

Hoch P. H., Cattell J. P., Strahl M. D., & Penness H. H. (1962) The course and outcome of pseudoneurotic schizophrenia. *American Journal of Psychiatry*, **119**, 106–15.

Hoffart A., Thornes K., Hedley L. M., & Strand J. (1994) DSM-III-R Axis I and II disorders in agoraphobic patients with and without panic disorders. *Acta Psychiatrica Scandinavica*, **89**, 186–91.

Høglend P. (1993) Personality disorders and long-term outcome after brief dynamic psychotherapy. *Journal of Personality Disorders*, **7**, 168–81.

Holmes D. (1990) The evidence for repression: an examination of sixty years of research. In J. Singer (Ed.) *Repression and dissociation: implications for personality theory, psychopathology, and health.* Chicago, University of Chicago Press, pp. 85–102.

Horney K. (1940) *The neurotic personality of our time.* New York, Norton.

Horwitz L. (1974) *Clinical prediction in psychotherapy.* New York, Jason Aronson.

Howard K. I., Kopta S. M., Krasue M. S., & Orlinsky D. E. (1986) The dose-effect relationship in psychotherapy. *American Psychologist*, **2**, 159–64.

Howard K. I., Orlinsky D. E., & Lueger R. J. (in press) The design of clinically relevant outcome research: some considerations and an example. In M. Aveline & D. Shapiro (Eds.) *Research foundations for psychotherapy services.* Sussex, Wiley.

Hwu H. G., Yeh E. K., & Change L. Y. (1989) Prevalence of psychiatric disorders in Taiwan defined by the Chinese Diagnostic Interview Schedule. *Acta Psychiatrica Scandinavica*, **79**, 136–47.

Hyler S. & Lyons M. (1988) Factor analysis of DSM-III personality disorder clusters: a replication. *Comprehensive Psychiatry*, **29**, 304–8.

Hyler S., Reider R., Williams J., Spitzer R., Hendler J., & Lyons, M (1988) The Personality Disorder Questionnaire: development and preliminary results. *Journal of Personality Disorders*, **2**, 229–37.

Ikuta N., Zanarini M. C., Minawaka K., Miyake Y., Moriya N., & Nishizono-Maher A. (1994) Comparison of American and Japanese outpatients with borderline personality disorder. *Comprehensive Psychiatry*, **35**, 382–5.

Inkeles A. & Smith D. H. (1974) *Becoming modern: individual change in six developing countries.* Cambridge, Harvard University Press.

Iwawaki S., Eysenck S. B. G., & Eysenck H. J. (1977) Differences in personality between Japanese and English. *Journal of Social Psychology*, **102**, 27–33.

Janet P. (1907) *The major symptoms of hysteria.* New York, MacMillan.

Jilek-Aall L. (1988) Suicidal behavior among youth: a cross-cultural comparison. *Transcultural Psychiatric Research Review* **25**, 87–105.

Johnson P. (1992) *The birth of the modern.* London, Vintage.

Jones E. (1953) *The life and work of Sigmund Freud.* New York, Basic Books.

Kagan J. (1989) *Unstable ideas: temperament, cognition and self.* Cambridge, MA, Harvard University Press.

Kagan J. (1994) *Galen's prophecy.* New York, Basic Books.

Kagan J., Resnick J. S., Snidman N., Gibbons J., & Johnson M. O. (1988) Childhood derivatives of inhibition and lack of inhibition to the unfamiliar. *Child Development*, **59**, 1580–9.

Kass F., Skodol A. E., Charles E., Spitzer R. L., & Williams, J. B. W. (1985) Scaled ratings of DSM-III personality disorders. *American Journal of Psychiatry*, **142**, 627–30.

Kaufman C. Grunebaum H. Cohler B., & Gamer E., (1979) Superkids: competent children of schizophrenic mothers. *American Journal of Psychiatry*, **136**, 1398–402.

Keitner I. G. & Miller I. W. (1990) Family functioning and major depression; an overview. *American Journal of Psychiatry*, **147**, 1128–37.

Kendler K. S., Gruenberg A. M., & Strauss, J. J. (1981): An independent analysis of the Copenhagen sample of the Danish Adoption Study of Schizophrenia, II: the relationship between schizotypal personality disorder and schizophrenia. *Archives of General Psychiatry*, **38**, 983–4.

Kendler K. S., Masterson C. C., Ungaro R., & Davis K. L. (1984) A family history study of schizophrenia-related personality disorders. *American Journal of Psychiatry*, **143**, 424–8.

Kendler K. S., Neale M., Kessler R., Heath A., & Eaves L. (1993) A twin study of recent life events and difficulties. *Archives of General Psychiatry*, **50**, 789–96.

Kernberg O. F. (1976) *Borderline conditions and pathological narcissism.* New York, Jason Aronson.

Kernberg O. F. (1987) *Severe personality disorders.* New York, Basic Books.

Kernberg O. F., Coyne L., Appelbaum A., Horwitz L., & Voth H. (1972) Final report of the Menninger Psychotherapy Research Project. *Bulletin of the Menninger Clinic,* **36**, 1–275.

Kessler R. C., McGonagle K. A., Nelson C. B., Hughes M., Eshelman S., Wittchen H. U., & Kendler K. S. (1994) Lifetime and 12–month prevalence of DSM-III-R psychiatric disorders in the United States. *Archives of General Psychiatry,* **51**, 8–19.

Kihlstrom J. F., Glisky M. L., & Anguilo M. J. (1994) Dissociative tendencies and dissociative disorders. *Journal of Abnormal Psychology,* **103**, 117–24.

Kirmayer L. (1991) The place of culture in psychiatric nosology: taijin kyofusho and DSM-III-R. *Journal of Nervous and Mental Disease,* **179**, 19–28.

Kirmayer L. (1994) Suicide among Canadian aboriginal peoples. *Transcultural Psychiatric Research Review,* **31**, 3–58.

Kleinman A. & Good B. (Eds.) (1985) *Culture and depression: studies in the anthropology and cross-cultural psychology of affective disorders.* Berkeley, CA, University of California Press.

Klerman G. (1986) Historical perspectives on contemporary schools of psychopathology, in Millon T. & Klerman G., (Eds.) *Contemporary psychopathology: towards the DSM-IV.* New York, Guilford, pp. 3–28.

Klerman G. L. (Ed.) (1986) *Suicide and depression among adolescents and young adults.* Washington, DC, American Psychiatric Press.

Klerman G. L. & Weissman, M. M. (1989) Increasing rates of depression. *Journal of the American Medical Association,* **261**, 2229–35.

Koenigsberg H. W., Kaplan R. D., & Gilmore M. M. (1985) The relationships between syndrome and personality disorder in DSM-III: experience with 2462 patients. *American Journal of Psychiatry,* **142**, 207–12.

Kohut H. (1970) *The analysis of the self.* New York, International Universities Press.

Kohut H. (1977) *The restoration of the self.* New York, International Universities Press.

Konner M. (1987) Anthropology and psychiatry. In H. Kaplan & B. Sadock (Eds.) *Comprehensive textbook of psychiatry,* 5th edition, Baltimore, Williams & Wilkins, pp. 283–99.

Kopta S. M., Howard K. I., Lowry J. L., & Beutler L. E. (1994) Patterns of symptomatic recovery in psychotherapy. *Journal of Consulting and Clinical Psychology,* **62**, 1009–16.

Kovess V., Murphy M. B. M., & Tousignant M. (1987) Urban-rural comparisons of depressive disorders in French Canada. *Journal of Nervous and Mental Disease,* **175**, 457–65.

Kraepelin E. (1905) *Lectures on clinical psychiatry.* London, Balliere Tindall.

Kramer M., Brown A., Skinner J. A., & German P. (1989) Changing living arrangements in the population and their potential effect on the prevalence of mental disorders. In B. Cooper (Ed.) *The epidemiology of psychiatric disorders.* Baltimore, Johns Hopkins University Press, pp. 3–26.

Kramer P. (1993) *Listening to prozac.* New York, Viking.

Kranzler H. R., Satel S., & Apter A. (1994) Personality disorders and associated features in cocaine-dependent inpatients. *Comprehensive Psychiatry,* **35**, 335–40.

Kroll J., Carey K., & Sines L. (1982) Are there borderlines in Britain? *Archives of General Psychiatry,* **39**, 60–3.

Lambert M. J. & Bergin A. E. (1994) The effectiveness of psychotherapy. In S. L. Garfield & A. E. Bergin (Ed.) *Handbook of psychotherapy and behavior change.* 4th edition, New York, Wiley, pp. 143–89.

Langer T. S. & Michael S. T. (1963) *Life stress and mental health: the Midtown Manhattan study.* London, Collier MacMillan.

Langs R. (1982) *Psychotherapy: a basic text.* New York, Jason Aronson.

Lasch C. (1979a) *Haven in a heartless world: the family besieged.* New York, Basic Books.

Lasch C. (1979b) *The culture of narcissism.* New York, Warner.

Lasch C. (1991) *The true and only heaven.* New York, Basic Books.

Laurence J. R. & Perry C. (1983) Hypnotically created memory among highly hypnotizable subjects. *Science,* **222**, 523–4.

Lazarus R. S. & Folkman S. (1984). *Stress, appraisal and coping.* New York, Springer.

Leary T. (1957) *Interpersonal diagnosis of personality.* New York, Ronald Press.

Lee K. C., Kovac Y. S., & Rhee H. (1987) The national epidemiological study of mental disorders in Korea. *Journal of Korean Medical Science,* **2**, 19–34.

Leff J. P. (1981) *Psychiatry around the globe: a transcultural view.* New York, Dekker.

Leighton A. H. (1959) *My name is legion: the Stirling County study of psychiatric disorder and sociocultural environment.* New York, Basic Books.

Leighton D. C., Harding J. S., & Macklin D. B. (1963) *The character of danger: psychiatric symptoms in selected communities.* New York, Basic Books.

Lepine J. P., Chignon J. M., & Teherani M. (1993) Suicide attempts in patients with panic disorder. *Archives of General Psychiatry,* **50**, 144–9.

Lerner D. (1958) *The passing of traditional society.* New York, Free Press.

Lerner H. E. (1974) The hysterical personality: a "woman's disease". *Comprehensive Psychiatry,* **15**, 157–64.

Lesage A. D., Boyer R., Grunberg F., Morisette R., & Vanier C. (1994) Suicide and mental disorders: a case control study of young males. *American Journal of Psychiatry,* **151**, 1063–8.

Lewis L. & Appleby L. (1988) Personality disorder: the patients psychiatrists dislike. *British Journal of Psychiatry*, **153**, 44–49.

Lewis-Fernandez R. & Kleinman A. (1994) Culture, personality, and psychopathology. *Journal of Abnormal Psychology*, **103**, 67–71.

Linehan M. M. (1993) *Cognitive behavioral treatment of borderline personality disorder.* New York, Guilford.

Lingiardi V., Madeddu F., Fossati A., & Maffei C. (1994) Reliability and validity of the personality functioning scale (PFS). *Journal of Personality Disorders*, **8**, 111–20.

Links P., Steiner M., Offord D. R., & Eppel A. (1988a). Characteristics of borderline personality disorder: a Canadian study. *Canadian Journal of Psychiatry*, **33**, 336–40.

Links P. S., Steiner B., & Huxley G. (1988b) The occurrence of borderline personality disorder in the families of borderline patients. *Journal of Personality Disorders*, **2**, 14–20.

Links P. S. & van Reekum R. (1993) Childhood sexual abuse, parental impairment, and the development of borderline personality disorder. *Canadian Journal of Psychiatry*, **38**, 472–4.

Livesley W. J. (1987) A systematic approach to the delineation of personality disorder. *American Journal of Psychiatry*, **144**, 772–7.

Livesley W. J. (Ed.) (1995a) *The DSM-IV personality disorders.* New York, Guilford.

Livesley W. J. (1995b) *Genotypic and phenotypic structure of personality disorder.* Society for the Study of Personality Disorders, Dublin, 1995.

Livesley W. J., Jackson, D. N., & Schroeder, M. L. (1992). Factorial structure of traits delineating personality disorders in clinical and general population samples. *Journal of Abnormal Psychology*, **101**, 432–40.

Livesley W. J., Jackson D. N., & Schroeder, M. L. (1989) A study of the factorial structure of personality pathology. *Journal of Personality Disorder*, **3**, 292–306.

Livesley W. J. & Jackson D. N. (1992) Guidelines for developing, evaluating and revising the classification of personality disorders. *Journal of Nervous Mental Disease*, **180**, 609–18.

Livesley W. J., Jang K., Schroeder M. L., & Jackson D. N. (1993) Genetic and environmental factors in personality dimensions. *American Journal of Psychiatry*, **150**, 1826–31.

Liveseley W. J. & Schroeder M. L. (1990) Dimensions of personality disorder: the DSM-III-R Cluster A diagnoses. *Journal of Nervous Mental Disease*, **178**, 627–35.

Liveseley W. J. & Schroeder M. L. (1991) Dimensions of personality disorder: the DSM-III-R Cluster B diagnoses. *Journal of Nervous Mental Disease*, **179**, 320–8.

Livesley W. J., Schroeder M. L., & Jackson, D. N. (1990) Dependent personality disorder and attachment problems. *Journal of Personality Disorders*, **4**, 131–40.

Liveseley W. J., Schroeder M. L., Jackson D. N., & Jang K. (1994) Categorical distinctions in the study of personality disorder: implications for classification. *Journal of Abnormal Psychology,* **103**, 6–17.

Loftus E. F. (1993) The reality of repressed memories. *American Psychologist,* **48**, 518–37.

Loftus E. & Ketcham K. (1994) *The myth of repressed memory.* New York, St. Martin's Press.

Loranger A. W. (1991) *Comorbidity of borderline disorder in 5000 patients.* Presented to American Psychiatric Association, New Orleans, May, 1991.

Loranger A. W., Hirschfeld R. M. A., Sartorius N., & Regier D. A. (1991) The WHO/ADAMHA International Pilot Study of Personality Disorders: background and purpose. *Journal of Personality Disorders,* **3**, 296–306.

Loranger A. W., Sartori N., Andreoli A., Berger P., Bucheim P., Channabasavanna S. M., Coid, B., Dahl A., Diekstra R. F. W., Ferguson B., Jacobsberg L. B., Mombour W., Pull C., Ono Y., & Regier D. A. (1994) The International Personality Disorder Examination. *Archives of General Psychiatry,* **51**, 215–24.

Loranger A. W., Susman V. L., Oldham J. M., & Russakoff L. M. (1987) The Personality Disorders Examination (PDE) a preliminary report. *Journal of Personality Disorders,* **1**, 1–13.

Luborsky L. (1963) Clinicians' judgment of mental health. *Archives of General Psychiatry,* **9**, 407–17.

Luborsky L. & Crits-Christoph P. (1990) *Understanding transference: the core conflict relationship theme method.* New York, Basic Books.

Luborsky L., Crits-Christoph P., Mintz J., & Auerbach A. (1988) *Who will benefit from psychotherapy?* New York, Basic Books.

Ludolph P. S., Westen, D., Misle B. E. (1990) The borderline diagnosis in adolescents. *American Journal of Psychiatry,* **147**, 470–6.

Lykken D. T., McGue M., Tellegen A., & Boucard T. J. (1992) Emergenesis: genetic traits which may not run in families. *American Psychologist,* **47**, 1565–77.

McCord J. (1978) A thirty year follow-up of treatment effects. *American Psychologist,* **33**, 284–9.

McCrae R. R. & Costa P. T. (1990) *Personality in adulthood.* New York, Guilford.

McFarlane A. C. (1993) PTSD: synthesis of research and clinical studies. In J. P. Wilson & B. Raphael (Eds.) *International handbook of traumatic stress syndromes.* New York, Plenum, pp. 421–9.

McGlashan T. H. (1984) The Chestnut Lodge Follow-up Study: long-term outcome of schizophrenia and the affective disorders. *Archives of General Psychiatry,* **41**, 573–85.

McGlashan T. H. (1986a) The Chestnut Lodge Follow-up Study: long-term outcomes of borderline personalities. *Archives of General Psychiatry,* **43**, 20–30.

McGlashan T. H. (1989b) The prediction of outcome in chronic schizophrenia. *Archives of General Psychiatry*, **43**, 167–334.

McGlashan T. H. (1986c) Implications of outcome, research for the treatment of borderline personality disorder. In J. Paris (Ed.) *Borderline personality disorder: etiology and treatment.* Washington, DC, American Psychiatric Press, pp. 235–60.

McGlashan T. H. (1986c) Chestnut Lodge Follow-up Study: long-term perspectives. *Archives of General Psychiatry*, **43**, 329–334.

McGlashan T. H. & Heinssen R. K. (1989) Narcissistic, antisocial, and non-comorbid sub-groups of borderline personality disorder. *Psychiatric Clinics of North America*, **12**, 653–70.

McGoldrick M., Pearce J. K., & Giordano J. (1982) *Ethnicity and family therapy.* New York, Guilford.

McGuffin P. & Thapar A. (1992). The genetics of personality disorder. *British Journal of Psychiatry*, **160**, 12–23.

McHugh P. R. (1992) Psychiatric misadventures. *American Scholar* **61**, 498–510.

McHugh P. R. (1994) Psychotherapy astray. *American Scholar*, **63**, 17–30.

McHugh P. R. & Slavney P. R. (1983). *The perspectives of psychiatry,* Baltimore, Johns Hopkins.

Maccoby E. E. & Jacklin C. N. (1974) *The psychology of sex differences.* Stanford, CA, Stanford University Press.

Maddocks P. D. (1970) A five year follow-up of untreated psychopaths. *British Journal of Psychiatry*, **116**, 511–15.

Maier W., Lichtermann D., Klingler T., & Heun R. (1992) Prevalences of personality disorders (DSM-III-R) in the community. *Journal of Personality Disorders*, **6**, 187–96.

Main M. & Hesse E. (1991) The insecure/disorganized attachment pattern in infancy: precursors and sequelae. In M. Greenberg, P. Ciccheti, & E. M. Cummings (Eds.) *Attachment in the preschool years: theory, research, intervention.* Chicago, University of Chicago Press.

Malinovsky-Rummell R. & Hansen D. J. (1993) Long-term consequences of physical abuse. *Psychological Bulletin*, **114**, 68–79.

Masters R. D. & McGuire M. T. (1994) *The neurotransmitter revolution: serotonin, social behavior, and the law.* Carbondale IL, South Illinois Press.

Mausner J. S. & Kramer S. (1986) *Epidemiology: an introductory text,* 2nd edition. Philadelphia, Saunders.

Mavissakalian M. R., Hamann M. S., Haidar S. A., & de Grott, CM (1993) DSM-III personality disorders in generalized anxiety, panic/agoraphobia, and obsessive-compulsive disorders. *Comprehensive Psychiatry*, **34**, 243–8.

Maziade M., Caron C., Coté R., Boutin P., & Thivierge J. (1990) Extreme temperament and diagnosis: a study in a psychiatric sample of consecutive children. *Archives of General Psychiatry*, **47**, 477–84.

Mednick S. A., Gabrieli, W. F., & Hutchings, B. (1984) Genetic influences in criminal convictions. *Science*, **224**, 891–4.

Mednick S. A., Machon R. A., & Huttunen M. O. (1988) Adult schizophrenia following prenatal exposure to an influenza epidemic. *Archives of General Psychiatry*, **45**, 189–92.

Mednick S. A. & Moffit T. (Eds.) (1985) *Biology and crime*. Cambridge, Cambridge University Press.

Meehl P. E. (1962) Schizotaxia, schizotypy, schizophrenia. *American Psychologist*, **17**, 827–38.

Meehl P. E. (1990) Toward an integrated theory of schizotaxa, schizotypy, and schizophrenia. *Journal of Personality Disorders*, **4**, 1–99.

Menninger K. (1963, reprinted 1983) *The vital balance*. New York, Peter Smith.

Merskey H. (1992) The manufacture of personalities. *British Journal of Psychiatry*, **160**, 327–40.

Merson S., Tyrer P., Duke P., & Henderson F. (1994) Interrater reliability of ICD-10 guidelines for the diagnosis of personality disorder. *Journal of Personality Disorders*, **8**, 89–95.

Meyer A. (1957) *Psychobiology*. Springfield, IL, Charles C Thomas.

Meyer-Williams L. (1994) Recall of childhood trauma: a prospective study of women's memories of child sexual abuse. *Journal of Consulting and Clinical Psychology*, **62**, 1167–1176.

Mezzich J. E., Fabrega H., & Coffman G. A. (1987) Multiaxial characterization of depressive patients. *Journal of Nervous Mental Disease*, **175**, 339–46.

Millon T. (1969) *Modern psychopathology*. Philadelphia, Saunders.

Millon T. & Davis R. (1981) *Disorders of personality: DSM-IV and beyond*. New York, Wiley.

Millon T. (1982, 1987, 1994) *Millon Clinical Multiaxial Inventory*. Minneapolis, National Computer Systems.

Millon T. (1987) On the genesis and prevalence of borderline personality disorder: a social learning thesis. *Journal of Personality Disorders*, **1**, 354–72.

Millon T. (1990) *Towards a new personology: an evolutionary model*. New York, Wiley.

Millon T. (1993) Borderline personality disorder: a psychosocial epidemic. In J. Paris (Ed.) *Borderline personality disorder: etiology and treatment*. Washington, DC, American Psychiatric Press, pp. 197–210.

Millon T. (1994) Personality disorders: conceptual distinctions and classification issues. In P. T. Costa & T. A. Widiger (Eds.) *Personality disorders and the five-factor model*. Washington, DC, American Psychological Association, pp. 279–303.

Monroe S. M. & Simons A. D. (1991) Diathesis-stress theories in the context of life stress research. *Psychological Bulletin*, **110**, 406–25.

Moos R. H. & Moos B. S. (1986) *Family environment scale: manual.* Palo Alto, CA, Consulting Psychologists Press.

Morey L. C. (1988) A psychometric analysis of the DSM-III-R personality disorder criteria. *Journal of Personality Disorders*, **2**, 109–24.

Morey L. C. (1993) Psychological correlates of personality disorder. *Journal of Personality Disorders*, **7** (Suppl.), 149–68.

Morey L. C. & Ochoa E. S. (1989) An investigation of adherence to diagnostic criteria: clinical diagnosis of the DSM-III personality disorders. *Journal of Personality Disorders*, **3**, 183–92.

Moriya N., Miyake Y., Minawaka K., Ikuta N., & Nishozono-Maher A. (1993) Diagnosis and clinical features of borderline personality disorder in the East and West: a preliminary report. *Comprehensive Psychiatry*, **34**, 418–23.

Murphy H. B. M. (1978) The advent of guilt feelings as a common depressive symptom. *Psychiatry*, **41**, 229–42.

Murphy H. B. M. (1982a) *Comparative psychiatry.* New York, Springer.

Murphy H. B. M. (1982b) Culture and schizophrenia. In I. Al-Issa (Ed.) *Culture and psychopathology.* Baltimore, University Park Press, pp. 221–49.

Murphy J. M. (1976) Psychiatric labelling in cross-cultural perspective. *Science*, **191**, 1019–28.

Nakao K., Gunderson J. G., Phillips K. A., Tanaka N., Yorifuji K., Takaishi J., Nishimura T. (1992) Functional impairment in personality disorders. *Journal of Personality Disorders*, **6**, 24–33.

Nandi D. N., Banerjee G., Nandi S., & Nandi P. (1992) Is hysteria on the wane? *British Journal of Psychiatry*, **160**, 87–91.

Nash M. R., Hulsely T. L., Sexton M. C., Harralson T. L., & Lambert W. (1993) Long-term effects of childhood sexual abuse: perceived family environment, psychopathology, and dissociation. *Journal of Consulting and Clinical Psychology*, **61**, 276–83.

Nestadt G., Romanovski A. J., Brown C. H., Chahal R., Merchant A., Folstein M. F., Gruenberg E. M., & McHugh P. R. (1991) DSM-III compulsive personality disorder: an epidemiological survey. *Psychological Medicine*, **21**, 461–71.

Nestadt G., Romanovski A. J., Brown C. H., Chahal R., Merchant A., Folstein M. F., Gruenberg E. M., & McHugh P. R. (1994) An evaluation of the structure of schizophrenia spectrum personality disorders. *Journal of Personality Disorders*, **8**, 288–98.

Nestadt G., Romanovski A. J., Chahal R., Merchant A., Folstein M. F., Gruenberg E. M., & McHugh P. R. (1990) An epidemiological study of histrionic personality disorder. *Psychological Medicine*, **20**, 413–22.

Nigg J. T. & Goldsmith H. H. (1994) Genetics of personality disorders: perspectives from personality and psychopathology research. *Psychological Bulletin*, **115**, 346–80.

Nurnberg G., Raskin M., Levine P. E., Pollack S., Siegel O., & Prince R. (1991) The comorbidity of borderline personality disorder with other DSM-III-R Axis II personality disorders. *American Journal of Psychiatry*, **148**, 1311–17.

Oakley-Browne M. A., Joyce P. A., Welss E., Bushnell J. A., & Hornblow, A. R, (1989) Christchurch psychiatric epidemiology study: six month and other period prevalences of specific psychiatric disorders. *Austrian and New Zealand Journal of Psychiatry*, **23**, 327–40.

Ofshe, R. & Watters, E. (1994) *Making monsters: false memories, psychotherapy, and sexual hysteria.* New York, Scribner.

Ogata S. N., Silk K. R., & Goodrich S. (1990a) The childhood experience of the borderline patient. In Links P. S. (Ed.) *Family environment and borderline personality disorder.* Washington, DC, American Psychiatric Press, pp. 85–104.

Ogata S. N., Silk K. R., & Goodrich S., Lohr N. E., Westen D., & Hill E. M. (1990b) Childhood sexual and physical abuse in adult patients with borderline personality disorder. *American Journal of Psychiatry*, **147**, 1008–13.

Oldham J. M., Skodol A. E., Kellman H. D., Hyler S. E., Doidge N., Rosnick L., & Gallagher P. E. (1995) Comorbidity of Axis I and Axis II disorders. *American Journal of Psychiatry*, **152**, 571–8.

Oldham J. M., Skodol A. E., Kellman D., Hyler S. E., Rosnick L., & Davies M. (1992) Diagnosis of DSM-III-R personality disorders by two structured interviews: patterns of comorbidity. *American Journal of Psychiatry*, **149**, 213–20.

Orlinksy D. E., Grave K., & Parks B. K. (1994) Process and outcome in psychotherapy. In S. L. Garfield & A. E. Bergin (Eds.) *Handbook of psychotherapy and behavior change*, 4th edition. New York, Wiley, pp. 270–8.

Orne M. T., Whitehouse W. G., Dinges D. F., & Orne E. C. (1988) Reconstructing memory through hypnosis: forensic and clinical implications. In H. M. Pettinati (Ed.) *Hypnosis and memory.* New York, Guilford, pp. 21–54 .

Paris J. (1983) Family theory and character pathology. *International Journal of Family Psychiatry*, **3**, 475–85.

Paris J. (1988) Follow-up studies of borderline personality: a critical review. *Journal of Personality Disorders*, **2**, 189–97.

Paris J. (1992) Social factors in borderline personality disorder: a review and a hypothesis. *Canadian Journal of Psychiatry*, **37**, 480–6.

Paris J. (1993) Personality disorders: a biopsychosocial model. *Journal of Personality Disorders*, **7**, 255–64.

Paris J. (1994) *Borderline personality disorder: a multidimensional approach.* Washington, DC, American Psychiatric Press.

Paris J. (1995) Memories of abuse in BPD: true or false? *Harvard Review of Psychiatry*, **3**, 7–10.

Paris J., Brown R., & Nowlis D. (1987) Long-term follow-up of borderline patients in a general hospital. *Comprehensive Psychiatry*, **28**, 530–5.

Paris J. & Frank H. (1989) Perceptions of parental bonding in borderline patients. *American Journal of Psychiatry*, **146**, 1498–9.

Paris J., Frank H., Buonvino M., & Bond M. (1991) Recollections. of parental behavior and Axis II cluster diagnosis. *Journal of Personality Disorders*, **5**, 102–6.

Paris J., Nowlis D., & Brown R. (1988) Developmental factors in the outcome of borderline personality disorder. *Comprehensive Psychiatry*, **29**, 147–50.

Paris J., Nowlis D., & Brown R. (1989) Predictors of suicide in borderline personality disorder. *Canadian Journal of Psychiatry*, **34**, 8–9.

Paris J., Zweig-Frank H., & Guzder J. (1994a). Psychological risk factors for borderline personality disorder in female patients. *Comprehensive Psychiatry*, **35**, 301–5.

Paris J., Zweig-Frank H., & Guzder J. (1994b). Risk factors for borderline personality in male outpatients. *Journal of Nervous and Mental Disease*, **182**, 375–80.

Parker G. (1983) *Parental overprotection: a risk factor in psychosocial development*. New York, Grune & Stratton.

Parnas J., Cannon T. D., Jacobsen B., Schlusinger H., Schlusinger F., & Mednick S. A. (1993) Lifetime DSM-III-R diagnostic outcomes in the offspring of schizophrenic mothers. *Archives of General Psychiatry*, **50**, 707–13.

Pepper C. M., Klein D. N., Anderson R. L., Rizo L. P., Ouimette P. C., & Lizardi H. (1995) DSM-III-R Axis II comorbidity in dysthymia and major depression. *American Journal of Psychiatry*, **152**, 239–47.

Perris C., Jacobsen L., Linstrom H., von Korring L., & Perris H. (1980) Development of a new inventory for assessing memories of parental rearing behavior. *Acta Psychiatrica Scandinavica*, **61**, 265–74.

Perry J. C. (1991) Use of longitudinal data to validate personality disorders. In J. C. Oldham (Ed.) *Personality disorders: new perspectives on diagnostic validity*. Washington, DC, American Psychiatric Press, pp. 23–40.

Perry J. C. (1992) Problems and considerations in the valid assessment of personality disorders. *American Journal of Psychiatry*, **149**, 1645–53.

Perry J. C. (1993) Longitudinal studies of personality disorders. *Journal of Personality Disorders*, (Suppl.), 63–85.

Perry J. C. & Cooper S. H. (1989) An empirical study of defense mechanisms. *Archives of General Psychiatry*, **46**, 444–52.

Pettinati H. M. (1988) Hypnosis and memory: integrative summary and future directions. In H. M. Pettinati (Ed.) *Hypnosis and memory*. New York, Guilford, pp. 277–92.

Pfohl B., Coryell W., Zimmerman M., & Stangl D. (1986) DSM-III personality disorders: diagnostic overlap and internal consistency of individual DSM-III criteria. *Comprehensive Psychiatry*, **27**, 21–34.

Pilkonis P. A. & Frank E. (1988) Personality pathology in recurrent depression: nature, prevalence, and relationship to treatment response. *American Journal of Psychiatry*, **144**, 485–8.

Plakun E. M. (1991) Empirical studies on narcissism. In S. M. Mirin, J. T. Gosssett & M. C. Grob (Eds.) *Psychiatric treatment: advances in outcome research*. Washington, DC, American Psychiatric Press, pp. 195–212.

Plakun E. M., Burkhardt P. E., & Muller J. P. (1986) 14 year follow-up of borderline and schizotypal personality disorders, *Comprehensive Psychiatry*, **27**, 448–55.

Plomin R. (1994) *Genetics and experience*. Thousand Oaks, CA, Sage.

Plomin R. & Bergeman C. (1991) Genetic influence on environmental measures. *Behavioral and Brain Sciences*, **14**, 373–427.

Plomin R., DeFries J. C., & McClearn G. E. (1990). *Behavioral genetics: a primer*. New York, Freeman.

Pollack J. (1987) Obsessive-compulsive personality: theoretical and clinical perspectives and recent research findings. *Journal of Personality Disorders*, **1**, 248–62.

Pollock V. E., Briere J., Schneider L., Knop J., Mednick S. A., & Goodwin D. W. (1990) Childhood antecedents of antisocial behavior: parental alcoholism and physical abusiveness. *American Journal of Psychiatry*, **147**, 1290–3.

Pope, H. G. & Hudson J. I. (1995) Can memories of childhood sexual abuse be repressed? *Psychological Medicine*, **25**, 121–6.

Poulton R. G. & Andrews G. (1992) Personality as a cause of adverse life events. *Acta Psychiatrica Scandinavica*, **85**, 35–8.

Prince R. & Tseng-Laroche F. (1990) Culture-bound syndromes and international disease classification. *Culture, Medicine and Psychiatry*, **11**, 1–49.

Propst A., Paris J., & Rosberger Z. (1994) Do therapist experience, diagnosis and functional level predict outcome in short-term psychotherapy? *Canadian Journal of Psychiatry*, **39**, 178–83.

Putnam F. W. (1989) *Diagnosis and treatment of multiple personality disorder*. New York, Guilford.

Raine A., Lencz T., & Scerbo A. (1995) Antisocial behavior, neuroimaging, neuropsychology, neurochemistry, and psychophysiology. In H. Ratey (Ed.) *Neuropsychiatry of personality disorders*. Cambridge, MA, Blackwell, pp. 50–78.

Raskin R. & Terry H. (1988) A principle components analysis of the Narcissistic Personality Inventory and further evidence of its construct validity. *Journal of Personality and Social Psychology*, **54**, 890–902.

Regier D. A. & Burke J. D. (1989) Epidemiology. In Kaplan H. &

Sadock B. (Eds.) *Comprehensive textbook of psychiatry*, 5th edition. Baltimore, Williams & Wilkins, pp. 308–26.

Reich J. (1989) Familiality of DSM-III dramatic and anxious personality clusters. *Journal of Nervous and Mental Disease*, **177**, 96–100.

Reich J. (1990a) Comparisons of males and females with DSM-III dependent personality disorder. *Psychiatry Research*, **33**, 207–14.

Reich J. (1990b) Relationship between DSM-III avoidant and dependent personality disorders. *Psychiatry Research*, **34**, 281–92.

Reich J. (1991) Avoidant and dependent personality traits in relatives of patients with panic disorder, with dependent personality disorder, and normal controls. *Psychiatry Research*, **39**, 89–98.

Reich J. & Green A. (1991) Effect of personality disorders on outcome of treatment, *Journal of Nervous and Mental Disease*, **179**, 74–82.

Reich J., Nduaguba M., & Yates W. (1988) Age and sex distribution of DSM-III personality cluster traits in a community sample. *Comprehesive Psychiatry*, **29**, 298–303.

Reich J. & Vasile R. G. (1993) Effect of personality disorders on the treatment outcome of Axis I conditions: an update. *Journal of Nervous and Mental Disease*, **181**, 475–84.

Reich J., Yates W., & Nduaguba M. (1989). Prevalence of DSM-III personality disorders in the community. *Social Psychiatry and Psychiatric Epidemiology*, **24**, 12–16.

Reich W. (1933, reprinted 1972) *Character analysis*. New York, Farrar, Strauss, & Giroux.

Rey J. M., Morris-Yates A., Singh M., Andrews G., & Stewart G. W. (1995) Continuities between psychiatric disorders in adolescents and personality disorders in young adults. *American Journal of Psychiatry*, **152**, 895–900.

Rich C. L., Fowler R. C., Fogarty L. A., & Young D. (1988) San Diego suicide study: relationships between diagnoses and stressors. *Archives of General Psychiatry*, **45**, 589–94.

Rich C. L. & Runeson B. S. (1992) Similarities in diagnostic comorbidity between suicide among young people in Sweden and the United States. *Acta Psychiatrica Scandinavica*, **86**, 335–9.

Riley G. (1991) *Divorce: an American tradition*. New York, Oxford University Press.

Robins E. & Guze S. B. (1970) Establishment of diagnostic validity in psychiatric illness: its application to schizophrenia. *American Journal of Psychiatry*, **126**, 107–11.

Robins L. N. (1966) *Deviant children grown up*. Baltimore, Williams & Wilkins.

Robins L. N. (1978) Sturdy childhood predictors of adult outcome. *Psychological Medicine*, **8**, 611–22.

Robins L. N. & Regier D. A., (Eds.) (1991) *Psychiatric disorders in America*. New York, Free Press

Robins L. N., Schoenberg S. P., & Holmes S. J. (1985) Early home environment and retrospective recall; a test for concordance between sibling with and without psychiatric disorders. *American Journal of Orthopsychiatry,* **55**, 27–41.

Robins L. N., Tipp J., & Pryzbeck T. (1991) Antisocial personality. In L. N. Robins & D. A. Regier (Eds.) *Psychiatric disorders in America.* New York, Free Press, pp. 258–90.

Romans S. E., Martin J. L., Anderson J. C., O'Shea M. L., & Mullen P. E. (1995) Factors that mediate between childhood sexual abuse and adult outcome. *Psychological Medicine,* **25**, 127–42.

Ronningstam E., Gunderson J. G., & Lyons M. (1995) Changes in pathological narcissism. *American Journal of Psychiatry,* **152**, 253–7.

Rose S. (1992) *The making of memory.* New York, Doubleday.

Rosenthal D. (1971) *Genetics of psychopathology.* New York, McGraw-Hill.

Rothbart M. K. & Ahadi S. A. (1994) Temperament and the development of personality. *Journal of Abnormal Psychology,* **103**, 55–66.

Rowe D. C. (1981) Environmental and genetic influences on dimensions of perceived parenting: a twin study. *Developmental Psychology,* **17**, 203–8.

Rutter M. (1971) Parent-child separation: psychological effects on the children. *Journal of Child Psychology and Psychiatry,* **12**, 233–60.

Rutter M. (1982) *Maternal deprivation reassessed,* 2nd edition. London, Penguin.

Rutter M. (1987a) Psychosocial resilience and protective mechanisms. *American Journal of Orthopsychiatry,* **57**, 316–31.

Rutter M. (1987b) Temperament, personality, and personality development. *British Journal of Psychiatry,* **150**, 443–8.

Rutter M. (1989) Pathways from childhood to adult life. *Journal of Child Psychology and Psychiatry,* **30**, 23–51.

Rutter M. (1993a) Developmental psychopathology as a research perspective. In D. Magnusson & P. Cusaer (Eds.) *Longitudinal research on individual development.* New York, Cambridge University Press, pp. 127–52.

Rutter M. (1993b) Developmental psychopathology course at Cape Cod Institute, Wellfleet, MA.

Rutter M. (1995) Mental disorders in childhood and adulthood. *Acta Psychiatrica Scandinavica,* **92**, 73–85.

Rutter M. & Madge N. (1976) *Cycles of disadvantage.* London, Heinemann.

Rutter M. & Quinton D. (1984) Long-term follow-up of women institutionalized in childhood. *British Journal of Developmental Psychology,* **18**, 225–34.

Rutter M. & Rutter M. (1993) *Developing minds: challenge and continuity across the life span.* New York, Basic Books.

Samuels J. F., Nestadt G., Romanovski A. J., Folstein M. F., & McHugh P. R. (1994) DSM-III personality disorders in the community. *American Journal of Psychiatry*, **151**, 1055–62.

Scarr S. & McCartney K. (1983) How people make their own environments: a theory of genotype-environment effects. *Child Development*, **54**, 424–35.

Schneider K. (1950) *Psychopathic personalities.* 9th edition. London, Cassell.

Sato T. & Takeichi M. (1993) Lifetime prevalence of specific psychiatric disorders in a general medicine clinic. *General Hospital Psychiatry*, **15**, 224–33.

Serban G. & Siegel S. (1984) Response of borderline and schizotypal patients to small doses of thiothixene and haloperidol. *American Journal of Psychiatry*, **141**, 1455–8.

Shea M. T., Pilkonis P. A., Beckham E., Collins J. F., Elikin E., Sotsky S. M., & Docherty J. P. (1990) Personality disorders and treatment outcome in the NIMH Treatment of Depression Collaborative Research Program. *American Journal of Psychiatry*, **147**, 711–18.

Shea M. T., Widiger T. A., & Klein M. H. (1992) Comorbidity of personality disorders and depression: implications for treatment. *Journal of Consulting and Clinical Psychology*, **60**, 857–68.

Shear M. K., Cooper A. M., Klerman G. L., Busch F. N., & Shapiro T. (1993) A psychodynamic model of panic disorder. *American Journal of Psychiatry*, **150**, 859–66.

Sheldon A. E. & West M. (1990) Attachment pathology and low social skills in avoidant personality disorder: an exploratory study. *Canadian Journal of Psychiatry*, **35**, 596–9.

Siever L. J. & Davis L. (1991) A psychobiological perspective on the personality disorders. *American Journal of Psychiatry*, **148**, 1647–58.

Siever L. J., Silverman J. M., Horvath T., Klar H., Coccaro E., Keefe R. S., Pinkham L., Rinaldi O., Mohs R. C., & Davis K. L. (1990) Increased morbidity risk for schizophrenia-related disorders in relatives of schizotypal personality disordered patients. *Archives of General Psychiatry*, **47**, 634–40.

Sigal J. J. & Weinfeld M. (1989) *Trauma and rebirth: intergenerational effects of the holocaust.* New York, Praeger.

Sigvardsson S., Cloninger R., Bohman M., & von Knorring A.-L. (1982) Predisposition to petty criminality in Swedish adoptees: III: sex differences and validation of the male typology. *Archives of General Psychiatry*, **39**, 1248–53.

Simonsen E. & Parnas J. (1993) Personality disorder research in Denmark. *Journal of Personality Disorders*, **7**, 187–95.

Skodol A. (1993) *Fears and inhibitions: a study of anxiety and personality disorder comorbidity.* Presented to the International Society for the Study of Personality Disorders, Cambridge, MA, Sept, 1993.

Skodol A. E., Buckley P., & Charles E. (1983) Is there a characteristic pattern in the treatment history of clinic outpatients with borderline personality? *Journal of Nervous and Mental Disease,* **171**, 405–10.

Smith M. L., Glass G. V., & Miller T. I. (1980) *The benefits of psychotherapy.* Baltimore, Johns Hopkins Press.

Soloff P. H. (1993) Psychopharmacological intervention in borderline personality disorder. In J. Paris (Ed.) *Borderline personality disorder: etiology and treatment.* Washington, DC, American Psychiatric Press, pp. 319–48.

Southwick S. M., Yehuda R., & Giller B. L. (1993) Personality disorders in treatment-seeking combat veterans with post-traumatic stress disorder. *American Journal of Psychiatry,* **150**, 1020–3.

Spanos N. P. (1982) Hypnotic behavior: a cognitive social psychological perspective. *Research Communications in Psychology, Psychiatry, Behavior,* **7**, 199–213.

Spence D. (1992) Interpretation: a critical perspective. In J. W. Barron, M. N. Eagle, & D. L. Wolitsky (Eds.) *Interface of psychoanalysis and psychology.* Washington, DC, American Psychological Association, pp. 558–72.

Spiegel D. & Cardena E. (1991) Disintegrated experience: the dissociative disorders revisited. *Journal of Abnormal Psychology,* **100**, 366–78.

Spitzer R. L., Endicott J., & Gibbon M. (1979) Crossing the border into borderline personality disorder. *Archives of General Psychiatry,* **36**, 17–24.

Spitzer R. L. & Williams J. B. W. (1986) *Structured clinical interview for DSM-III-R personality disorders.* New York, Biometric Research Department, New York State Psychiatric Institute.

Spitzer R. L., Williams J. W., & Sodol A. E. (1983) *International perspectives on DSM-III.* Washington, DC, American Psychiatric Press.

Srole L. & Fischer A. K. (1980) The Midtown Manhattan Longitudinal Study vs. "The Mental Paradise Lost Doctrine". *Archives of General Psychiatry,* **37**, 209–18.

Stangl D., Pfohl B., Zimmerman M., Bowers W., & Corenthal C. (1985) A structured interview for the DSM-III personality disorders. *Archives of General Psychiatry,* **42**, 591–6.

Stein D. J., Hollander E., & Skodol A. E. (1993) Anxiety disorders and personality disorders: a review. *Journal of Personality Disorders,* **7**, 87–104.

Stern A. (1938) Psychoanalytic investigation of and therapy in the borderline group of neuroses. *Psychoanalytic Quarterly,* **7**, 467–89.

Stevenson J. & Meares R. (1992) An outcome study of psychotherapy for patients with borderline personality disorder. *American Journal of Psychiatry*, **149**, 358–62.

Stone M. H. (1990) *The fate of borderline patients.* New York, Guilford.

Stone M. H. (1993) *Abnormalities of personality.* New York, Norton.

Storr A. (1988) *Solitude.* New York, Free Press.

Stravynski A., Belisle M., Macouiller M., Lavallée Y.-V., & Elie R. (1994) The treatment of avoidant personality disorder by social skills training in the clinic or in real-life settings. *Canadian Journal of Psychiatry*, **39**, 377–83.

Sudak H. S., Ford A. B., & Rushforth N. B. (1984) *Suicide in the young.* Boston, John Wright.

Sutker P. B., Bugg F., & West J. A. (1993) Antisocial personality disorder. In P. B. Sutker & H. E. Adams (Eds.) *Comprehensive textbook of psychopathology.* New York, Plenum, pp. 337–69.

Swanson D. W. (1970) *The paranoid.* Boston, Little, Brown.

Swartz M., Blazer D., George L., & Winfield I. (1990) Estimating the prevalence of borderline personality disorder in the community. *Journal of Personality Disorders*, **4**, 257–72.

Taylor C. (1992) *The malaise of modernity.* Toronto, Anisna.

Tellegen A., Lykken D. T., Bouchard T. J., Wilcox K. J., Segal N. L., & Rich S. (1988) Personality similarity in twins reared apart and together. *Journal of Personality and Social Psychology*, **54**, 1031–9.

Tennant C. (1988) Parental loss in childhood to adult life. *Archives of General Psychiatry*, **45**, 1045–50.

Terr L. (1994) *Unchained memories.* New York, Basic Books.

Terr L. C. (1988) What happens to early memories of trauma? *Journal of the American Academy of Child and Adolescent Psychiatry*, **27**, 96–104.

Terr L. C. (1991) Childhood traumas: an outline and an overview. *American Journal of Psychiatry*, **148**, 10–20.

Thompson R. A., Connell J. P., & Bridges L. J. (1988) Temperament, emotion, and social interactive behavior in the strange situation. *Child Development*, **56**, 1106–10.

Thorslund J. (1990) Inuit suicide in Greenland. *Arctic Medical Research*, **49**, 25–33.

Tillman J. G., Nash M. R., & Lerner P. M. (1994) Does trauma cause dissociative pathology? In S. J. Lynn & J. W. Rhue (Eds.) *Dissociation: clinical and theoretical perspectives.* New York, Guilford, pp. 395–414.

Toffler A. (1970) *Future shock.* New York, Random.

Torgersen S. (1980) The oral, obsessive and hysterical personality syndromes, A study of heredity and environmental factors by means of the twin method. *Archives of General Psychiatry*, **37**, 1272–7.

Torgersen S. (1983) Genetic factors in anxiety disorders. *Archives of General Psychiatry*, **40**, 1085–9.

Torgersen S. (1984) Genetic and nosological aspects of schizotypal and borderline personality disorders: a twin study. *Archives of General Psychiatry*, **41**, 546–54.

Torgersen S. (1991) *The psychometric-genetic structure of DSM-III personality disorder diagnostic criteria.* Presented to the International Society for the Study of Personality Disorders, Oslo, Norway.

Torgersen S. & Alnaes R. (1989) Localizing DSM-III personality disorders in a three-dimensional structural space. *Journal of Personality Disorders*, **3**, 274–81.

Torgersen S., Onstad S., Skre I., Edvardsen J., & Kirnglen, E (1993) "True" schizotypal personality disorder: a study of co-twins and relatives of schizophrenic probands. *American Journal of Psychiatry*, **150**, 1661–7.

Torrey E. F. (1992) *Freudian fraud*, New York, Harper Perennial.

True W. R., Rice J., Eisen S. A., Heath A. C., Goldberg J, Lyons M. J., & Nowak J. (1993) A twin study of genetic and environmental contributions to liability for post-traumatic stress symptoms. *Archives of General Psychiatry*, **50**, 257–64.

Trull T. J. & McRae R. R. (1994) A five-factor perspective on personality disorder research. In P. T. Costa & T. A. Widiger (Eds.) *Personality disorders and the five-factor model.* Washington, DC, American Psychological Association, pp. 59–71.

Tyrer P. (1987) Problems in the classification of personality disorders. *Psychological Medicine*, **17**, 15–20.

Tyrer P. (1988) *Personality disorders.* London, Wright.

Tyrer P., Casey P., & Ferguson B. (1991) Personality disorder in perspective. *British Journal of Psychiatry*, **159**, 463–71.

Tyrer P., Ciccheti D., & Casey P. (1984) Cross-national reliability study of a schedule for assessing personality disorders. *Journal of Nervous and Mental Disease*, **172**, 718–21.

Tyrer P. & Ferguson, B. (1988). Development of the concept of abnormal personality. In P. Tyrer (Ed.) *Personality disorders.* London, Wright, pp. 1–11.

Tyrer P., Seivewright N., & Ferguson B. (1990) The Nottingham study of neurotic disorder: relationship between personality status and symptoms. *Psychological Medicine*, **20**, 423–31.

Tyrer P. & Stein G. (Eds.) (1993) *Personality disorder reviewed.* London, Royal College of Psychiatrists.

Vaillant G. E. (1977) *Adaptation to life.* Cambridge, MA, Little, Brown.

Vaillant G. E. & Vaillant C. O. (1981) Natural history of male psychological health X: work as a predictor of positive mental health. *American Journal of Psychiatry*, **138**, 1433–8.

Vaillant G. E. & Vaillant C. O. (1990) Natural history of male psychological health XII: a 45 year study of predictors of successful aging at age 65. *American Journal of Psychiatry*, **147**, 31–7.

van der Kolk B. A., Perry J. C., & Herman J. L. (1991) Childhood origins of self-destructive behavior. *American Journal of Psychiatry*, **148**, 1665–71.

van Reekum R., Links P. S., & Boiago I. (1993) Constitutional factors in borderline personality disorder. In Paris J. (Ed.) *Borderline personality disorder: etiology and treatment*. Washington, DC, American Psychiatric Press, pp. 13–38.

Wachtel P. L. (1977) *Psychoanalysis and behavior therapy*. New York, Basic Books.

Wachtel P. L. (1994) Cyclical processes in personality and psychopathology. *Journal of Abnormal Psychology*, **103**, 51–4.

Wallerstein J. (1989) *Second chances: men, women, and children a decade after divorce*. New York, Ticknor and Fields.

Wallerstein R. (1986) *Forty-two lives in treatment*. New York, Guilford.

Walton H. J. (1986) The relationship between personality disorder and psychiatric illness. In T. Millon & G. Klerman (Eds.) *Contemporary directions in psychopathology*. New York, Guilford, pp. 553–70.

Weiss G. & Hechtman L. T. (1992) *Hyperactive children grown up*, 2nd edition. New York, Guilford.

Weiss M., Zelkowitz P., Vogel J., Guzder J., Heyman M., Feldman R., & Paris J. (1995) Children of mothers with borderline personality disorder. (submitted for publication).

Weissman M. W. (1974) The epidemiology of suicide attempts, 1960 to 1971. *Archives of General Psychiatry*, **30**, 737–46.

Weissman M. M. (1993) The epidemiology of personality disorders: a 1990 update. *Journal of Personality Disorders*, **7** (Suppl.), 44–62.

Weissman M. M., Myers J. M., & Ross E. (Eds.) (1986) *Community surveys of psychiatric disorders*. New Brunswick, NJ, Rutgers University Press.

Weisz J. R., Sigman M., Weiss B., & Mosk J. (1993) Parent reports of behavioral and emotional problems among children in Kenya, Thailand, and the United States. *Child Development*, **64**, 98–109.

Werner E. E. & Smith R. S. (1992) *Overcoming the odds: high risk children from birth to adulthood*. New York, Cornell University Press.

West D. J. & Farrington D. P. (1973) *Who becomes delinquent?* London, Heinemann.

West M., Rose S., & Sheldon-Keller A. (1994) Assessment of patterns of insecure attachment in adults with application to dependent and schizoid personality disorders. *Journal of Personality Disorders*, **8**, 249–56.

West M. O. & Prinz R. J. (1987) Parental alcoholism and childhood psychopathology. *Psychological Bulletin*, **102**, 204–24.

Westen D. (1985) *Self and society: narcissism, collectivism and the development of morals*. New York, Cambridge University Press.

Whiting B. B. & Edwards C. P. (1988) *Children of six cultures*. Cambridge, MA, Harvard University Press.

Widiger T. A., Trull T. J., Clarkin J. F., Sanderson C., & Costa P. T. (1994) A description of the DSM-III-R and DSM-IV personality disorders with the five factor model of personality. In P. T. Costa & T. A. Widiger (Eds.) *Personality disorders and the five-factor model*. Washington, DC, American Psychological Association, pp. 41–58.

Widom C. S. (1989) The cycle of violence. *Science*, **244**, 161–6.

Wiggins J. S. (1982) Circumplex models of interpersonal behavior in clinical psychology. In P. S. Kendall & J. N. Butcher (Eds.) *Handbook of research methods in clinical psychology*. New York, Wiley, pp. 183–221.

Wiggins J. S. & Pincus A. L. (1989) Conceptions of personality disorders and dimensions of personality. *Psychological Assessment*, **1**, 305–16.

Winokur G., Clayton P., & Reich T. (1969) *Manic-depressive illness*. St. Louis, Mosby.

Winston A., Laikin M., Pollack J., Wallner Samstag L., McCullough L., & Muran J. C. (1994) Short-term psychotherapy of personality disorders. *American Journal of Psychiatry*, **151**, 190–4.

Woody G. E., McLennon T., Lubursky L., & O'Brien C. P. (1985) Sociopathy and psychotherapyy outcome. *Archives of General Psychiatry*, **42**, 1081–6.

World Health Organization. (1992) *International classification of diseases*, 10th edition. Geneva.

Wright L. (1994) *Remembering Satan*. New York, Knopf.

Yeung A. S., Lyons M. J., Waternaux C. M., Faraone S. V., & Tsuang M. T. (1993) The relationship between DSM-III personality disorders and the five-factor model of personality disorders. *Comprehensive Psychiatry*, **34**, 227–34.

Yochelson S. & Samenow S. (1976) *The criminal personality*. New York, Jason Aronson.

Young A. (in press) *Harmony of illusions*. Princeton, NJ, Princeton University Press.

Young J. E. (1990) Cognitive therapy for personality disorders: a schema-focused approach. Sarasota, FL, *Professional Resources Exchange*.

Zakinofsky I. & Roberts R. (1987) The ecology of suicide in the provinces of Canada. In B. Cooper (Ed.) *The epidemiology of psychiatric disorders*. Baltimore, Johns Hopkins University Press, pp. 27–42.

Zanarini M. C., Gunderson J. G., & Frankenburg F. R. (1990) Cognitive features of borderline personality disorder. *American Journal of Psychiatry*, **147**, 57–63.

Zanarini M. C., Frankenburg F. R., Chauncey D. L., & Gunderson J. G. (1987). The diagnostic interview for personality disorders: interrater and test-retest reliability, *Comprehensive Psychiatry*, **28**, 467–480.

Zanarini M. C., Gunderson J. G., Marino M. F., Schwartz E. O., & Frankenburg F. R. (1989a). Childhood experiences of borderline patients. *Comprehensive Psychiatry*, **30**, 18–25.

Zanarini M. C., Gunderson J. G., Frankenburg F. R., & Chauncey D. L. (1989b) The revised diagnostic interview for borderlines: discriminating BPD from other Axis II disorders. *Journal of Personality Disorders*, **3**, 10–18.

Zanarini M. C., Gunderson J. G., & Frankenburg F. R. (1989c) Discriminating borderline personality disorder from other Axis II disorders. *American Journal of Psychiatry*, **147**, 161–7.

Zimmerman M. (1994) Diagnosing personality disorders. *Archives of General Psychiatry*, **51**, 225–45.

Zimmerman M. & Coryell W. (1989) DSM-III personality disorder diagnoses in a nonpatient sample. *Archives of General Psychiatry*, **46**, 682–9.

Zoccolillo M., Pickles A., Quixton D, & Rutter M. (1992) The outcome of childhood conduct disorder. *Psychological Medicine* **22**, 971–86.

Zweig-Frank H. & Paris J. (1991) Recollections of emotional neglect and overprotection in borderline patients. *American Journal of Psychiatry*, **148**, 648–51.

Zweig-Frank H. & Paris J. (in press) The five factor model of personality in borderline personality disorders. *Canadian Journal of Psychiatry*.

Zweig-Frank H., Paris J., & Guzder J. (1994a) Psychological risk factors for dissociation in female patients with borderline and non-borderline personality disorders. *Journal of Personality Disorders*, **8**, 203–9.

Zweig-Frank H., Paris J., & Guzder J. (1994b) Psychological risk factors for disssociation and self-mutilation in female patients with personality disorders. *Canadian Journal of Psychiatry*, **39**, 259–65.

Zweig-Frank H., Paris J., & Guzder J. (1994c) Dissociation in male patients with borderline and non-borderline personality disorders. *Journal of Personality Disorders*, **8**, 210–18.

Zweig-Frank H., Paris J., & Guzder J. (1994d) Psychological risk factors for self-mutilation in male patients with personality disorders. *Canadian Journal of Psychiatry*, **39**, 266–8.

Index